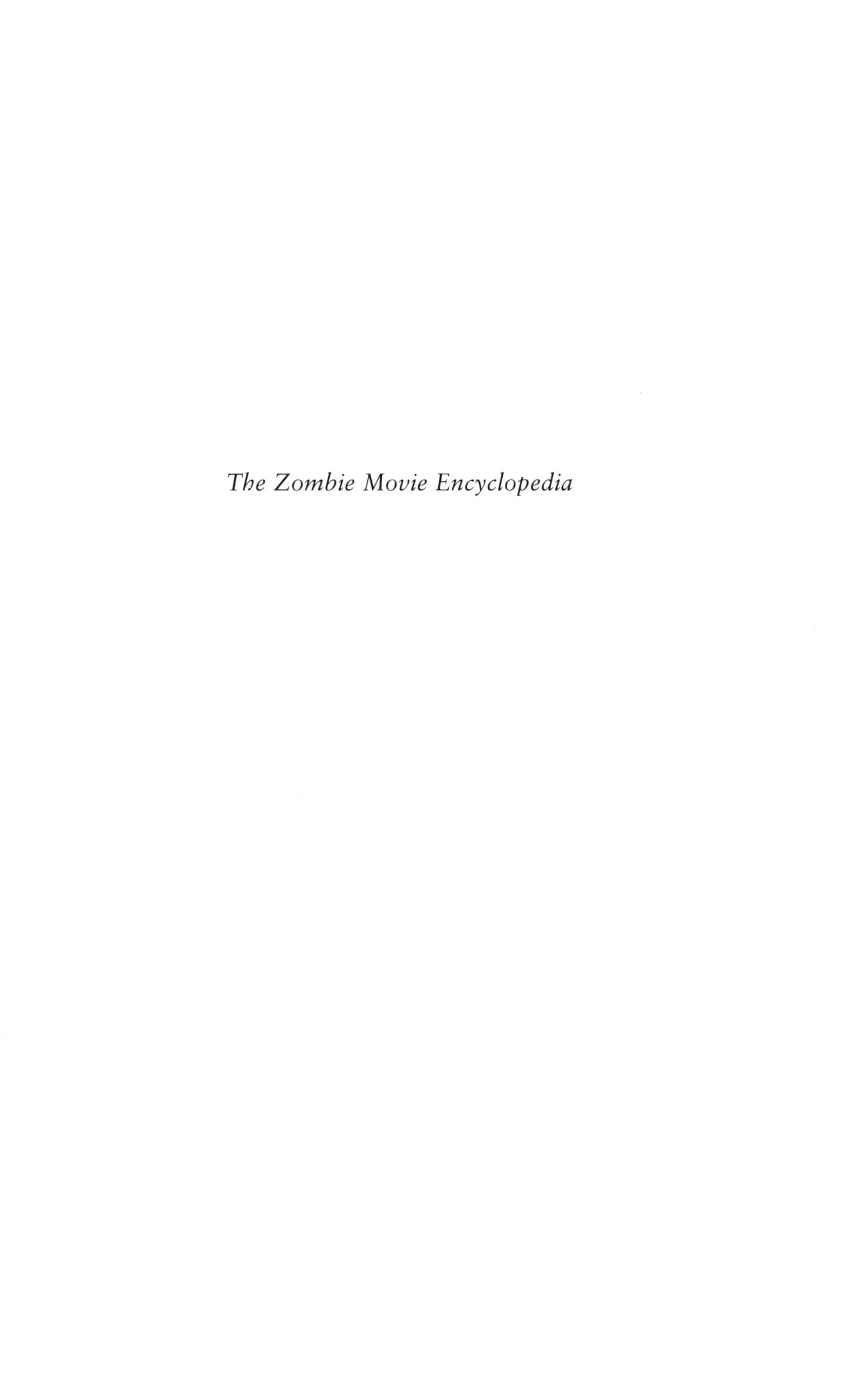

The Zombie Movie Encyclopedia

The Zombie Movie Encyclopedia

by
PETER DENDLE

McFarland & Company, Inc., Publishers
Jefferson, North Carolina, and London

Library of Congress Cataloguing-in-Publication Data

Dendle, Peter, 1968–
The zombie movie encyclopedia / by Peter Dendle.
p. cm.
Includes bibliographical references and index.
ISBN 0-7864-0859-6 (illustrated case binding : 50# alkaline paper) ∞
1. Zombie films—Catalogs. 2. Zombie films—History and criticism.
I. Title.
PN1995.9.Z63 D46 2001
016.79143'675—dc21 00-56062

British Library cataloguing data are available

Manufactured in the United States of America

McFarland & Company, Inc., Publishers
Box 611, Jefferson, North Carolina 28640
www.mcfarlandpub.com

For "Bub"—
we're right behind you

Acknowledgments

The Lexington crew:

Amy Goff-Yates.

Michael Kim, Susan Adams, Tom Arnold, Diane Timmons, Jim Shaw, Vida Vitagliano, Amy Baxter, John Mayfield, Erik Siegel, Joe "Mr. Friendly" Conkwright, Buck Reynolds, Blake "Flipper" Cox, Mike Joyner, Joel Glenn, J.J. Haws, Becca Stormcrowe, Bill Baxter III, Scott Hand, Lisa Brandenburg, Shelby Thacker, Steve Heiner, Ernesto Delgado, Claudia Silvy, Lalana Powell, and The Kentucky Theater—a place of initiation.

The Toronto ghouls:

Lisa Fox.

Brian Catlos, Richard Raiswell, Mary Catherine Davidson (the vase!), Steve Giles, Diane Blair, Jessica Wakefield, David Winter, Kim McGhee, Elizabeth Schoales, Carrie Hintz, Karin Peterson, Sarah Winters, and Marc Plamondon.

Giridhar Chukkapalli (sorry about *City of the Walking Dead*), Paul Feenstra (sorry about all of them), and Santhi.

My brother Mark has always been supportive of my sundry schemes, and this was no exception. I also owe a great deal to my father Brian and my mother Catherine, Julie Dendle, Sylvain Coucharrière, Gildas Coucharrière, *et grandmère*.

For information, advice, research assistance, and general encouragement I am indebted to David Wilke, Janet Layman, Danice Nutter, Barbara Hale, Tom Weaver, Derek Neito, Faith Shaffer of

ZombieJuice.com, Jesse Mark Cesario, Liana Martin, Bill Hellfire, Michael Weldon, Ken Kish, and Jerry Ohlinger.

Special thanks to Bryan Senn, for proofreading and moral support, for generously making his private collection of stills available to me, and (can such a gift be measured?) for *War of the Zombies*, which had impishly eluded me for so many years.

James O'Neill's *Terror on Tape*, Michael Weldon's *Psychotronic Encyclopedia of Film*, and Phil Hardy's *Aurum Film Encyclopedia: Horror* have been my constant companions in this project, and their influence appears throughout. I have also gleaned much from Bryan Senn's *Drums of Terror: Voodoo in the Cinema* and Tom Weaver's *Poverty Row Horrors!*

Contents

Acknowledgments vii

Introduction 1

THE FILMS 17

Appendix A: Movies Listed by Year 217

Appendix B: Foreign Movies by Country 222

Bibliography 225

Index 231

"I can't bear those empty, staring eyes!"
—*White Zombie*

"It's hard to believe such monstrous things..."
—*Ouanga*

"Don't bother me ... can't you see I's a has-been?"
—*King of the Zombies*

"Oh, the whole thing has me ... confused!"
—*White Zombie*

Introduction

"The evil that men do lives after them"
—*Julius Caesar*

The zombie remains, for the most part, unappreciated. Zombie films are relegated to the last page of every horror movie guide, saved from utter obscurity only by the dubious *Zontar, the Thing from Venus*. There are almost no serious studies of TV and movie zombies, as there are for vampires in abundance. Nevertheless, the sheer volume of zombie movies attests to their enduring cult popularity and contemporary relevance. *The Zombie Movie Encyclopedia* suggests something of this relevance.*

This book is not only about movies but also about a peculiar motif of contemporary suburban Western mythology. I am not as interested in the quality of the films as in the attention and creativity they devote to their particular treatment of the zombie. Technically correct movies may feature unimaginative zombies, while even some of the worst sometimes have glimpses of genius, deliberate or accidental. I have simply tried to be an objective zombie ethologist, observing them in their natural habitat, and recording their nature and behavior.

**Prior panoramic treatments of zombie films include Pierre Gires' detailed overview in* L'Ecran Fantastique *(1983), Rose London's* Zombie: The Living Dead *(1976), and Leslie Halliwell's chapter "A Note on Zombies" (1986,* The Dead That Walk*). Also useful are Yves Bérard's "Les Morts-Vivants" (1977), Steve Thrower's entry for "zombies" in the* BFI Companion to Horror *(ed. Kim Newman, 1996), and the catalogue entry in Howard Maxford's* A–Z of Horror Films *(1996). Allan Bryce's excellent collection of essays on zombie movies (simply called* Zombie, *2000) gives brief entries on 141 movies, and includes chapters on key directors and film cycles.*

History and Evolution

Early Caribbean travel literature occasionally mentioned voodoo rites and transmitted snippets of zombie lore, but even as late as 1928 folklorist Elsie Parsons mentioned that the "zombi" was virtually unknown outside of Haiti. William Seabrook catapulted them to instant fame with his 1929 travel book *The Magic Island*, and after Kenneth Webb's 1932 New York stage production *Zombie* the creature fell irrevocably under the auspices of the entertainment industry. A month after the play opened, the Halperin brothers began work on a film adaptation, *White Zombie*, and despite a suit brought against them by Webb, the movie opened in the summer of 1932.

Bela Lugosi was still riding on the wave of his ground-breaking performance in *Dracula* (1930), which had stunned audiences still not fully used to talkies, and his presence in *White Zombie* graced that film with a reflected brilliance it might not have enjoyed had there been no such film as *Dracula* first. The zombie didn't immediately gain the popularity of the other undead monsters to spring up after *Dracula—Frankenstein* (1931) and *The Mummy* (1932)—or of other fiends such as *The Invisible Man* (1933) and the belated *Wolfman* (1941). However, while the occasional filmmaker risked a zombie-centered movie that generally flopped, the creature was to some extent kept current after its original fifteen years or so of independent existence by its presence in vampire movies, as the subordinate minions of the main vampire.

Though derivative in some respects, the zombie has nonetheless survived as an independent mythological creature in its own right. Moreover, zombies have organically given rise to a number of recognizable sub-species, such as Nazi zombies, underwater zombies, and zombie monks.* After all, their roots are to be found in African and African-Caribbean folklore, and so they are one of the few screen creatures in the Hollywood menagerie not of European origin. Zom-

**Underwater zombies:* Zombies of Mora-Tau *(1957),* Shock Waves *(1977),* The Fog *(1979),* Zombie Lake *(1980),* The Alien Dead *(1980),* Creepshow *(1982); see also* Erotic Nights of the Living Dead *(1979) and* Zombie *(1979). Nazi zombies:* King of the Zombies *(1941),* Revenge of the Zombies *(1943),* Shock Waves *(1977),* Zombie Lake *(1980),* Gamma 693 *(1981),* Oasis of the Zombies *(1982),* Hard Rock Zombies *(1984),* Ginseng King *(1989). Zombie monks:* Tombs of the Blind *series (1971–1975),* Cross of the Devil *(1975),* Burial Ground *(1980),* Mansion of the Living Dead *(1982). Other noteworthy subspecies include redneck zombies, yuppie zombies, and the rare but captivating dock-worker zombie.*

bies are, furthermore, the only creature to pass directly from folklore to the screen, without first having an established literary tradition.

The Early Film Zombie (1932–1952)

The film zombie of the '30s and '40s is essentially a backdrop figure, an atmospheric detail added to supplement a more dramatic human villain. Though continuously menacing and potentially fierce, early zombies are seldom exploited for violence. This is true to their folkloric roots: as Wade Davis and Maya Deren make clear, the fear in Haiti is not of being harmed by a zombie, but of becoming one. Early Hollywood zombies are primarily objects of visual horror rather than genuine threats to the protagonists—the camera focuses on them for a moment while thunderingly eerie music plays. If they kill anyone of importance, it's their own master, the villain, at the movie's climax.

Early film zombies are robotic. There is grace in their unwavering pace and fluidity of motion. When they walk in a group their gait is perfectly synchronized, and if they talk at all, it's in a monotone. They exhibit no passions or drives, bearing little resemblance to the increasingly animalistic zombies of recent decades. In fact, their utter lack of concern for humans, or for anything at all, was what originally made zombies frightening. No zombie movie since the early decades has sustained the complete depersonalization that is the source of fear in Haitian folklore.

Early zombie movies are most obviously concerned with the appropriation of female bodies, and the annihilation of female minds, by male captors. Time and again the villains learn that to possess the woman's mindless body is unsatisfying. This relatively safe—almost saccharine—theme pales next to the charged racial tensions that permeate these films at a less explicit level, however. The earliest zombie movie, *White Zombie* (1932), draws attention by its title to the fact that the hypnotized heroine is a white woman, and not one of the native dead who form Legendre's zombie army. *Ouanga* (1935) is patently racist in its presentation of natives as monsters, and continually plays on a symbolic identification of black with ignorance and evil, and white with light and purity. These relatively simplistic racial dynamics are redeemed by the powerful *I Walked with a Zombie* (1943), which sustains a thoughtful juxtaposition of black and white imagery in a setting fraught with racial tension. The wooden figurehead from a slave ship erected in front of the plantation house looms over the dominant European aristocracy that originally brought the native population's ancestors to the island in shackles. More recently, movies such as *Sugar Hill* (1974) and *Demoni 3* (1991) have shown a rekindled interest in the slave substratum of zombie folklore, featuring reanimated slave zombies that still wear their chains and manacles.

The '50s and '60s: Tension and Transition (1952–1966)

The '50s and early '60s represent a strange transitional time for the screen zombie, as though the concept were ready to move beyond its stagnant, two-decade-old paradigm, but experienced some confusion in exactly which direction to go. People stayed fascinated with the word long after they had tired of the original referent, and it's interesting to observe the range of creatures and altered states of consciousness that passed under the term "zombie" in this period. *Zombies of the Stratosphere* (1952), for instance, insists on calling human-looking Martian invaders "zombies," though they think, feel, talk, and plot to take over the earth. *Zombies of Mora-Tau* (1957) returns to the classic zombie conceptualization, but curiously resituates the zombies under water. In *Teenage Zombies* (1957) the term refers to the wholesome, middle-class, fun-loving protagonists, who are simply under the effect of a hypnotizing drug. Ray Dennis Steckler's suspect *The Incredibly Strange Creatures Who Stopped Living and Became Mixed-Up Zombies* (1964) cheekily offers as "zombies" the embittered and ferocious ex-lovers of Madame Estrella, now crazed, homicidal fiends horribly disfigured by acid and deranged by imprisonment (but who, for all that, have not stopped living and are not zombies). *The Astro-Zombies* (1968) peddles synthetic cybernetic androids as zombies. Most outrageous of all, perhaps, is Del Tenney's delightful *The Horror of Party Beach* (1963), which freely attaches the term "zombie" to its irradiated, humanoid, mutated fish antagonists. But even in this conceptual potpourri, certain coherent threads of exploration and development are discernible.

The '50s were preoccupied with individuality, the privacy of human consciousness, and the potential for depersonalization. Movies such as *Plan Nine from Outer Space* (1958) and *Invisible Invaders* (1959) share a common anxiety in insisting that the revived dead are not sentient in any way, and that the ambulatory loved ones are not really themselves (space aliens are the culprits in both of those pictures). The animated bodies are kept radically distinct from any conception of mind or soul. The issues of human dignity and family relations that inherently arise from images of the mindless, walking dead are suppressed, though clearly rippling beneath the surface, in these and other ostensibly safe and sanitized movies of the period. With *The Last Man on Earth* (1964), issues such as the disposal of bodies and the residual feelings for the deceased reach the surface, paving the way for the genuinely disturbing themes that emerge in the late '60s.

Though Halliwell calls "The Incredible Doktor Markesan" (a 1962 episode of the TV series *Thriller* hosted by Boris Karloff) "possibly the last of the old-style zombies to emanate from Hollywood" (246), what it in fact represents is a taste of the new-style zombie that would come into its own increasingly in the '60s: the visibly rotting cadaver. This trend actually took root in Mexico in advance of other countries, especially in such gems as Rafael Portillo's *The Aztec Mummy* series (starting in 1957). England decisively established the convention, however, with *Doctor Blood's Coffin* (1960) and especially *Plague of the Zombies* (1966). Though deformed and disfigured villains, monstrous aliens, and radiated creatures are commonplace throughout motion picture history, there was clearly some unspoken taboo against portraying human cadavers as visibly decomposing. Early Hollywood features revive the dead often enough—even those many centuries dead—but always rest content with making them sullen and gaunt. The '60s thus mark a transitional period in the evolution of the conception of human dignity, a transformation whose completion is perhaps signaled most decisively by the graveyard art in the opening scene of *The Texas Chainsaw Massacre* (1974). Through this period, screen zombies thus serve as key symbolic gauges for the trivialization of humans as individuals and for the declining insistence that life is sacred.

The Stabilizing of the Contemporary Zombie Mythos (1966–present)

The protean zombie concept crystallized into its currently recognizable form with two movies in the late '60s, one in England and one in America: *The Plague of the Zombies* (1966) and *Night of the*

Living Dead (1968). *Plague* established the zombie's decaying appearance and nasty temper, while *Night* established its motives and limitations. In earlier presentations, the zombie was a derivative creature, always under the control of some other more intelligent being (voodoo master, mad scientist, vampire). Romero liberated the zombie from the shackles of a master, and invested his zombies not with a function (a job or task such as zombies were standardly given by voodoo priests), but rather a drive (eating flesh). He conflated the "zombie" with the "ghoul," a cannibal creature that (despite a couple of '30s movies) had never really caught on by itself. Zombies thus become endowed with a highly physical, biological craving; they are no longer robotic machines, but gluttonous organisms demanding representation in the food chain. More than 60 movies follow *Night* in presenting zombies as cannibals.

Night of the Living Dead's most peculiar zombie innovation is the idea that zombies can be destroyed only by being shot in the head or by otherwise deactivating the brain core.* This is consistent with the implied physicalism of the trilogy: however aberrant, the life force inhabiting the errant bodies is intrinsically connected with the physical brain processes. *Day of the Dead* (1985) provides more detail: the brain is slowly rotting, and when the decomposition consumes the brain core entirely, the zombie will cease functioning. Two to three dozen movies follow *Night* in making the head the zombie's only vulnerable part.

What stands out most about post–1960s zombie cinema is not so much the violence or the horror as the gore. The gore in *Night* shocked Roger Ebert when he first saw the movie at a Saturday matinee, surrounded by horrified children: "They had seen horror before, but this was something else. This was ghouls eating people—you could actually see what they were eating." Blood and guts were coming into their own in the '60s with Herschell Gordon Lewis' free-for-alls, and though the visceral element was relatively subdued in the '70s, horror movies in the '80s were often little more than two-dimensional slaughterhouses. This development particularly complemented the essentially corporeal and biological themes of the zombie mythos, in which the living organism is unceremoniously revealed to be a

**The idea actually appeared earlier in* Revenge of the Zombies *(1943) and* Creature with the Atom Brain *(1955)—though in each of those movies it's only mentioned casually—and in* Dr. Orloff's Monster *(1964), where it is put to the test.*

temporary and convenient accumulation of cell clusters, which subsists for a time and then deteriorates when the individual cells no longer derive benefit from the arrangement. A major concern of zombie movies is the stripping away of surface ornament, such that the insides are out, in body no less than in mind. The skin is unable to confine the organs, just as the cerebral cortex is no longer capable of controlling the reptile brain.

The Golden Age (1968–1983)

With the Romero paradigm in place, zombie film entered its golden age, the classical period of zombie invasions. *Night of the Living Dead* appeared in 1968 and slowly gained notoriety on the midnight movie circuit. More than 30 zombie movies appeared between 1969 and 1977 in Spain, Mexico, Italy, England, and the States, representing the first post–Romero wave. Horror favorites such as Peter Cushing, Christopher Lee, and Paul Naschy suddenly found themselves pitted against zombies rather than the more conventional '60s monsters (e.g., the mummies and vampires of Hammer or Amicus). This first wave is characterized by a wide variety of zombie types and settings: the dream zombies of *A Virgin Among the Living Dead* (1971), the skeletal monks of de Ossorio's *Tombs of the Blind Dead* series (1971–75), the African-American slave zombies in the blaxploitation *Sugar Hill* (1974), the remote-control family members in *Shanks* (1974), and the slick techno-zombies of *Shock Waves* (1977). In general, these movies are pensive and cloaked in a delirious—almost narcotic—surrealism. The initial enthusiasm waned somewhat between 1975 and 1978, but the mid–'70s zombie recession ended with an explosion in 1979 following Romero's *Dawn of the Dead*. The decade that followed (1979 to 1989) boasted an average of six zombie movies per year, or about one every eight weeks.

When zombie movies began reappearing in 1979, however, they no longer exhibited the scattered range of topics that the initial wave did. The stories aren't isolated yarns about a small group of people overcoming a localized monster attack, but focus specifically on the larger theme of utter apocalypse. Zombies carry a powerful and unholy contagion that spreads with dizzying speed, and the undead threaten nothing less than global Armageddon. Italy secured a position at the forefront at this time, quickly producing an abundance of apocalyptic zombie invasions such as *Burial Ground* (1980), *City of the Walking Dead* (1980), *The Gates of Hell* (1980), and *Night of the Zombies* (1981). Romero's *Dawn of the Dead* initiated this trend, just as *Night* initiated the first wave, but Lucio Fulci's *Zombie* (1979)—made and released within a matter of months after *Dawn*—is on the whole more representative of the second wave. Some notable contributions came from France and Spain as well, such as *Zombie Lake* (1980) and *Oasis of the Zombies* (1982), but America's offerings at this time were few and unimpressive.

These Southern European movies are generally characterized by exotic settings, often a tropical island inhabited by natives of ill-defined ethnicity. There is sometimes an unfortunate colonial brutality implicit in the endless scenes of European survivalists gunning down native zombies, but on the whole these movies concentrate their energies precisely on those aspects of zombie film that have proven the most aesthetically powerful: provocative settings, the restrained appearance and blocking of the zombies, a mounting sense of claustrophobia and helplessness, and the careful pacing and rhythm of the escalating apocalypse. Uncomplicated but engaging synthesizer scoring lends the best of these invasions a hypnotic, dream-like ambience. To my mind, it is perhaps these second-wave French, Spanish, and especially Italian movies—low-budget, badly acted, but resolutely sincere—that represent the apex of the zombie film golden age. What zombie movies do well, these movies do best, pushing the themes inherent in the genre to their logical conclusions. They are parables of entropy, presenting global devastation with maddening patience and relentlessness. Zombie movies after this time are sometimes excellent, but rarely recapture the naïve charm that makes these Mediterranean visions of apocalypse fascinating. When America at last appropriated the genre in 1983 with *Thriller* and in 1985 with *Re-Animator* and *Return of the Living Dead*, the shoddy sets were replaced with slick, fully funded studios, the synthesizer scores were supplanted by rock and pop, and the sincerity gave way to camp.

The Mid-'80s Spoof Cycle

The final crossover from cult to mainstream popularity came with Michael Jackson's *Thriller* video (1983). Following that point, zombie invasion motifs were familiar enough to allow for the zombie spoof cycle. The very titles suggest a detached, tongue-in-cheek attitude: *Bloodsuckers from Outer Space* (1984), *Hard Rock Zombies*

(1984), *I Was a Teenage Zombie* (1986), *Redneck Zombies* (1987), and *Chopper Chicks in Zombietown* (1989). From low-budget backyard movies to professional productions, the interest in the mid– to late–'80s was in applying the accepted body of zombie lore to unique and bizarre situations, or occasionally in expanding the mythology itself in light-hearted ways. Thus, whereas in *Night* there's only a remote hint that the ghouls feast on non-human flesh (one woman zombie picks a bug from a tree and eats it), the spoof cycle picks up the ball and runs with it: a zombie eats a lamb in the bucolic *Bloodsuckers from Outer Space*, another eats a pig in the equally rustic *Redneck Zombies*, one zombified dwarf eats a live cow and another eats himself (!) in *Hard Rock Zombies*, and the undead ravage an entire pet store filled with poodles and cute furry animals in *Return of the Living Dead Part II* (1987).

The year 1985 was a capital one for zombies. Romero completed his trilogy with the excellent *Day of the Dead*, but his slower, more contemplative brand of horror was no longer in fashion, and *Day* couldn't hope to spark off a third zombie wave as *Night* and *Dawn* had done. Instead, two other movies of the same year, *Re-Animator* and *Return of the Living Dead*, moved to the fore by satisfying mid–'80s horror expectations such as high-impact gore, frequent shocks, memorable one-liners, and above all, a sense that none of it should be taken too seriously.

Return of the Living Dead in particular exerted a tremendous influence on the general stock of zombie lore. *Return* is the obvious inspiration, for instance, behind the zombie conceptualization in the Itchy Kitchen song "Corpse Rock" (1985), the third *Simpsons* Halloween special (1992), and the first-season *South Park* Halloween episode (1997). Most importantly, whereas Romero's zombies only eat the flesh of victims in a general way, the zombies of *Return* specifically eat the brains. The undead don't view the living simply as undifferentiated meat samples, but specifically target the intellectual center itself. Thus the zombies crave the consciousness (metonymically literalized as the brain) that they so sorely lack.

The spoof cycle ran its course quickly, but the popularity of the zombie—particularly the zombie invasion—weathered the comic sidetrack. By the late '80s there was a notable tendency to incorporate the accepted zombie motifs into larger productions whose main concern isn't the zombie or zombie invasion itself. Thus the zombie invasion becomes a sort of detachable subplot, kept hovering on the periphery throughout most of the film but only coming to the forefront at the climax (*Curse of the Blue Lights*, *The Vineyard*, *The Dead Pit*). Throughout the spoof cycle, however, the zombies are generally presented as serious, even when the rest of the movie is tongue-in-cheek. Zombies are, understandably, the ideal "straight men."

There were few major studio attempts after the mid–'80s to center an entire movie around a zombie invasion. Peter Jackson's *Dead Alive* (1992) is one successful venture, but this splatterpunk epic is quite far in spirit from the subdued and shadowy tropical chases of the zombie invasion golden age. The zombie romantic-comedy—an unlikely combination, one would think—proved one of the more enduring off-shoots in the late '80s and early '90s (*Deadly Friend*, *I Was a Teenage Zombie*, *My Zombie Lover*, *My Boyfriend's Back*, *Return of the Living Dead Part III*).

Local filmmakers, however, took up the zombie invasion with a vengeance in the early '90s, which saw the appearance of a number of no-budget apocalypses (such as the direct-to-video releases from Troma, Suburban Tempe, and Trustinus Productions), many only videographed. Though these are sometimes clever and attest to the zombie's enduring cult popularity, they have little to offer the broader movie-watching public. At the time of this writing, a movie is in production based on the video game *Resident Evil*, Rob Cohen is negotiating a remake of *I Walked with a Zombie* with Dimension Films, and Todd Sheets is still grinding out his assembly line home-movie zombie invasions in Kansas City, Missouri.

Significance

Zombies are an unashamed mockery of humankind's most universally cherished ideal: life after death.

By way of comparison, consider Dracula: a being of supernormal intelligence and pathos, whose complicated psychological gears embody conflicts between animalistic impulses on the one hand (thirst for blood, repressed sexual cravings, etc.), and on the other, an aristocratic breeding and politeness associated with only the most polished of literature's great villains. The vampire is dashing, smooth-complexioned, sexy, and erudite with centuries of selective reading. Painfully self-reflective of the tragedy of his condition, he is poised at the threshold between an id and a superego, both of exaggerated proportions.

The zombie—the ragged, unkempt, rotting corpse sorely lacking in psychological machinery and social presentability—is the antithesis of this aristocratic figure. Domestically set vampire movies (that is, those not set in exotic foreign forests or Eastern European villages) are usually urban-cosmopolitan efforts, taking place in high-profile centers such as Los Angeles or New York. Domestically set zombie movies, by contrast, are from the heartland: Louisiana (*Revenge of the Zombies*, *The Beyond*); Louisville, Kentucky (*Return of the Living Dead*); Akron, Ohio (*The Dead Next Door*); backwoods Alabama (*The Supernaturals*) and Tennessee (*Toxic Zombies*); rural Pennsylvania (*Night*, *Dawn*) and Maryland (*Redneck Zombies*); Florida swamplands (*Day*, *Alien Dead*); and Kansas City, Missouri (*The Chilling*, *Zombie Bloodbath*). Zombies are blue-collar undead, banding together in loose mobs and endeavoring to compensate in sheer numbers for what they lack in individual speed or strategy. From the plantation and mine slaves in *White Zombie* (1932) and *The Plague of the Zombies* (1966) to the shopping mall slaves of declining Western civilization in *Dawn* (1979), zombies embody the ultimate Marxist working-class society. Finally, with *Shatter Dead* (1993), even the zombie's role as the oppressed worker is deromanticized: here zombies are simply another disenfranchised and marginalized sector of the population, threatening to unionize but mostly just panhandling.

Pretty much everyone has commented that *Night of the Living Dead* documents middle-class America's eating of itself and the death of the nuclear family, and that *Dawn of the Dead* exposes the vacuousness of contemporary consumer society. Caputi sees *Night*'s apocalypticism as atomic-age disquietude, and compares the "psychic numbing" associated with the victims of Hiroshima with screen portrayals of zombies (103). Higashi discusses such recurring motifs as military organization, media involvement, and particular images such as helicopters in the context of the Vietnam War (178–86), while Hoberman and Rosenbaum also point out other late '60s social concerns such as racial tension in *Night* (112). Ed Lowry and Louis Black see in *Dawn* a '70s parable of environmental deterioration and the "postindustrial catastrophe" (17), and Beard reads zombie films in terms of Ford–era labor economics and the obsolescence of the American worker (30). In an age of increasing life expectancy and decreasing employment possibilities, the fear of aging indefinitely and parables of overpopulation resound throughout zombie movies (Bérard 27, Boss 15–20). Finally, Linda Badley reads films such as

Re-Animator as explorations of late twentieth-century biomedical and health care worries such as the commoditization of the human body, the fragmentation of the individual into organs and body parts, and other forbidding issues raised by medical and genetic technology: "but as the language and iconography revealed most dramatically in the 1980s, the horror and the real monster had become the body itself" (73–4).

Underlying these cultural strata, deeper, more timeless tensions between the living and the dead simmer as well. Throughout the world, pre-modern societies exhibit an acute anxiety of the dead, envisioned variously as spirits, ghosts, or physical revenants. (Sir James Frazer's *Fear of the Dead* is still the most comprehensive overview.) The primordial fear of the dead even forms a part of certain pre-modern initiation rites, as in the following account from Fiji:

> Beginning with puberty, boys were taken at night to an area where the adult men had placed a group of bloody supposedly dead and decaying bodies covered with intestines. The boys were forced to crawl through the "dead" bodies, which suddenly "came to life." Boys who showed fear were denied manhood [Miller, cited in Zillmann and Gibson 23].

In zombie movies since Romero, these fears are compounded with archetypal fears of contagion and of uncleanness in the abstract. Plague anxiety comes in many forms, from the classical and biblical revulsion against leprosy to the modern media fascination with invasive–A streptococcus, the "flesh eating disease"; screen zombies find themselves connected with a range of ailments including bubonic plague (*Terror Creatures from the Grave*), cancer (*After Death*), AIDS (*Zombie '90: Extreme Pestilence*), and even teen acne (*I Was a Teenage Zombie*, *My Boyfriend's Back*). This pestilence anxiety is almost always non-specific, however, because ultimately it isn't leprosy or plague or AIDS, but death itself that is the disease. Death is a comma in the midst of a cursed existence, gone from mediocre to horrible, rather than a period at the end of it.

Zombies are people reduced to the lowest common denominator. The zombie is simply the hulk, the rude stuff of generic humanity, the bare canvas; passion, art, and intellect are by implication reduced to mere ornament. There is an existential component inherently built into the genre if it's read with even a minimum of allegory. The zombie just is.

Definition, Scope, and Principles of Selection

The substantial overlap among the various movie monsters precludes the possibility of an all-encompassing definition of a zombie. The soulless, reanimated corpse under the control of a voodoo master from Caribbean lore serves as a useful starting point, since that's where the zombie film finds its own beginning (*White Zombie*, 1932), but complications arise quickly: how much soul or personality is permissible in the resurrected person? What if there is no voodoo master, as in the Romero trilogy? Once the zombie becomes a familiar screen monster with certain fixed features, what are we to make of similar movies, whose creatures exhibit most of the familiar traits but are not actually reanimated corpses? The irradiated or diseased hordes of Cronenberg's *Rabid* (1977), Rollin's *The Grapes of Death* (1978), Eberheardt's *Night of the Comet* (1984), and others fall within the broader zombie genre, in a loose sense, but this book will limit coverage to movies in which the creatures are actually revived corpses, or are explicitly referred to as zombies.

The zombie first appeared as the revived corpse of *vodou* religion, and most of the early zombie films sustain a religious connection.* But screen zombies have evolved to something quite different in their long and varied history, and have largely left their voodoo origins behind. In the late '60s and early '70s, *The Plague of the Zombies* (1966) and *Night of the Living Dead* (1968) redefined their appearance and behavior entirely. The zombie today is a limping, shambling, decaying ghoul in search of human flesh, utterly distinct from the robotic, deadpan zombie of early voodoo thrillers. The basic definition of a revived corpse with diminished mental faculties generally holds true through this evolution, though, and unites zombies from before the late–'60s metamorphosis with those after it.

Due to the volume of material, I have not attempted to cover

**Contemporary practice employs the spelling* vodou *or* vodoun *instead of* voodoo, *a practice that in part reflects a more accurate linguistic rendering of the word, but more importantly, serves to distinguish the living religion from the mockery Hollywood has made of it. It is a sad truth of our subject that in oversimplifying, decontextualizing, and demonizing* vodou *rites and beliefs, popular books and films throughout the Western world have encouraged ignorance and fostered misconceptions about the African and Caribbean religion. This book uses the term* voodoo, *however, because that's the term familiar from the movies themselves, and use of the term emphasizes the fact that it is the Hollywood caricature, rather than the actual religion, that is at issue.*

"zombie" in the broader colloquial sense of "willless, obedient person," e.g., a living person simply hypnotized or possessed (unless the film title specifically identifies such persons as zombies). Though an important thread of zombie genealogy, such classics as *Village of the Damned* (1960), *Invaders from Mars* (1953), and *Invasion of the Body Snatchers* (1956) are beyond the scope of the present work, which considers the physical death and (partial) resurrection of the body integral to the core definition.

Resurrected bodies that retain all previous personality and mental ability don't constitute zombies. Zombies are dim-witted, with ideally no more than the thinnest shred of continuity connecting the present animating principle (mind, soul, etc.) with the former. As Ecclesiastes 9:5 states, "The dead know not anything." Ghost movies that deny the gross corporeality of the corpse aren't zombie movies, either. Though the maimed soldiers of the early French *J'Accuse!* (1938) provide excellent zombie analogues, for example, the superimposed photography of the hordes of risen dead doesn't really elicit the same tensions as resurrected, physical hulks. In ghost movies, editing room nonsense is often paraded as psychological horror, the facile camera trickery and disrupted narrative logic representing internal fragmentation. Zombie movies, in contrast, generally adhere to strict narrative logic of time and space; if the zombie is to get from point A to B, the story must provide for the physical traversing of points in between.

Mummies are close cousins; in fact, a mummy is arguably only a zombie with bandages. Mexican mummies, which never had bandages to begin with, form obvious parallels with the Hollywood zombie. But the Egyptian mummy, noble and timeless, is altogether different. It is supported by, and vestigially defends, the hieratic civilization of the ancient Egyptians, whose stately gods still empower the mummy, and whose long-dead priests have woven into the sarcophagus their laments and curses. Nothing could be more antithetical to the anonymous zombie, chosen at random from working-class corpses for menial ends by two-bit witch doctors.

This book does not cover demon-zombies, such as those of *Evil Dead* (1982), *Demoni* (1985), or *Demon Wind* (1989), since they exhibit enhanced rather than impaired mental faculties, and enjoy a wide range of other powers incommensurate with common notions of a zombie. Demons are autonomous spiritual entities from other planes or worlds, a clear distinction being maintained between them and the bodies they inhabit. If the zombie suffers from a lack of soul or spirit, the demon suffers from an overabundance.

Zombies share certain features with robots and androids—slow and relentless pursuit, for instance, and immunity from many weapons. Although both zombies and robots evoke the terror of a mindless foe who shows no regard for self-preservation, pre-cybernetic mechanical foes such as 1950s robots are biologically antiseptic: they don't dangle before us the rotten carcasses that we inhabit, and don't allow for the exploration of peeled-away levels of body tissue alongside the peeled-away levels of intellect and consciousness. The obstinate corporeality of zombies audaciously flaunts what Joseph Campbell has called "the fullness of that pushing ... malodorous, carnivorous, lecherous fever which is the very nature of the organic cell" (121).

I have tried to cover full-length zombie feature films as exhaustively as possible, as well as TV movies and (when available) significant episodes of TV serials. Movies explicitly advertising "zombies" in the original title, alternate title, or in an English-language release title are also included, even when the term is applied with the most wanton license and the film has nothing to do with actual zombies, so that the work can serve effectively as a reference tool. The history of the term "zombie" and the evolution of its meaning through different generations is itself telling and worthy of documentation.

As the zombie mania trickled down into backyard film operations in the late '80s and early '90s, a profusion of very low-budget films appeared, including videographed features and film school projects, many of which are virtually (and mercifully) unobtainable. This book includes those that have come to my attention; doubtless there are others.

The list of titles is compiled from horror movie guide books, articles and reviews, video catalogues, on-line databases and fan sites, and consultation with other zombie hounds. Only movies that I have been able to track down and see are included, to ensure that a consistent, personal reading of the genre as a whole emerges. Literal English translations of titles are provided for foreign movies that have never been dubbed or subtitled into English; otherwise movies are listed by their most commonly recognized English language title. (An exception is *La Cage Aux Zombies*; to render this title in English is to lose the obvious reference to the popular cross-dressing comedy *La Cage Aux Folles*.)

The Films

A comme apocalypse see *A Virgin Among the Living Dead*

Absurd see *Zombie 6: Monster Hunter*

After Death

Dir: Claudio Fragasso. *Story and Screenplay*: Rossella Druddi. *Cast*: Chuck Peyton, Candice Daly, Alex McBride, Jim Gaines, Don Wilson, Adrianne Joseph. Flora Film (Italy), 1988.

Long after the main flood of Italian zombie movies had dissipated in the early '80s, Flora Film continued to crank them out. This Philippines-shot outing presents atmospheric zombies in authentic jungle settings, supported by up-beat synthesizer scoring and a high body count of both zombies and humans. Fun-seekers marooned on a desert island confront the living-dead remnants of the island's population, which was long ago wiped out by an epidemic. Barricading themselves in the old hospital, the group dwindles in numbers as bitten characters join the swelling undead army. At last, Jenny (Daly), one of the two survivors, discovers through some suspect "Book of the Dead" that she can close the gate of hell by relinquishing her own soul. The mournful cries of wailing souls echo throughout the jungle, but inept choreography of close-combat scenes and inconsistent treatment of zombies undercut the elegant atmosphere.

The dead natives who crawl from their shallow graves to feast on the flesh of the living all wear black cloaks with hoods, which give them an ominous homogeneity of appearance, almost like an order of monks. They have the standard issue splotchy skin, drip with the requisite gore, and follow the usual specs (only deanimated by destroying the head, etc.). In certain scenes they're slow as cold molasses: in fact, whenever certain ritual candles are lit, they come to a stop altogether (until one enterprising zombie finally knocks the candle table over). In other scenes, though, they leap and tumble stealthily, the black-cloaked figures amounting to a veritable ninja army. Characters who are bitten and who rise as undead retain more human characteristics than the inscrutable zombie natives. Thus they wield guns and speak, even taunting their former friends: "Don't you want to be like us?" The zombie "Bub" delighted audiences in 1985 by lethargically wielding a revolver in *Day of the Dead*, but he wouldn't last a round against these character zombies packing M-16 assault rifles.

Alternate title: *Zombie 4: After Death*.

L'Aldilà see ***The Beyond***

The Alien Dead

Dir: Fred Olen Ray. *Prod*: Chuck Sumner, Fred Olen Ray. *Screenplay*: Fred Olen Ray, Martin Alan Nicholas. *Cast*: Buster Crabbe, Raymond Roberts, Linda Lewis, Mike Bonavia, George Kelsey, Dennis Underwood, Ellena Contello. Firebird Pictures, 1980.

Fred Olen Ray somehow cajoled doddering Buster Crabbe (the original Flash Gordon) in his declining years to appear in this backwoods Florida fiasco. A sparkling, flaming red meteorite lands in the swamps, destroying a houseboat and transforming the partiers onboard into zombies. Uninteresting reporter Tom (Roberts) teams up with dull local woman Shawn (Lewis) to uncover the mystery behind the recent murders and disappearances plaguing the area, which cranky Sheriff Kowalski (Crabbe) attributes to "gators." A slightly off-beat and promising opening scene soon gives way to serious tedium; everyone runs around pointlessly, periodically falling prey to the aquatic swamp zombies. The sound and film quality of the low-budget affair may be excusable, but the acting, make-up, and affected Southern accents are ordeals. The most advanced gore effect is a small trickle of blood that pours from the victims' mouths.

Some of the zombies are only pale-faced, dark-eyed figures, while others have completely oozing, blackened, mutated heads. But their clothes are suspiciously clean, and some parade around disingenuously in bleached white shirts and shorts that look pressed (and look for the zombie with perfect hair and his shirt neatly tucked into his pants). They tend to travel in packs, usually walking with slow, studied steps.

They're clearly supposed to be tearing and biting at their victims, but manifestly the actors are only pushing and nudging their fellow actors half-heartedly. There's only one faint hint of intelligence: in a tour de force of cooperative strategy and communication, one zombie who spots a victim points him out to his chums.

Most remarkably, these zombies are fully amphibious: they navigate under water and drag swimmers down, and leap out of the water to snag people from boats. Somewhat reminiscent of *Shock Waves*, there's a scene in which two of them slowly raise their heads above the water's surface in sync, and then lower them again at the same time. Though there aren't any underwater combat scenes, there are numerous glimpses of the fiends prowling around underwater, trailing some sort of swamp-weed. Coming at the height of the zombie invasion craze, these tepid zombies are a decidedly sad contribution to the genre. You and a few friends could probably put together something better than this sorry lot in, say, the next few hours.

Alternate titles: *It Fell from the Sky*, *Swamp of the Blood Leeches*.

Almost Human see ***Shock Waves***

Among the Living Dead see ***A Virgin Among the Living Dead***

And You'll Live in Terror! The Beyond see ***The Beyond***

Anthropophagus II see ***Zombie 6: Monster Hunter***

Apocalipsis canibal see ***Night of the Zombies***

The Astro-Zombies

Dir: Ted V. Mikels. *Prod*: Ted V. Mikels. *Screenplay*: Ted Mikels, Wayne Rogers. *Cast*: John Carradine, Wendell Corey, Tom Pace, Joan Patrick, Tura Satana, Rafael Campos, Joseph Hoover, Victor Izay, William Bagdad, Vincent Barbi. RAM Ltd., 1968.

This action-lacked goulash of horror, science-fiction, and spy film elements revolves about three factions: mad scientist DeMarco (Carradine) with his stooped assistant, a foreign spy team (Satana, Campos) out to obtain his discovery, and a bunch of morons from the CIA (Corey, Pace) trying to stop them. What DeMarco has discovered is a method of wiping the human brain clear of all emotions, leaving a pure "calculating machine." The deceased cells are reactivated electronically, and thought waves are transmitted by remote—thus creating the perfectly obedient servant. The skin and most vital organs are also replaced by synthetic parts for greater endurance and performance. DeMarco has already built a prototype, and sends the creature out on forays to mine for fresh organs in the bodies of hapless victims. After much running around, everybody kills everybody else in the climactic confrontation, except for the CIA clods who survive and close with a Captain Kirk–like sermon to the effect that DeMarco couldn't entirely quench the basic element of human life: the emotions. Mikels churned out flimsy movies like this for next to nothing, mostly releasing them in the deep South to fill out triple bills. At least executive producer and co-writer Wayne Rogers would go on to better things, as Trapper on *M*A*S*H.*

The mostly-synthetic Astro-men are equipped with skull-face masks, for no apparent reason other than shock value. The only working prototype is accompanied on-screen by a heavy heartbeat sound, and lurks in dark corners waiting for victims. He strangles one victim, but his preferred M.O. is to hack repeatedly with whatever sharp object is at hand. He is speedy, mentally alert, and resourceful. Particularly, when the solar power storage-cell is torn from his forehead, and he requires light to avoid running out of power, he quickly grabs a flashlight and runs back to the scientist's laboratory, holding it over the receptor-spot on his forehead the entire time. It's hard to take a mutant cybernetic robot-fiend seriously when he runs around holding a flashlight to his forehead. The Astro-zombie is impervious to bullets, however, and doesn't even bleed, thanks to a special instantly-coagulating synthetic blood replacement DeMarco has also created (he seems to have gone to the same eclectic educational institution as the Professor from *Gilligan's Island*). At the end he loses control and goes on the predictable killing rampage, until DeMarco deactivates him from a central control unit. A second Astro-man is activated at the last minute, just long enough to kill a villain and accidentally electrocute himself. Mad scientists will presumably have an easier time taking over the world when they finally develop robots or zombies that, at the very least, refrain from killing them.

Alternate title: *Space Zombies.*

El Ataque de los muertos sin ojos see ***Return of the Evil Dead***

The Atomic Brain see ***Monstrosity***

Attack of the Blind Dead see ***Return of the Evil Dead***

Attack of the Eyeless Dead see ***Return of the Evil Dead***

Baron Blood

(Orig. *Gli orrori del castello di Norimberga*). *Dir:* Mario Bava. *Prod:* Alfred Leone. *Story and Screenplay:* Vincent Forte. *Cast:* Joseph Cotten, Elke Sommer, Massimo Girotti, Rada Rassimov, Antonio Cantafora, Humi Raho, Alan Collins, Dieter Tressler. Euro International Films/Dieter Geissler/Leone International Production (Italy, West Germany), 1972.

Peter (Cantafora) travels to Austria to visit his ancient ancestral castle, and accidentally resurrects cruel Baron von Kleist (Cotten). Art restorer Eva (Sommer) raises the corpses of the Baron's bloody, mutilated torture victims, who crowd around him at the climax and subject him to his own instruments of pain. They're only on-screen for a minute or two, and Mario Bava—the grandfather of Italian horror—doesn't quite get in on the Italian zombie racket.

Alternate titles: *The Blood Baron*, *Chamber of Tortures*, *The Thirst of Baron Blood*, *The Torture Chamber of Baron Blood.*

Beverly Hills Bodysnatchers

Dir: Jon Mostow. *Prod*: P.K. Simonds, Jr., Jon Mostow. *Screenplay*: P.K. Simonds, Jr. *Story*: Jon Mostow, P.K. Simonds, Jr. *Cast*: Vic Tayback, Frank Gorshin, Art Metrano, Rodney Eastman, Warren Selko, Seth Jaffe. Busybody Productions, 1989.

Out-of-work surfer brats Vincent (Selko) and Freddie (Eastman) can't pay their debts, so their "Uncle" Vito (Metrano), a mafioso, forces them to work at the Eternal Palms Mortuary. (No contrived premise here.) There they team up with funeral home directors Lou (Tayback) and Doc (Gorshin), who are secretly perfecting an enzyme that reactivates neurotransmission in deceased tissue. They have only had partial success so far, bringing back corpses as mindless simpletons. Things turn zany when they unwittingly bring back choleric mafia kingpin Don Carlo (Jaffe) and when Doc himself dies and comes back at half-capacity. When Doc finally perfects the serum that restores perfect mental faculties, the entire cast becomes rich and famous for conquering death, and they resurrect Elvis and Napoleon to hang out with them at the pool. Slick production values don't save the movie from its mediocre script and assembly line plot-twists, though Generation X–ers may get a kick out of seeing Mel from "Alice" (Vic Tayback) look stressed and yell at people one last time, even sans spatula.

Before Doc perfects his serum, the reanimated corpses exhibit only the most primitive motor skills, and next to no signs of intelligence. The simple coordination and aptitude tests they are given reveal some promise—they can at least walk a treadmill and place a peg in the correctly shaped hole (well, after trying to eat it). Though docile and listless, they occasionally show some curiosity and object play as well: a certain zombie plays with his spaghetti like a one-year-old, for instance, and then tries to stick his knife in his nose. At least these isolated zombie gags provide a couple of good moments, and it's admittedly diverting to watch the half-revived zombie Doc try to mix chemicals and consult his notes with wildly unresponsive motor skills.

The Beyond

(Orig. *...E tu vivrai nel terrore! L'aldilà*). *Dir*: Lucio Fulci. *Prod*: Fabrizio de Angelis. *Screenplay*: Dardano Sacchetti, Giorgio Marluzzo, Lucio Fulci. *Story*: Dardano Sacchetti. *Cast*: Katherine MacColl, David Warbeck, Sarah Keller, Antoine Saint John, Veronica Lazar. Fulvia Film (Italy), 1981.

Fulci's third zombie foray (following *Zombie* and *Gates of Hell*), a dark and lyric atmosphere-piece, is the most artistic, if not the most exciting, of Fulci's series. Liza (MacColl) comes to New Orleans from New York to renovate an old hotel she has just inherited, but a plumber accidentally breaches the ancient gateway to the underworld on which the hotel is built. With the help of a supportive but skeptical doctor (Warbeck), Liza struggles to cope with the zombies that pour from the ruptured portal to hell. At last the two wander unstrategically into the cursed gateway themselves, and the closing scene finds them tentatively entering the bleak, grey wasteland to face (as the narrator explains) the sea of darkness and all that may be explored therein. With sharp cinematography, the film relies largely on sound, color, and composition rather than dialogue or plot. There are numerous successful horror scenes, such as a little girl watching while acid pours on her dead mother's face from a jar above (and then having to avoid the frothy acid-flesh goop that subsequently spreads across the floor), and a paralyzed man watching helplessly and wide-eyed as his own face is eaten by tarantulas. The narrative coherence is repeatedly distorted for surreal effect, but Fabio Frizzi's score, alternately nostalgic and grandiose, helps connect the disparate scenes and images into a unified, dream-like vision. Nonetheless, slow-paced and heavily burdened with its recurring, poorly explained images, *The Beyond* suffocates under the weight of its own grandeur.

The zombies in the hotel behave differently from those in a nearby hospital. Very ancient and badly damaged, the hotel zombies are corrupt in the extreme. They are more like ghosts than zombies in their nebulousness and caprice, appearing only when a character is alone, and retreating mysteriously after a single, conscientiously planned encounter. In one memorable scene, these zombies assume an unparalleled, sinister dignity when they surround blind Emily (Keller), staring at her while she screams for mercy—not advancing or attacking, just staring.

The zombies in the hospital, by contrast, don't make mysterious entrances and exits, but are resolutely physical. Too recently dead to be decomposed, they mill about the white, sterile corridors in their hospital gowns with downcast expressions. They are painfully slow—in fact, often they don't so much advance as sway gently back and forth from foot to foot (the Templars would be proud). Though the build-up is far more deliberate and polished than that of Fulci's other zombie movies, on the whole he doesn't do much interesting with his zombies once he gets them on-screen. The hotel zombies are employed for a few elegant visual shots, while the hospital zombies are just there for target practice.

Alternate titles: *And You'll Live in Terror! The Beyond*, *L'aldilà*, *Seven Doors of Death*.

Beyond the Living Dead see ***Return of the Zombies***

Biohazard see ***Warning Sign***

Black Magic II see ***Revenge of the Zombies*** (1981)

Black Zombies see ***Demoni 3***

The Blind Dead see ***Tombs of the Blind Dead***

The Blood Baron see ***Baron Blood***

Bloodeaters see ***Toxic Zombies***

Bloodfeast of the Blind Dead see ***Night of the Seagulls***

Blood of Ghastly Horror

Dir: Al Adamson. *Prod*: Al Adamson. *Screenplay*: Dick Poston, Chris Martino. *Story*: Al Adamson, Samuel Sherman. *Cast*: John Carradine, Kent Taylor,

Tommy Kirk, Regina Carrol, Roy Morton, Tacey Robbins, Arne Warda, Richard Smedley. Hemisphere/Independent-International/TAL, 1971.

In 1969 Adamson reworked his own earlier film, *Psycho-a-Go-Go* (1965), to create *The Fiend with the Electronic Brain*, and then in 1971 reworked that to produce this patchwork confusion. Both times he extracted isolated sequences, and shot new scenes around them involving different characters and story lines. The result is a brisk-paced if scattered potpourri of hammy acting and beehive hair-dos. The composite film even yields *two* mad scientists. The first, Dr. Howard Vanard (Carradine, in distractingly oversized glasses), implants an experimental device into the brain of wounded Vietnam vet Joe Corey (Morton), turning him into a homicidal maniac. This plot appears in lengthy flashback sequences (the mind reels to think that these are probably the most exciting scenes from the earlier versions). Now, the second mad scientist, Joe's father Dr. Elton Corey (Taylor), attempts to track down and kill those responsible for his son's death, with the help of his disfigured zombie Akro (Smedley). Absolute chaos. Good luck sorting it all out. The opening credits announce that the feature is presented in enigmatic "Chill-O-Rama."

Dr. Corey, who supposedly learned the secrets of voodoo in the Caribbean, turns two people into zombies. Akro is meant to be a fairly gruesome zombie (if we overlook the sketchy make-up effects)—cadaverous, splotchy, and sore-covered—but this can't be from decomposition. It's an instantaneous effect of Corey's zombie-making potion, since Susan Vanard (Carrol), upon being given the potion, becomes similarly splotchy and zombie-like in only a matter of seconds. A stiff-limbed monster who strangles people, Akro obeys Dr. Corey's every command—at least until Corey unwisely drops in conversation his plan to cut off Akro's life-sustaining fluid. Akro breaks from his locked cell and strangles the doctor. He then collapses to the floor, pathetically trying to lick up the last few drops of the spilled vitality potion from the floor (recalling a great scene from the end of the 1940 *The Mummy's Hand*). Susan is a slightly more intelligent zombie, speaking a few words in a scratchy and uneven voice: "What's ... hap ... pened ... to ... me?" She completely returns to normal after taking an antidote, however. The entire zombie component of the film is tacked-on footage at the beginning and end, only thinly connected with (though far more interesting than) the intermediate plot. This woeful attempt on Adamson's part to salvage his docile and outdated '60s horror footage is not unlike Akro licking at the dregs of his zombie potion on the floor.

Alternate titles: *The Fiend with the Atomic Brain*, *The Fiend with the Synthetic Brain*, *The Man with the Synthetic Brain.*

Bloodsuckers from Outer Space

Dir: Glen Coburn. *Prod*: Rick Garlington. *Screenplay*: Glen Coburn. *Cast*: Thom Meyers, Laura Ellis, Dennis Letts. One-of-Those Productions, 1984.

Corny jokes and obvious visual gags officially launch the mid–'80s zombie spoof cycle in this primitive production—by all rights the whole trend should have fallen stillborn. An energy field from outer space, which economically manifests itself as a gust of wind, descends on a rural Texan farming town, turning all who inhale it into zombie-like bloodsucking mutants. Jeff (Meyers) and Julie (Ellis) try to elude the spreading menace while a paranoid military general (Letts) itches to nuke the entire area. The alien wind at last descends upon Jeff and Julie, but they're able to neutralize the effects by sniffing nitrous. The movie ends with a scene of everyday life in the fully-zombified town, where a bloodsucking mutant reads the paper, another remarks what a nice day it is, and children mutants play toss in the street. *Bloodsuckers* is a lot like the following year's *Return of the Living Dead*, except that it isn't funny or exciting. Best line: "When are you going to learn that art is shit?"

Only those who breathe in the alien wind become bloodsuckers; the condition isn't spread through bites or wounds. They can move quickly and stealthily when they want to, but more often they just lurch around, hunched over in an Igor–like manner. An anomalously civilized zombie gives a complicated speech in a lecture hall, claiming that a certain "intergalactic energy" is glad at last to have found a physical form in which to manifest itself, so that it can know time and death and finally come to an end. That's all well and good, but it's entirely askew with the coarse, animalistic zombies out in the streets, who rely entirely on shooting jets of blood and Gilligan-esque gags for their intended humor.

Bloodsucking Nazi Zombies see ***Oasis of the Zombies***

The Boneyard

Dir: James Cummins. *Prod*: Richard F. Brophy. *Screenplay*: James Cummins. *Cast*: Ed Nelson, Deborah Rose, James Eustermann, Denise Young, Norman

Fell, Phyllis Diller, Willie Stratford, Jr., Robert Yun Ju Ahn, Sallie Middleton Kaltreider, Janice Dever, Cindy Dollar-Smith. Backbone Productions, 1990.

In this energetic but directionless fiend-fest, Police Lieutenant Jersey Callum (Nelson) and his skeptical partner (Eustermann) recruit the reluctant aid of a burnt-out psychic (Rose) to help identify the bodies of three children whose apparent killer, mortuary owner Mr. Chen (Yun Ju Ahn), has turned himself in. Chen says that for three centuries his ancestors have fed the ghouls human flesh to keep the world safe from them. Lately the "kyoshi"—the demon children—have been getting restless, however, and since he has no wife or progeny to continue the line, he has come to the authorities out of desperation. Phyllis Diller appears as vitriolic Miss Poopinplatz, who becomes a towering monster with skanky, mottled skin and fake ping-pong ball eyes. Meanwhile her white poodle Floofsoms licks up some of the goop from a dead ghoul and turns into a humongous Poodle–zilla creature. The film has excellent acting (especially from leads Nelson and Rose) and a professional feel, capturing some of the spirit of *Re-Animator* and *Return of the Living Dead* while generally avoiding obvious shocks and surprises. The first hour, which has a serious tone, is engaging and thoughtful, but things just get silly as the genuinely creepy ghouls give way to the phony Poopinplatz creature and the comic poodle monster.

The ghoulish "kyoshi" gremlins (Kaltreider, Dever, Dollar-Smith) are superbly conceived and visually effective: they are hunched over, brutish, and naked, but so covered from head to toe with dirty, black, slimy skin that even their sexes are indistinguishable. They growl and gurgle, squatting contentedly over the cadavers they feast on; they even eat from the remains of each other. They move quickly and have nasty grips, attacking with their mouths or claw-like hands (one has a very long pinky finger with what for all the world appears to be a coke nail). Since the evil is centered in their hearts, destroying the chest is the only way to deanimate them. One of the twisted demon-goblins carries a nice doll with her.

Bowery at Midnight

Dir: Wallace Fox. *Prod*: Sam Katzman, Jack Dietz. *Screenplay*: Gerald Schnitzer. *Cast*: Bela Lugosi, Wanda McKay, John Archer, Lew Kelly, Tom Neal, Vince Barnett, Anna Hope. Monogram, 1942.

What it lacks in action, *Bowery at Midnight* tries to make up with increasingly improbable levels of plot complications. Bela Lugosi leads three lives—by day renowned psychologist Professor Brenner, by night the manager of the charitable New York "Bowery Friendly Mission," and somewhere in between, the loving husband of a wife who wonders why he's never around. Furthermore, the mission is only a front for Brenner's underground crime racket. His hallmark is to leave the body of an accomplice at every crime site. It turns out that Brenner's live-in basement lackey "Doc" (Kelly), once a great doctor but now a snivelling derelict, has been reviving the corpses of Brenner's victims instead of burying them as instructed, and keeps them in a secret pit under a grave marked "Hilton." Psychology student Richard (Archer) and mission worker Judy (McKay) help the police uncover Brenner's operation. The horror is mild and quickly defused by the closing scene, in which Richard—after being killed and revived as a zombie earlier in the movie—is inexplicably healthy once again, laughing merrily with Judy. More of a cops and gangsters movie than a horror piece, *Bowery* is just spunky and unpredictable enough to sustain interest.

There are only two brief scenes in which the revived corpses enter the story line; villain Brenner doesn't even know of their existence until his final seconds. In the first scene Doc opens the fake grave that covers the dark pit, telling them that it's feeding time, and promising them a new companion (Brenner has just killed another assistant). Looking a little scruffy and disheveled, the restless stiffs gather expectantly around the ladder, and start to climb it until Doc closes the trap on them. Then we don't see them again until the climax, when they crowd around Brenner himself and violently drag him off-screen to kill him in some unspeakable manner. Though the word never comes up, these revived bodies are clearly zombies—inarticulate, minimally aware of their surroundings, incapable of resistance or expression, slowly shuffling around in the dark. Set in Manhattan, *Bowery* is the first movie to place zombies in a domestic rather than a tropical island location.

Bracula—The Terror of the Living Dead see ***Return of the Zombies***

Braindead see ***Dead Alive***

Breakfast at the Manchester Morgue see ***Let Sleeping Corpses Lie***

Bride of Re-Animator

Dir: Brian Yuzna. *Prod*: Brian Yuzna. *Screenplay*: Woody Keith, Rick Fry. *Cast*: Jeffrey Combs, Bruce Abbott, Claude Earl Jones, Fabiana Udenio, David Gale, Kathleen Kinmont, Mel Stewart. Wildstreet Pictures, 1991.

The *Re-Animator* team is back to peddle a pointless and forgettable sequel to their 1985 classic, but without director Stuart Gordon—Brian Yuzna (who produced the original) takes the helm this time. Eight months after the events of the first movie, West (Combs) and Dan (Abbott) are back at their old experiments, despite the fact that West died at the end of the original. Not content merely to revive the dead, West now aspires to create new life altogether by stitching body parts together. Meanwhile the disembodied head of Carl Hill (Gale) turns up again, acquires bat wings, and summons the aid of another army of maimed cadavers to seek vengeance on his old nemesis. In the over-burdened climax, Dan and West's patchwork creation is unhappy with her restored life and pulls out her own heart, while the protagonists are attacked by Hill's zombies and a host of other Clive Barker–inspired anatomical abominations from West's reject room. The pedestrian script sidesteps the most interesting questions, leaving the fragments of scientific and philosophical insight as unconnected as West's monstrous offspring. Even West himself is less charismatic, his innocent self-indulgence and pointed sarcasm coming across more as belligerence this time around.

The created woman (who is supposed to be Megan from the first movie) falls in line with the standard Frankensteinian "Why did you bring me back just to make me a monster?" paradigm. None of the other reanimated cadavers—all under Hill's telepathic control—have any intrinsic drive or autonomy. Little of the first movie's zombie conceptualization is really expanded, except that when a cadaver begins to break through a door with a fireplace poker, West exclaims, "My god—they're using tools!" We've already been through all this with Romero's *Day of the Dead*, of course.

Alternative title: *Re-Animator II*.

Brides of Dr. Jekyll see ***Dr. Orloff's Monster***

El Buque maldito see ***Horror of the Zombies***

Burial Ground

(Orig. *Le notti del terrore*). *Dir*: Andrea Bianchi. *Prod*: Gabriele Crisanti. *Screenplay*: Piero Regnoli. *Cast*: Karin Well, Gian Luigi Chirizzi, Simone Mattioli, Antonietta Antinori, Roberto Caporali, Peter Bark, Maria Angela Giordano. Esteban Cinematografica (Italy), 1980.

"The earth shall tremble ... graves shall open ... they shall come among the living messengers of death and there shall be the nights of terror."

Bianchi's contribution to the Italian zombie torrent is a high-impact, somber dirge that sustains tension mercilessly and wastes little time on plot and circumstance. A professor working in the cemetery grounds of a rural Italian estate raises the dead by means of ancient Etruscan magic, and becomes their first victim. A group of people without backgrounds or character development come to visit the estate for a vacation, but the undead hordes swarm them straight away, terrorizing them throughout the night and into the next day. A brotherhood of zombie monks joins the Etruscan crew to finish off the survivors. The gore is heavy, the violence untamed, and frustrations are augmented rather than relieved. *Burial Ground* is widely dismissed as a cheap clone of Fulci's *Zombie* (1979), but actually Bianchi succeeds not only in capturing but even enhancing many of *Zombie*'s strong points. Bizarre, cosmic synthesizer music accompanies the slow-motion invasion, which concentrates almost entirely on blocking and pacing. There is no moral—no anti-colonial or ecological subtext—only an abstract apocalypse, painted in earth-tones and black. Few zombie films attain such clarity of vision.

The blackened, skeletal zombies are soiled, worm-infested corpses similar to de Ossorio's zombie monks, except that these have no malign intelligence or ritual order. Some of the masks are lame, but there are also good dry, crumbling effects when their heads are smashed with rocks (make-up artist de Rossi also did effects for *Zombie*). The famous scene in which a zombie child bites off his mother's nipple is often cut from video releases. The zombies walk and move with almost painful torpor, every gesture taking a small eternity. In one scene, when a victim moves her leg out of a zombie's grasp, there's something perfectly sinister in the way he doesn't react but simply watches her pull away from him, without budging. So dull are this zombie's wits that, thrown off by his failure to grab the intended leg, he has effectively stopped altogether. Unparalleled in patience and relentlessness (except perhaps for de Ossorio's), these undead are exquisite.

Alternate titles: *Zombie 3, Zombie Horror.*

La Cage aux Zombies **see under** ***La***

Cannibal Virus see ***Night of the Zombies***

El Castillo de las momias de Guanajuato see ***Castle of the Mummies Guanajuato***

Castle of the Mummies of Guanajuato

(Orig. *El castillo de las momias de Guanajuato*). *Dir*: Tito Novaro. *Screenplay*: Rogelio Agrasánchez. *Cast*: Superzán, Blue Angel, Tinieblas, Zulma Faiad, Mara Salomé. Producciones Fílmicas Agrasánchez (Mexico), 1973.

The Mummies of Guanajuato was widely popular, and sequels had to follow. Forget everything about the first movie, except that it was funny in a painful sort of way and had some masked wrestlers. Forget Guanajuato, even—this was shot entirely in Guatemala. Now we meet glittery Superzán, Blue Angel, and Tinieblas, who tour the country without luggage in a VW minivan until running afoul of evil Dr. Donner. To supplement the shady dwarves in his employ, the superannuated doctor raises scraggly-haired zombies from the cemetery by means of black magic. The inept, creaky-limbed corpses claw their way out of their graves (through what must be half an inch of loose straw) to abduct and torture locals, as part of Donner's occult experiments to find the secret of eternal youth. Controlled by a silent whistle—like dogs—the ugly zombies slap feebly at the wrestling heroes for half the movie, at last turning to dust once Donner is destroyed. Only for diehard appreciators of Mexican wrestling movies and other shiny objects.

Cemeterio del terror see ***Zombie Apocalypse***

The Cemetery Man

(Orig. *Della morte, del'amore*). *Dir*: Michele Soavi. *Prod*: Tilde Corsi, Gianni Romoli, Michele Soavi. *Screenplay*: Gianni Romoli. *Original novel*: Tiziano Sclavi. *Cast*: Rupert Everett, Francois Hadji-Lazaro, Anna Falchi, Mickey Knox, Fabiana Formica, Clive Riche, Katja Anton, Stefano Masciarelli. Audifilm/Urania Film (France, Italy), 1994.

Picture a Beckett play, add sex and gore, and set it against a zombie-invasion backdrop. This French-Italian production combines the best of both traditions: quirky interpersonal dynamics and existential meditations from the French side, and sumptuous cinematography and primal zombies from the Italian. Francesco Dellamorte is the burnt-out, drop-dead handsome caretaker at the Buffalora cemetery, where impish blue will-o'-the-wisps dance in the night, and where the dead rise from their graves to seek the flesh of the living seven days after they're buried (sometimes a little sooner, sometimes a little later). Though he doesn't know why the phenomenon occurs, he doesn't care quite enough to report it to the authorities: "It's easier just to shoot them," he shrugs. Francesco and his simpleton friend Gnagi make a terrific pair of heroes as they search for meaning, perplexed at every turn by unmanageable relationships, remote and incompetent authorities, and the restless dead. The twisted vision of life and love is at first stylish, then turns increasingly campy, and at last crosses over into pure allegory. Soavi's tour de force is one of the more complex zombie movies, and one of the few that may speak to more than the normal exploitation audience.

The dead decompose quickly in the hot climate and are in bad shape by the time they return to the surface world—pock-marked, bluish, and covered with leaves and dirt from clawing their way out of the ground. Camp moments include a rebel biker zombie driving his motorcycle out of the grave (in an echo of the off-beat 1963 movie *Psychomania*), but the funniest zombie scene involves an entire Boy Scout troop going off a cliff in a bus and coming back en masse. Sometimes Francesco kills off a few locals who aren't dead yet, just to get ahead in his work. After accidentally killing a living person along with the intended zombie, he muses, "The living dead and the dying living are all the same, cut from the same cloth. But disposing of dead people is a public service, whereas you're in all sorts of trouble if you kill someone when they're still alive." Can't sort it all out? Neither can he.

Alternate title: *Demons '95*.

Chamber of Tortures see ***Baron Blood***

The Child

Dir: Robert Voskanian. *Prod*: Robert Dadashian. *Screenplay*: Ralph Lucas. *Cast*: Laurel Barnett, Rosalie Cole, Frank Janson, Richard Hanners, Ruth Ballen. Panorama Films, 1977.

Slow-paced but atmospheric, *The Child* domesticates the zombie apocalypse, portraying familial rather than societal tensions through the metaphor of the undead. Unsuspecting governess Alicianne (Barnett) comes to serve as substitute mother for creepy Rosalie (Cole), who exhibits strange telekinetic powers. Having no friends, the spoiled girl makes some (literally) in the cemetery next to the house: she animates corpses and goes out at night to play with them. As Rosalie's frustration grows, she has her "friends" eliminate people who displease her, including her father and the rest of the cast. The film offers a moody score and capable cinematography for such a low-budget effort. Though it's a little hampered by wooden acting, it nonetheless sustains an unmistakable, lingering charm.

It isn't clear whether Rosalie uses her powers to reanimate the spirits of the dead or simply moves their soulless bodies around telekinetically, but in general her undead chums seem to behave as autonomous agents. The bald cadavers are cruddy and earthen, with black, moldering clothes, loamy flesh, and long, Max Schreck–like claws, and on top of it all they take on a mournful bluish tint in the movie's budget lighting. They lurk about the forest behind the trees and in the bushes, feeding on local specimens of wildlife. The zombies don't speak, emote, or show any intellectual awareness, though strange calls are sometimes heard at night. They attack only with their claws and teeth, and can be easily deanimated by being stabbed in the neck or axed in the head, for instance. They're also unusually sensitive to noise, and the sound of a car horn continuously sounding drives them away holding their ears. These zombies are interesting mainly in their pet-like relationship with their animator, the innocent Rosalie, who draws schoolgirl sketches of her killings and brings the zombies litters of kittens to snack on.

Alternate titles: *Kill and Go Hide*, *Zombie Child.*

Children Shouldn't Play with Dead Things

Dir: Bob Clark. *Prod*: Bob Clark, Gary Coch. *Screenplay*: Benjamin Clark, Alan Ormsby. *Cast*: Alan Ormsby, Valerie Mamches, Jeffrey Gillen, Anya Ormsby, Paul Cronin, Jane Daly. Geneni/Brandywine/Motionarts, 1972.

Bob Clark and Alan Ormsby gained a minor cult following with this quirky labor of love. Egoistic and melodramatic director Alan (Ormsby) brings a group of his occult-curious actors to an island cemetery, where he spooks them with pre-planned pranks and stages a ceremony to raise the dead with a joke Satanic spell from his ancient

Druid grimoire. The grimoire turns out to be legitimate, of course, and the dead promptly rise from their graves to feast on the living. The movie becomes an encapsulated replay of *Night* from this point on: the group barricade themselves inside the house, board up the windows, and devise a plan to escape that fails tragically. There's even a catatonically unhelpful woman hovering at the periphery. Once all the characters are dead, a group of zombies board their boat and set off for the mainland. The suspense is poorly balanced: too much build-up prevents the actual zombie sequence from mounting adequate suspense of its own, while the killings come late and rapidly. The attempts at humor fizzle, but the movie flaunts an eccentric audacity that keeps it from becoming predictable. Unquestionably the scariest thing about it all is Alan's pants. Best line: "The dead are losers."

These surprisingly convincing ghouls aren't your glassy-eyed blank starers; they're savages. Clearly they're trying too much to be zombie-like, though, grasping exaggeratedly with arms outstretched. There's no evidence that their victims rise again, and at least one of them would certainly have had time to. On the other hand, their intelligence is hard to determine: they don't use tools, but one figures out how to climb on a roof to get in through a second-story window. Even more impressively, they calmly board a boat and take off from the marina—thus they at least know how to untie the mooring, and are clearly seen working at the riggings. Of course, these undead aren't autonomous agents but are driven by the powers of Satan. The lighthearted tone of the first hour disappears altogether for the closing zombie assault sequence, which is played seriously.

Alternate title: *Revenge of the Living Dead.*

The Chilling

Dir: Deland Nuse, Jack A. Sunseri. *Prod*: Jack A. Sunseri. *Screenplay*: Jack A. Sunseri. *Cast*: Linda Blair, Dan Haggerty, Troy Donahue, Jack A. de Rieux, Ron Vincent, John Flanagan, Michael Jacobs. Trans-Bay Pictures, 1989.

All is not well at Universal Cryogenic Labs, Inc., in Kansas City, Missouri, where bodies are kept frozen for possible future resuscitation pending technological breakthroughs. For one thing, corrupt president Dr. Miller (Donahue) is actually selling his subjects' organs on the black market; and for another, direct bolts of lightning strike the body storage cannisters and cause the dead occupants to burst out as savage zombies. On hand are security guard Vince (Haggerty, star of *Grizzly Adams*) and customer relations agent Mary (Blair, famous for her possession in *The Exorcist*). The zombie "cryonoids" run around killing and eating the servicemen and other unlucky after-hours visitors at the plant, until Vince discovers that cooling them keeps them at bay. He douses them with liquid nitrogen. The end sequence relates, "Vince retired to the mountains of Colorado with Luke, the dog, and his pet bear." The film is belabored and obvious, but it's not every day you see Grizzly Adams fend off a horde of zombies with a forklift.

The cannibal cryonoids go around wearing the silver foil body suits in which they were initially frozen. Their black, shrivelled bodies reflect a variety of hideous deaths and reveal the half-hearted nature of their preservation, rendered even more unsightly by the charring they suffered from the lightning. They don't speak or show signs of intelligence, but at the end they put Miller in a cryogenic cannister and operate the controls to freeze him. (Say, how do they know which buttons to push?) The freezing effect of liquid nitrogen slows them down, but actually they die in a variety of ways: burning, shotgun wounds, and falling onto pavement from a great height. Though they don't really do anything interesting, the cryonoids do look sharp with their glowing white eyes, wearing their sleek, TV dinner foil suits.

Chopper Chicks in Zombietown

Dir: Dan Hoskins. *Prod*: Maria Snyder. *Screenplay*: Dan Hoskins. *Cast*: Jamie Rose, Catherine Carlen, Lycia Naff, Vicki Frederick, Kristina Loggia, Gretchen Palmer, Nina Peterson, Whitney Reis, Ed Gale, Don Calfa. Chelsea Partners, 1989.

Leather-clad biker women called the "Cycle Sluts," led by Joan Jett–styled, whip-cracking Rox (Carlen), hit the small desert town of Zariah with a bad attitude and a host of appetites, but are soon the target of town mortician Ralph Willum's (Calfa) evil plans. Willum is reviving the dead by means of a battery implant in the head, and forcing them to dig for radioactive substances in an old mine. Though driven out of town by local citizens, the cycle women agree to help them fend off the zombie attack anyway. Ensuing antics include rescuing a besieged school bus full of blind orphans, and saving a baby by tossing it around and then out the window like a football. The bikers at last trap all the zombies in the town church and blow them up, using the blind orphans singing hymns for bait. The interesting camp free-for-all has strong gore effects, some fun moments, and a few good one-liners (with many more failed attempts), though on the whole it's forced and overdone. The few serious moments and moralizations are sadly out of place, and the derisive treatment of Bob the dwarf (Gale) is tasteless. The premise suggests interesting opportunities to explore gender roles and alternate sexualities, which are utterly passed over. Best line (son to zombie father): "Ah geez, Dad—look—maybe if you don't eat anybody, no one'll notice."

The zombies play it straight, but slapstick polka music and slide-whistles accompany their on-screen appearances, and everyone plays pranks on them. The mildewy departed crave flesh, though they aren't terribly picky: it doesn't have to be human or even living, and one clueless ghoul even tries to eat a hand grenade. The major inconsistency is the discrepancy between the zombie masses and character zombie Lucile (Reis), who has voracious sexual appetites for the living but doesn't hunger for them otherwise. The zombies can only be stopped by removing the battery in their brains—in other words, as usual, by destroying the head. After overrunning the town, the zombies engage in normal small-town activities for a brief period: one pushes along a rotary lawn mower, for instance, and a couple of good ol' undead boys in rocking chairs sip hooch. Though the movie's nothing special, more thought than usual admittedly goes into exploring zombie spoof possibilities.

Christina chez les morts vivants see ***A Virgin Among the Living Dead***

Christina, Princess of Eroticism see ***A Virgin Among the Living Dead***

Christina, princesse de l'érotisme see ***A Virgin Among the Living Dead***

Christina, Sex Princess see ***A Virgin Among the Living Dead***

Cinque tombe per un medium see ***Terror Creatures from the Grave***

City of the Dead see ***The Gates of Hell***

City of the Living Dead see ***The Gates of Hell***

City of the Walking Dead

(Orig. *Incubo sulla città contaminata*). *Dir*: Umberto Lenzi. *Prod*: Diego Alchimede, Luis Mendez. *Screenplay*: Piero Regnoli, Antonio Corti, José Luis Delgado. *Cast*: Hugo Stiglitz, Laura Trotter, Maria Rosaria Omaggio, Francisco Rabal, Mel Ferrer. Dialchi Films/Lotus International Film (Italy, Spain), 1980.

The veritable Waterloo of zombie cinema, this lamentable reel-stain is, at its best moments, a forced and pointless test of endurance. Squelchy lunatics suffering from radiation poisoning pour out of an airplane and storm a major urban center. News reporter Miller (Stiglitz) and love interest Anne flee from the rapidly spreading zombie catastrophe, eventually winding up in an undead-infested amusement park atop a roller coaster. The movie is essentially a lot of running around punctuated by occasional moralizing, while the gore effects and suspense sequences are trite to the point of insult. The best part is watching one of the major protagonists fall to her death, bouncing ignominiously through the beams of the roller coaster structure.

The mutant zombies are utterly unconvincing; some black goop applied to the face passes for make-up. The atomic radiation apparently attacks subjects' blood cells, such that they have to replenish their supply continually by drinking that of their victims. In a hospital, they even slurp directly from the blood plasma bags. The zombies generally don't kill with their hands or teeth, but employ a number of handy implements: chains, knives, axes, sickles, bars, and even a machine gun. Of course they target women's breasts, sometimes tearing away the shirt before stabbing or biting at the victim, and one cuts off a woman's nipple with a knife for no apparent reason. Unlike the standard late '70s to early '80s zombie fare, these zombies aren't slow or clumsy—they run, aim, jump, and all but perform on the uneven bars. They're also highly intelligent, cutting phone lines and driving cars, and one zombie artist is even found working on her sculpture. In fact, their concerted attack against media centers, power stations, and military installations bear all the marks of an organized urban assault. Ugly people in lounge suits with shoe polish on their faces running around in every direction hardly constitutes a proper zombie movie, however.

Alternate titles: *La invasión de los zombies atómicos*, *Invasion of the Atomic Zombies*, *Nightmare*, *Nightmare City*.

The Corpse Vanished see *Revenge of the Zombies* (1943)

Creature with the Atom Brain

Dir: Edward L. Cahn. *Screenplay*: Curt Siodmak. *Story*: Curt Siodmak. *Cast*: Richard Denning, Angela Stevens, Michael Granger, S. John Launer, Gregory Gay, Tristram Coffin. Columbia Pictures, 1955.

Cahn's fascinating mid–'50s science-fiction feature basks lovingly in the two miracle technologies of the period, electronics and nuclear power. Deported mob leader Frank Buchanan (Granger, with the help of reluctant German scientist Wilhelm Steig) raises the dead with atomic power and brain circuitry implants, sending them out as unstoppable assassins against those who originally had him convicted. Police Captain David Harris becomes a zombie and unwittingly leads the authorities back to Buchanan's hide-out. Domestic security is once again restored for the nuclear family, represented by Walker (Denning) and his Betty Crocker wife and daughter. Good '50s fun abounds, with all the twisted gender ideology and antiseptic social ideals that that implies, packed in a tightly-wrought action film with strong (if entertainingly dated) conceptual support.

Buchanan procures bodies from the morgue, and Steig reanimates them with brain implants after replacing their blood with a radioactive chemical composition (the resulting bodies are said to be "charged" with "atom rays"). The zombies' power source is a bar of radium that Dr. Steig keeps in a containment chamber but blithely waves around in his hand once in a while, when he wants to emphasize a point. The creatures all wear suits and ties, like good upstanding businessman zombies, though most have sutures across their foreheads from the brain surgery. They walk mechanically, staring straight ahead and keeping all movements to a bare minimum. From their laboratory, Buchanan and Steig can observe on a screen what the zombies see, via "light-sensitive implants" behind the eyes, and they direct the creatures' activities by speaking instructions into a microphone. The zombies don't even flinch when shot repeatedly, but continue following instructions so long as the brain isn't too damaged. Buchanan and Steig "feed" the creatures in the lab, as part of their daily routine, with radiation charging.

The brain is the first part of the body to die, while the rest of the body takes longer—this is why it's possible to raise the bodies without the minds. Steig can only keep his specimens going for a few days until they disintegrate, however. Although it's repeatedly insisted that the creatures have no awareness of anything, and that all former memories and personality are wiped out, they still seem to figure out certain things on their own, such as driving a car without being given any instructions more detailed than: "Now drive the car." The zombie creatures, in the midst of their climactic hand-to-hand melee against the army and police, all fall to the ground lifelessly when Walker destroys the computers in the lab.

Creature wears its anxieties on its sleeve. On the one hand, it betrays a studied avoidance of death: the Walkers go to great lengths to avoid letting their seven-year-old daughter know that such a thing as death exists, hiding newspapers and telling her that the deceased Harris, with whom she was close, "has to be away for awhile ... on business." On the other hand, the movie parades the mangled cadavers about almost with relish: sometimes they press their faces right up to the camera. The zombies here look meaner than those of '40s movies, and they're also white instead of African-American. As in *Invaders from Mars* (1953) or *Invasion of the Body Snatchers* (1956), the enemy is internalized: the "other" turns out to emerge from the very heart of the American workplace and home. Though the script is at pains to rationalize and sterilize the creatures, insisting in every possible way that they are not "us," the images on the screen plainly imply the opposite.

Creeps see *Night of the Creeps*

Creepshow

Dir: George A. Romero. *Prod*: Richard P. Rubinstein. *Screenplay*: Stephen King. *Cast*: Stephen King, Hal Holbrook, Adrienne Barbeau, Fritz Weaver, Leslie Nielsen, Carrie Nye, Viveca Lindfors, Ed Harris, Ted Danson, John Amplas, E.G. Marshall. Laurel Show/Warner Bros., 1982.

George Romero and Stephen King collaborate on a popular and spirited horror anthology, based on the eponymous comic book. In "Father's Day," a wealthy heiress (Lindfors) accidentally resurrects her father (Amplas) by spilling a bottle of Jim Beam on his grave. He goes around killing everyone on the estate in search of a Father's Day cake, at last settling for a victim's head on a platter. Forced and mechanical, this is the weakest of the five episodes.

The third segment, "Something to Tide You Over," is much

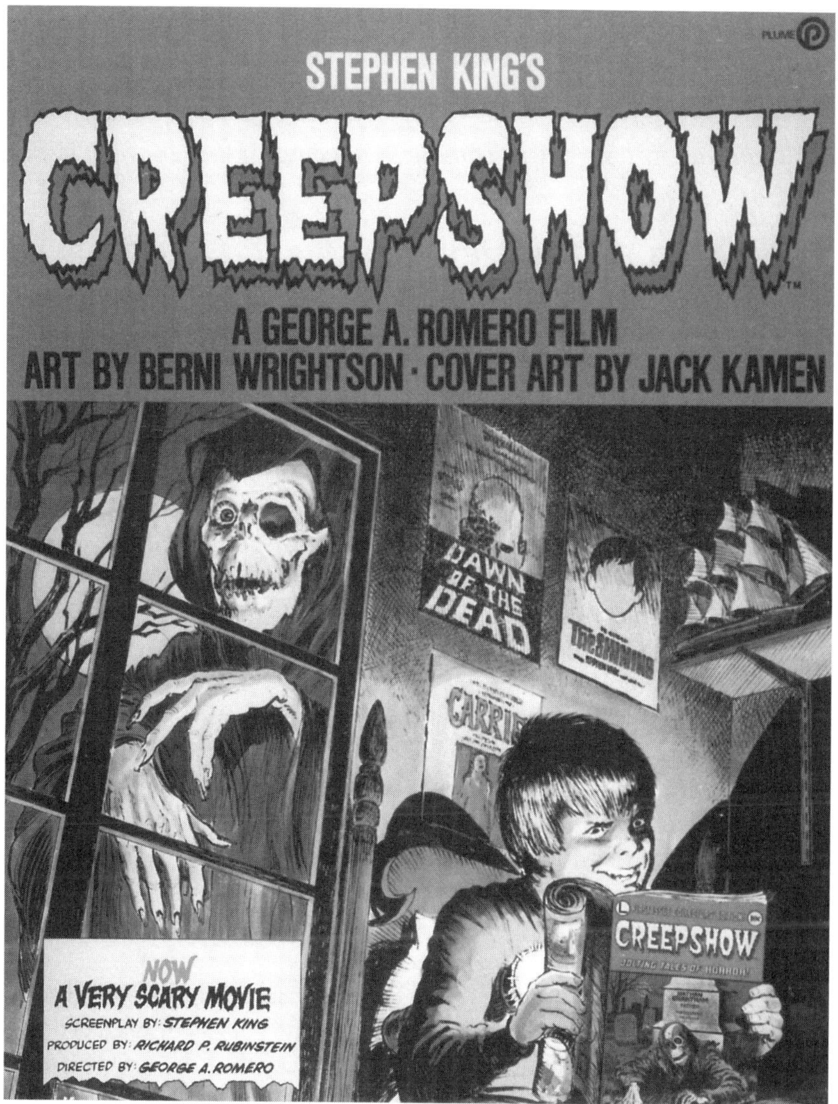

George Romero and Stephen King attempt to resurrect the waning horror anthology trend in 1982 with *Creepshow*.

zestier. Jealous husband Richard (Nielsen) buries wife Rebecca and her lover Harry (Danson) in the sand at his beach house, and videotapes them dying as the tide comes in. They return later as zombies—bluish white, with tightly drawn skin and bloated features, covered with seaweed. These water-logged undead speak with absurdly distorted voices that resound with a gurgling bubble effect, and are accompanied by haunting, echoing "Song of the Whale" sounds.

Crime of Voodoo see ***Ouanga***

Los Crímines de Usher see ***Zombie 5: Revenge of the House of Usher***

The Cross of the Devil

(Orig. *La cruz del diablo*) *Dir*: John Gilling. *Screenplay*: Juan José Porto, Jacinto Molina. *Cast*: Ramiro Oliveros, Carmen Sevilla, Adolfo Marsillac, Eduardo Fajaro, Emma Cohen, Mónica Randall. Bulnes (Spain), 1975.

Though ostensibly based on stories by Gustavo Adolfo Bécquer, this snoozy tale of murder and mysticism set in nineteenth-century Spain is more obviously modeled after the de Ossorio Templar monk series. Washed-up writer Alfred Dawson (Oliveros) travels from London to Spain to visit his sister Justine (Randall), only to find her dead. He charitably suspects everyone: Justine's husband Enrique (Fajaro), who looks vaguely like Lorne Greene; Enrique's sinister assistant César del Río (Marsillac), who may or may not be the devil; and evil Templar ghost monks from the Middle Ages. He at last arrives at the shunned Iron Cross at the foot of the Mountain of Souls, where he releases a trapped, immortal soul from a curse, only to be hauled off by the police. As the intricate details of an ancient and predestined drama unfold, Dawson has trouble sorting out reality from his prophetic dreams and hash stupors, and the movie watcher is no better off. A disappointing final film for ex–Hammer Studios director John Gilling (most famous for *Plague of the Zombies* and *The Reptile*), who moved to Spain in 1970.

The long-awaited zombie monks themselves only come out briefly at the end, emerging from the shadows in white robes with red crosses on the front. They are completely covered except for their dark skeletal faces, which are only barely glimpsed in passing. A few seconds of Gregorian chant and a tolling bell accompany their appearance. Though no one has yet fought the Templars and lived, somehow this drugged up, has-been writer easily defeats them with a few parries and thrusts. The flimsy Templar monk scene owes everything to de Ossorio save its lamentable lack of suspense or artistry.

La Cruz del diablo see ***The Cross of the Devil***

Crypt of the Blind Dead see ***Tombs of the Blind Dead***

Cult of the Damned see *The Snake People*

Curse of the Blue Lights

Dir: John Henry Johnson. *Prod*: John Henry Johnson. *Screenplay*: John Henry Johnson. *Story*: Bryan Sisson, John Henry Johnson. *Cast*: Clayton McCaw, Patrick Keller, Deborah DeVencenty, Becky Golladay, Brent Ritter, Marty Bechina, James Asbury, Bettina Julius, Kent Fritzell, Willard Hall. Tamarack Productions/Blue Lights Partners, 1988.

A bunch of meddling kids in rural Dudley stumble across Loath (Ritter), leader of the ghoul clan Kwa, and his ghoul minions (Fritzell, Hall). These trollish flesh-eaters attempt to fulfill an ancient ghoul prophecy by reincarnating a demon gargoyle. Under this Anti-Messiah, Loath and the ghouls hope to usher in a new era of darkness that will reign forever over humankind. But once he arrives the demon gargoyle doesn't particularly seem to know anything about any era of darkness—the first thing he does is to crush Loath's head. The limited budget effects and talentless acting cripple an atmosphere otherwise served well by close attention to lore.

The first zombie scene occurs in an old house, when two women stumble across the ghouls' larder of bodies. The peckish undead come after the squealing damsels, only to be fended off at the last moment by a ghoul with a whip. Then toward the end of the movie, Loath casts a dark spell to awaken all the dead in the cemetery for devastation-spreading purposes. The segment owes a lot to *Return of the Living Dead*, right down to a familiar police barricade scene. The zombies are unobjectionable, if conventional—certainly more interesting than the actors in the fake ghoul masks.

The Curse of the Doll People

(Orig. *Muñecos infernales*). *Dir*: Benito Alazraki. *Prod*: William Calderón Stell/Pedro Calderón, Guillermo Calderón. *Story and Screenplay*: Alfred (Abel) Salazar. *Cast*: Elvira Quintana, Ramón Gay, Robert G. Rivera, Quintin Bulnes, Alfonso Arnold. Cinematográfica Calderón (Mexico), 1960.

Unstoppable K. Gordon Murray, who imported Portillo's inestimable *Aztec Mummy* series, smuggles more Mexican horror over the border. After four tourists invoke the curse of a voodoo priest (Bulnes) by witnessing sacred rites in Haiti, oversized animated dolls (actually creepy-looking dwarfs in suits) begin stabbing them and their families. The priest, whose lair features a rotating disco ball, has a zombie named Sabud to deliver the dolls and perform various odd jobs. At last the heroine Karina (Quintana) and some others trace him to his hide-out, where they keep him and his evil minions at bay with a cross and then destroy them all with fire. Like Jerry Warren, K. Gordon Murray bought up cheap Mexican thrillers, picked out the murder or monster footage, shot extra English language scenes to ensure incoherence, and distributed the resulting abominations on the children's matinee circuit. Many of them are now notorious cult favorites, virtually unobtainable in the States except in these re-edited versions.

Sabud is the grim-looking, shriveled—almost mummified—zombie slave kept in an upright sarcophagus. He wears a wide-brimmed hat over his long, bedraggled hair and wears a black shirt, pants, and a belt. Since his soul has fled the body, he's obedient to the bitter end (one of the doll people, by contrast, retains sufficient autonomy to rebel against the priest). It's said that Sabud is afraid of fire because it represents the awful, eternal fate that awaits him in hell. Geez—what did he ever do?

Dark Eyes of the Zombie see ***Raptors***

Dawn of the Dead

Dir: George A. Romero. *Prod*: Richard Rubinstein. *Screenplay*: George A. Romero. *Cast*: David Emge, Ken Foree, Scott H. Reiniger, Gaylen Ross. Laurel Group/Dawn Associates, 1979.

Romero waited eleven years before making his sequel to *Night*, and just when it seemed the zombie craze had all but died out, he inaugurated a second one of even larger proportions with this thoughtful and entertaining social allegory. This zombie outing provides a radical contrast to *Night*, forsaking austere, black-and-white horror for a brightly-colored, gore-packed feature permeated with a wry, sardonic humor and tightly choreographed action sequences. Here the zombie epidemic has spread beyond control, and society is in the process of total collapse. Isolated groups band together to mount desperate stands. Traffic reporter Stephen (Emge), Fran (Ross), and SWAT team soldiers Peter (Foree) and Roger (Reiniger) flee in a helicopter, at last alighting on an abandoned shopping mall complex. Finding the mall still operative and filled with supplies, they manage

Passed-on patrons bargain shop for brains (and other morsels) in George Romero's influential *Dawn of the Dead* (1979).

to empty it of zombies and seal off the entrances. For a time they enjoy all the cornucopic comforts that the consumer wonderland can offer, struggling to build a self-contained, microcosmic civilization, before the neon Eden is finally penetrated by a band of traveling redneck bikers. The zombies enter and disperse themselves evenly throughout the mall once again, as though subject to laws of gaseous diffusion. *Dawn* avoids the usual sequel pitfalls by successfully exploring a new range of settings and extending the zombie mythos in intriguing ways. The movie was an immediate commercial success, especially in Europe, where it sparked off a host of imitations starting with Fulci's *Zombi 2*. In fact, *Dawn* represents a watershed in the evolution of horror film, linking the subdued strains of talky '70s domestic horror with the in-your-face, tongue-in-cheek action of '80s splatter.

Romero's living dead have evolved in appearance and behavior since the first movie. The restrained lethargy of the zombies in *Night* gives way to a stiffer, more apoplectic twitchiness in *Dawn*, and the undead are now decidedly more damaged and decayed. Tom Savini's dry-skinned zombies have an unmistakable sky-blue tint, matching the pastels of the mall decor. They are laudably slow and even-paced—the unforgettable Hare Krishna zombie takes half the movie to make it a few hundred yards. Tripping over each other and randomly riding up and down the escalators, these clueless ghouls are humorous as often as menacing. They even get pies and seltzer water in the face. But the humor is steeped in social commentary; Stephen surmises that the zombies are led to the mall by "some kind of instinct. Memory. What they used to do. This was an important place in their lives." Thus they go through the shadowy pantomime of their former lives, trudging past mirrors and store displays, picking up change in the fountains, and aimlessly batting a puck around with a hockey stick. The zombies are cleverly blended with the mannequins abounding in the mall, as well—thus the complex teems with glassy stares and detached limbs; human and plastic are one and the same.

Zombie fans are rewarded with fresh insights into the nature of the condition. A radio broadcast refers elliptically to "experiments with hallucinogens," and notes that "Scientists fear that the creatures function on a subconscious, instinctive level." One such scientist, the almost inhumanly rational Dr. Millard Rausch, states in a TV broadcast that the living dead have "seemingly little or no reasoning power, but basic skills remain—and more remembered behaviors from normal life.... These creatures are nothing but pure, motorized instinct." Furthermore, Rausch explains that the zombies only eat five percent or so of the food available in the human body—that's why the victim is still sufficiently intact, usually, to rise again and become a zombie. *Dawn* no longer refers to the revived corpses as "ghouls," the preferred term in *Night*. Consistent with the film's tendency to dehumanize the undead, the most common terms in *Dawn* are "creature" and "thing." But Peter, offering a spiritual interpretation of the apocalypse to counterbalance the scientific one filling the airwaves, suggests the term "zombie"—the only time the word appears in the trilogy.

Alternate titles: *Dawn of the Living Dead*, *Zombie*, *Zombies*.

Dawn of the Living Dead see ***Dawn of the Dead***

Dawn of the Mummy

Dir: Frank Agrama. *Prod*: Frank Agrama. *Screenplay*: Daria Price, Ronald Dobrin, Frank Agrama. *Story*: Ronald Dobrin, Daria Price. *Cast*: Brenda King, Barry Sattels, George Peck, John Salvo, Ibrahim Khan, Joan Levy,

Ellene Faison, Diane Beatty, Ali Gohar. Harmony Gold (U.S., Italy, Egypt), 1981.

A mummy-zombie invasion hybrid isn't a half-bad idea, unless it's burdened by predictable scripting and unremarkable acting, and backed by an incongruous slasher score (picture frenetic music accompanying low-speed mummy chases). A team of American models on a photo shoot in Egypt run into mad-as-a-hatter American grave robber Rick, who is in the process of plundering the tomb of cruel Pharaoh Seferaman. They decide to hold their shoot in the tomb, but the heat of the bright lights—combined with an ancient curse—reanimate the mummy. His "armies of the undead" (the ministers and slaves who were originally buried with him) rise shortly afterwards, and members of the photo expedition begin disappearing rapidly. The mummy and his cannibal undead army converge on the local village, spreading death and mayhem indiscriminately. The attempt to bring the mummy mythos up to contemporary horror expectations of violence and gore only has the effect here of robbing the mummy of his sober dignity, and of crippling the slasher conceit with a particularly lethargic murderer.

There is little interaction and no visible communication between Seferaman and his zombie minions. The bald zombie slaves emerge from the desert surrounding the tomb, blackened hands thrusting up through the sand. They stumble around in dirty shredded rags, their flesh swarthy and glistening. Though they first appear halfway through the movie, they really do nothing but stand around, concealed among the reeds and cacti of the oasis, until the invasion scene at the end. They enter the town unseen during a public wedding, and when the groom pulls aside a curtain during the ceremony, he finds a handful of them noshing on his bride. There are some nice shots of them climbing out of the sand and then walking across the dunes against a glorious desert sunrise, in a scene reminiscent of *Oasis of the Zombies*.

Day of the Dead

Dir: George A. Romero. *Prod*: Richard P. Rubinstein. *Screenplay*: George Romero. *Cast*: Lori Cardille, Terry Alexander, Joe Pilato, Richard Liberty, Jarlath Conroy, Antone DiLeo, Howard Sherman, G. Howard Klar, John Amplas. Laurel, 1985.

Romero's third zombie sortie, though the least popular, is in many

All walks of life stumble in death in George Romero's undead cross-section of America. Besieged protagonists wish the gate hadn't been left open in *Day of the Dead* (1985).

ways the most polished and sophisticated of the trilogy. Horror and action elements are eclipsed by explorations into the physiology and social psychology of the zombies, and into the interpersonal relations among humans. The zombie invasion that began in *Night* and spread uncontrollably in *Dawn* is all but complete, and *Day* focuses on a small handful of survivors who may be the only ones left in the world. A makeshift scientific outfit led by Sarah (Cardille) and Ted (Amplas) in an underground bunker in Florida attempts to research the zombie epidemic, while pressured for results by an unsympathetic military troop. Helicopter pilot John (Alexander) and radio operator McDermott (Conroy) try to stay out of the way, but are increasingly drawn into the quarrel as the new leader of the military outfit, Captain Rhodes (Pilato), tightens his despotic regime. On the fringes of all, the slightly psychotic but eminently likable Dr. Logan (Liberty) busies himself with experiments ranging from neurophysiology to behavioral conditioning. The film delves into the nature of civilization, encapsulating at the microcosmic level the inability of people to agree on even basic priorities and values. The abstruse inquisitiveness (and in the case of Logan, the inhumanly detached objectivity) of the scientific community fares no better than the brutish territoriality and aggression of the military one. Only McDermott, who likes to drink whiskey, and John, who likes to chill, make any sense amidst the chaos.

Here the zombies are juicier than ever, more vivacious and animalistic than in the earlier movies. They're never called "ghouls" or "zombies"—the scientists call them "beings" or "specimens," while the soldiers only refer to them with a wide range of rude invectives. Logan determines that the R-complex of the brain core—the prehistoric reptile brain—is what drives the ghouls even after the outer brain has completely eroded. A specimen could function up to 10 or 12 years, he speculates, before decay would threaten mobility. Quite simply, then, the brain begins to rot from the outside in, and the zombie, with increasingly reduced mental capacity, continues to function until the central core has wasted away. Logan tries to condition specimens through controlled positive reinforcement, achieving modest success with a promising pupil he calls "Bub" (Sherman), who exhibits unequivocal signs of learning and recollection from his former life. Presented with a series of objects, Bub tosses aside a toothbrush (it's probably a bit late for one anyway), but flips through a book curiously, and somewhat clumsily scrapes a razor across his face. He enjoys Beethoven's "Ode to Joy" on a Walkman, and Logan even teaches him to rasp into a phone, very dryly and imperfectly, "Hello, Aunt Alicia." Bub's moment of glory, however, comes at the end when the wryly charismatic zombie chases Captain Rhodes through the corridors at a pace that is fiendishly—almost knowingly—slow, leisurely picking away at him with a pistol.

Dead Alive

Dir: Peter Jackson. *Prod*: Jim Booth. *Screenplay*: Stephen Sinclair, Frances Walsh, Peter Jackson. *Cast*: Timothy Balme, Diana Peñalver, Elizabeth Moody, Ian Watkin, Stuart Devenie, Brenda Kendall, Jed Brophy. WingNut Films (New Zealand), 1992.

This absolutely over-the-top splatter opera from New Zealand by talented Kiwi director Jackson bristles with creativity. An evil Sumatran "rat-monkey" bites fussy Vera (Moody), the overprotective mother of clean-cut hero Lionel (Balme), turning her into a cannibal demon whose victims rise again as flesh-eating zombies. Aided by love interest Paquita (Peñalver), Lionel tries to keep the escalating epidemic at bay, finally confronting an entire houseful of infected

Resourceful "Uncle Les" (Ian Warkin) pauses for a break in the middle of a particularly moist zombie assault in the New Zealand splatter classic *Dead Alive* (1992).

party-goers. The gore makes *Evil Dead* look like *Brideshead Revisited*, but even in the comic book violence and fountains of blood there is nuance, as the movie takes pokes at countless slasher and splatter movies and abounds with inside references.

The demon zombies are some of the most visceral on record—gurgling, sputtering, and leaking unwholesome organic syrups from the seams. One zombie seated at table attempts to eat with a spoon, but inadvertently jams it into his mouth with too much force and runs it through the back of his head. Only dismemberment renders them powerless, and only complete pulverization or burning deanimates them altogether. Perhaps the movie's greatest contribution to zombie lore is its creative exploration of ways to messily maim and dismember them, including scissors, hedge clippers, a frying pan, chair, meat cleaver, lawn mower, and Cuisinart. Lionel is the *real* lawnmower man.

Alternate title: *Braindead.*

Dead and Buried

Dir: Gary A. Sherman. *Prod*: Ronald Shusett, Robert Fentress. *Screenplay*: Ronald Shusett, Dan O'Bannon. *Cast*: James Farentino, Melody Anderson, Jack Albertson, Dennis Redfield, Lisa Blount. Avco Embassy, 1981.

This unobjectionable suspense movie from Gary Sherman, whose first film was the outstanding *Raw Meat* (1972), is the story of a Mayberry gone awry. Out-of-towners are being murdered in Potter's Bluff, and sheriff Dan Gillis (Farentino) can't get the facts to add up. It turns out that most of the town are in fact dead (oops, sorry!), and local funeral home director Mr. Dobbs (Albertson) has revived them with the black arts ("satanism and voodooism") and reconstructed their skin with plastic surgery. The townspeople, who brutally kill strangers for community recreation, must come to him periodically to have their skin retouched. A *Rosemary's Baby*–style satanic conspiracy movie, this builds suspense effectively and plays its genuine twists well, so long as you don't ask too many questions of the everyone-is-in-on-it-but-one-person plot. Shusett reportedly paid O'Bannon to use his name as a co-writer, though O'Bannon never wound up contributing to the script.

A significant portion of the population of Potter's Bluff are Dobbs' custom-made zombies, all of them clinically dead. They are explicitly connected with the walking dead of voodoo lore, but as the schoolteacher tells her class, the popular conception of the zombie as slow and mindless is a myth. Dobbs explains that they have no memory but those he has implanted in them, though he's also given Dan's wife Janet (Anderson) emotions and passions, as a special favor to

Dan. The zombies are under Dobbs' control, but he doesn't require anything from them other than that they go about their normal lives. They never age or get sick, and enjoy an artificial beauty that Dobbs finds superior to transient, natural beauty. They only conform to the expectations of zombie behavior in a few isolated stalking contexts, and even then there is relish rather than emptiness in their expression. These aren't especially satisfying as zombies; they're simply good ol' small-town, undead citizens who happen to commit group murder once in a while.

The Dead Don't Die

Dir: Curtis Harrington. *Prod*: Henry Colman. *Teleplay*: Robert Bloch. *Cast*: George Hamilton, Linda Cristal, Ray Milland, Joan Blondell, Ralph Meeker, James McEachin, Reggie Nalder, Jerry Douglas. Douglas S. Cramer Productions, 1975.

Though tightly directed and well acted, this made-for-TV, '40s–style detective picture is an unlikely setting for post–Romero zombies. Only moments before innocent Ralph (Douglas) dies in the electric chair, his brother Don (Hamilton) promises to find out who framed him. He befriends schmoozy dance club owner Moss (Milland) as well as misty Vera (Cristal), who turns out to be a zombie. Don eventually learns that a crime kingpin called Varick is a voodoo master raising the dead in an effort to conquer the world. The horror of *The Dead Don't Die* doesn't come from its diluted zombies, but from human cruelty that is pointedly graphic for a TV movie. Some highlights include a drawn-out depiction of a man going to the electric chair, including the preliminary scalp shaving; and dance marathon competitors as haggard as those in *They Shoot Horses, Don't They?* (1969), who are no less Depression-era zombies than Varick's corpses. Scriptwriter Robert Bloch also wrote the novel *Psycho*.

Varick raises his army of the undead through the worship of Damballah Awede, the Haitian Lord of the Zombies, and controls them by remote with voodoo dolls. He hopes to rule the earth by placing his zombie puppets in international positions of power. Some have already established themselves in such positions, but most are still waiting in Varick's deep freeze. Generally the crusty undead walk slowly and evenly, and don't say anything, but rebellious Vera, who has managed to free herself from Varick's control to some extent, speaks perfectly normally and exhibits a full range of human emotions. Zombie Ralph also retains a certain degree of autonomy, since he rather predictably turns on his master at the climax. On the whole the movie offers a wide range of inconsistent zombie types and behaviors, introduced *ad hoc* to make each scene quirky and surprising, but not unified in a coherent zombie conceptualization.

Dead Heat

Dir: Mark Goldblatt. *Prod*: Michael Meltzer, David Helpern. *Screenplay*: Terry Black. *Cast*: Treat Williams, Joe Piscopo, Lindsay Frost, Darren McGavin, Vincent Price, Clare Kirkconnell. New World Entertainment, 1988.

In this flat action-comedy, two wisecracking Los Angeles cops, ladies' man Roger Mortis (Williams) and boorish partner Doug (Piscopo), stumble onto a case involving resurrected corpses committing crimes. Roger dies and is himself revived, but has only ten hours to solve the case with Doug before his cells deteriorate completely into goop. The two put a stop to Arthur P. Loudermilk's (Price) evil scheme to swindle rich folk out of their fortunes, but Doug dies and becomes a deteriorating zombie too. The pair walk out yukking it up, presumably to become goop over the next few hours and thus leave the entire cast dead. By the '80s, horror icon Price found himself in a number of embarrassing films (such as this one) beneath his talents, while ex-SNLer Piscopo is always this obnoxious. In one genuinely unnerving scene, though, all the dead animals and animal sections in a butcher shop come to life—the cold cuts, chicken parts, and hanging specimens writhing and twitching horribly.

Fresh corpses revived by Loudermilk's machine generally keep their memories and personality, but if the brain has been dead too long the subject only comes back as a complacent vegetable zombie. This explains why the revived protagonists retain some autonomy and personality, while the ugly decaying goons working for villain McNab (McGavin) are mindless thugs. The revived dead can't be deanimated with bullets, but that doesn't stop them from blasting away at each other with automatic weapons for minutes on end anyway. It's conceivable that shooting them in the head would work, but no one ever thinks to try it—didn't any of the characters ever see a Romero movie?

The Dead Next Door

Dir: J.R. Bookwalter. *Prod*: J.R. Bookwalter. *Screenplay*: J.R. Bookwalter. *Cast*: Peter Ferry, Bogdan "Don" Pecic, Michael Grossi, Jolie Jackunas, Robert Kokai, Floyd Ewing Jr., Roger Graham, Maria Markovic, Jon Killough, Michael Todd, Bill Morrison. Suburban Tempe Company/Amsco Studios, 1989.

Heavily indebted to a handful of zombie classics, most obviously *Day* and *Dawn*, and awash with other horror homages, this shoestring-budget ode to gore from independent filmmaker J.R. Bookwalter nonetheless offers some interesting variations on the usual themes. Five years after the unleashing of an experimental virus, zombies have all but taken over America. The population has been almost completely reduced to refugee survival in a landscape dominated by the restless ghouls, although there are still pro-zombie protesters who picket for zombie rights in Washington. Law enforcement agencies have mobilized "zombie squads," which drive around in special station wagons bearing Zombie Squad insignia, looking for survivors and clearing away pockets of the undead. Raimi (Ferry) and Kuller (Jackunas) travel to Akron with a special team to find the original formula for the virus in the hopes of synthesizing an antidote. The final scene is of Raimi—now a zombie himself—climbing into his patrol wagon, with the word "zombie" crossed out in "Zombie Squad" and the word "human" scrawled over it. The movie is tighter and more thoughtful than other backyard zombie efforts of the period (such as *Zombie Cop*), and Bookwalter's script interacts craftily with other zombie movies, but starchy acting and obvious production limitations plague the feature throughout. *Evil Dead* architect Sam Raimi helped finance the picture.

Dr. Moulsson (Pecic) fills in technical details about the rampant epidemic: it's a virus that feeds on the host, devouring living cells. Then when it runs out of these cells, and the virus is the only living thing in the body, it uses the host as a slave to procure more living cells as food—hence the zombies turn cannibalistic. If no food is available, the virus is forced to devour itself, at last completely consuming the host body in a month or so. Though the medical explanation for the epidemic is completely reconceptualized, the zombies follow those of Romero to the letter (seek human flesh, transmit the condition through wounds, and must be shot or hacked in the head to be deanimated). Moments of note include zombies being rounded up and led around with dog collars and muzzles, a zombie singing the "Star Spangled Banner," and a decapitated zombie head biting off someone's finger, only to have it pass out a moment later through its open, stumpy neck.

Dead of Night

Dir: Bob Clark. *Prod*: Bob Clark. *Screenplay*: Alan Ormsby. *Cast*: Richard Backus, John Marley, Lynn Carlin, Anya Ormsby, Henderson Forsythe, Jane Daly, Michael Mazes. Europix International/Impact Quadrant Films (Canada), 1972.

Clark and Ormsby follow up their *Children Shouldn't Play with Dead Things* with a mournful and nostalgic adaptation of "The Monkey's Paw." After being killed in Vietnam, irritable Andy Brooks (Backus), shows up back home to greet his grateful but bewildered family. He has no pulse or heart beat, and in fact he doesn't deny that he's dead—but he doesn't much like to talk about it either. He maintains an absolute minimum of surface courtesy and speaks sparingly, until his antisocial behavior deteriorates into violence and savagery. It slowly comes out that he also feeds on the blood of the living, which gives him a fix like heroin. He is so openly contemptuous of the "Happy Days" community in which he lives that he can barely trouble himself to cover up his murders. His family lapses into madness as he sits in his room all day long in the dark, staring blankly and rocking back and forth with sinister regularity. The final scene in which the decaying, unresponsive zombie is dragged along on a double date to a hamburger joint and a drive-in is perfectly delicious. There are some raw moments, especially a scene in which he strangles his dog with one hand in the air before a group of horrified children. Though not very lively and ultimately anti-climactic, the movie sustains a calculated mood of off-centered awkwardness from start to finish, and is buttressed by strong acting and plausible dialogue. *Dead of Night* was Tom Savini's first make-up assignment, as assistant to Ormsby.

Andy is half vampire, half zombie—he requires blood for sustenance, but otherwise stares blankly and feels nothing. Though he looks normal for most of the film, by the climax his eyes are blanched, his hands and face have turned, and his head starts dripping ooze as his girlfriend watches aghast. He is rational, however, and can generally reason enough to keep himself from getting caught (when he bothers).

In the final scene he heads for the graveyard and attempts to bury himself, apparently desiring to be at rest. Though several zombie movies have Vietnam War associations, this Canadian production offers the most explicit tie-in between zombies and post-traumatic stress disorder.

Alternate titles: *Deathdream*, *The Night Andy Came Home*, *Night Walk*, *The Veteran*.

Dead People see ***Messiah of Evil***

The Dead Pit

Dir: Brett Leonard. *Prod*: Gimel Everett. *Screenplay*: Brett Leonard, Gimel Everett. *Cast*: Cheryl Lawson, Danny Gochnauer, Steffen Gregory Foster, Jeremy Slate, Joan Bechtel, Geha Getz. Cornerstone Production, 1989.

Leonard's uninvolving psychological horror revels in shock effects and disrupted narrative logic, poured into the tried dreamworld and asylum settings of *Nightmare on Elm Street* and *Hellbound*. Twenty years after his death, ghostly doctor Colin Ramzi (Gochnauer) still haunts the insane asylum where he once performed gruesome experiments on patients. He especially targets amnesiac heroine Jane Doe (Lawson), who must team up with fellow inmate Christian (Foster) to combat the fiendish aggressor. The psychological horror-drama transforms into a zombie invasion movie for the final third, when Ramzi summons his formaldehyde-soaked patients from their mass grave (the "dead pit") to wreak vengeance on the living. Omnipresent Ramzi toys with his victim gloatingly while making clever wisecracks, thus coming across as a sort of Freddie Kruger or Dr. Channard, a villain-type that was pretty stale by the late '80s. Though cinematographically correct, this isn't very inspired in its handling of the familiar Tarr and Fether themes. Leonard and Everett went on to create the equally gimmicky *The Lawnmower Man* (1992). Best line: "The brain is a parasite."

Still wearing their hospital robes, the pale, wet, and bloody undead follow Ramzi's bidding and slaughter anyone they meet. Their frenzied twitching and jerking look more like neural fits than anything else. They kill by crushing the skull, since what they want is the brain—which, curiously enough, they don't eat, but simply sit around fondling and admiring with unfailing fascination. They are momentarily stunned by gunshots and blows to the head, but only one thing deanimates them permanently: holy water. This leads to perhaps the only innovative scene in the film, the grandiose climax in which a crazed nun (Getz) blesses an entire water tower, which is then toppled over with explosives such that the holy water drenches the entire army of undead.

The Dead That Walk see ***Zombies of Mora-Tau***

Deadly Friend

Dir: Wes Craven. *Prod*: Robert M. Sherman. *Screenplay*: Bruce Joel Rubin. *Original novel*: Diana Henstell. *Cast*: Matthew Laborteaux, Kristy Swanson, Michael Sharrett, Anne Twomey, Anne Ramsey, Richard Marcus. Warner Bros. (Pan Arts/Layton Production), 1986.

Wes Craven attempts to cross *Frankenstein* with *Short Circuit* and maybe half a dozen other movie types in this yawny genre-mongrel uniquely designed to fit no particular audience or mood. Brainiac Paul Conway (Laborteaux) resurrects sweetheart Samantha (Swanson), recently killed by her abusive father, by implanting the microprocessor from his annoying robot chum in her head. She spends the rest of the film looking clueless and killing off people she didn't like in life. The dumb surprise ending is no surprise, coming from shock-happy Craven. A screen presence like Herbert West of *Re-Animator* would be required to pull off the absurdities attempted here. Despite some horror elements and a strange basketball-related death, the movie still winds up feeling like an after-school special.

Though robot-zombie Sam follows some simple directions and reacts to situations, she never seems to understand any of them fully. She doesn't answer Paul, but does follow some of his simpler instructions. The main identity tension she struggles with isn't living vs. dead, but robot vs. human. In many ways she's simply an android: she opens a padlock by trying every possible combination in a matter of seconds, for instance, and the point-of-view shots showing her field of vision are digitally discretized (and not with very high resolution, either—she's like the Terminator with "Pong"-level technology). On the other hand, she obviously retains many of Sam's memories and former feelings, and nostalgically rubs a silky fabric against her cheek. At the end, the digitized robot-vision starts to give way to normal perception, as though her human personality is breaking through at last. Actually, this is all far more speculation than the movie really merits.

Undead Kristy Swanson doesn't appreciate being kept in her boyfriend's closet in Wes Craven's *Deadly Friend* (1986).

Death Corps see *Shock Waves*

Deathdream see *Dead of Night*

Della morte, del'amore see *The Cemetery Man*

Demoni 3

Dir: Umberto Lenzi. *Prod*: Giuseppe Gargiulo. *Screenplay*: Olga Pehar. *Cast*:

Keith Van Hoven, Joe Balogh, Sonia Curtis, Philip Murray, Juliana Texeira, Maria Alves. Filmakers (Italy), 1991.

Lenzi, guilty of *City of the Walking Dead* (1980), returns to the scene of the genre with a slightly more disciplined, if still not very exciting, Amazon zombie adventure. Taping folkloric music in Brazil, Jessica, Dick, and Kevin come face to face with the macumba black magic rampant among the African-Brazilian population. When their Jeep breaks down deep in the jungle, they find shelter at a nearby plantation that suffers from an ancient curse. It seems that six black slaves were executed there a hundred years earlier for trying to flee from their cruel master, and now they're back to slaughter six whites in return. At last Jessica and Kevin burn the predatory undead with Molotov cocktails. Though made in the '90s, Lenzi's Brazilian odyssey looks and feels fifteen years earlier. Highly charged tensions of race and class hover at the forefront, but the black African slaves are demonized in a largely unreflective manner (they don't even get their six white victims, after a hundred years of waiting). Despite the title, *Demoni 3* is utterly unrelated to the Argento–produced *Demoni* movies of Lamberto Bava.

Visually the shackled undead are among the finest in the tradition of African slave zombies (that is to say, they're vaguely better than those in the 1974 *Sugar Hill*). Their skin glistening with wet slime, they're still dressed in the white cotton work-clothes of the plantation fields, and drag around with them the remnants of chains and manacles. They hack at their victims with a host of farm implements, including a machete, knife, hook, hand-ax, and sickle. Their eyes are blank and white; occasionally there are disorienting scenes in which only the white eyes can be seen glowing in the darkness, like those of a jungle cat. They coordinate their nocturnal assaults carefully, waiting until characters are alone and then stealthily surrounding them. They lurk patiently in dark corners, and duck quickly behind things to avoid detection. Aside from these rather well-developed strategic skills, the macumba magic affords them some sort of intuitive resource allowing them to locate a specific victim even many miles away. Though conceptually rich, however, the zombies' screen presentation is undermined repeatedly by the posturing of the undead in artificial, stylized poses, holding their weapons out before them at unnatural angles, as though posing for a photographer. Actually, the slave zombies in *Sugar Hill* suffer from the same problem.

Alternate title: *Black Zombies*.

Demons '95 see ***The Cemetery Man***

El Desierto de los zombies, see ***Oasis of the Zombies***

Diabolical Dr. Voodoo see ***The Incredibly Strange Creatures Who Stopped Living and Became Mixed-Up Zombies***

Dial "Z" for Zombies

(Episode, *The Simpsons*). *Creator*: Matt Groening. *Story Editors*: Bill Oakley, Josh Weinstein, Dan McGrath. *Voices*: Dan Castellaneta, Julie Kavner, Nancy Cartwright, Yeardly Smith, Hank Azaria, Harry Shearer. 20th Century–Fox, 1992.

Matt Groening's *Simpsons*, which offered a welcome alternative to industry sit-coms in the early '90s and opened prime time to animation, features a zombie invasion as one of the three segments in the third Halloween special. Driven to the library by a class assignment, Bart finds a spell book in the hitherto-unnoticed "occult" section. He and Lisa attempt to raise their ex-pet cat Snowball I, but accidentally reanimate all the human corpses in the cemetery instead. Lisa yells "Zombies!" but Bart notes that they prefer to be called the "living impaired." The zombies spread and quickly take over Springfield, while our yellowish heroes make a break for the school library to retrieve the spell book. Finding the proper counter-spell, Bart sends the fiends back to their graves. As they stroll back to the graveyard the zombies chat politely: "See you in hell," and "Still pushing that boulder?" The final scene is a back-to-normal evening with the Simpsons in front of their TV, mindlessly grunting at some idiotic show that has them transfixed.

Following Romero, the zombies can be killed by destroying the head, and following *Return of the Living Dead*, they feast specifically on brains. Rational and somewhat articulate, they stumble around expressing this culinary preference: "Brains!" say they. There are cameos by an undead George Washington, Einstein, and Shakespeare, but the best zombie gag is when Homer turns on the car radio and finds the station has been taken over by zombies. The announcer identifies the station as "KZMB: all-zombie radio"—and then launches into the new format, which is the continuous sound of low-key groaning.

Doctor Blood's Coffin

Dir: Sidney J. Furie. *Prod*: George Fowler. *Screenplay*: Jerry Juran, James Kelly, Peter Miller. *Cast*: Kieron Moore, Hazel Court, Ian Hunter, Kenneth J. Warren, Paul Stockman. Caralan (England), 1960.

Though dated and watery in most respects, this British biomedical horror by Canadian director Furie offers the first glimpse of the modern screen zombie—decayed and violent, rather than simply pale and aloof. Medical student Peter Blood (Moore) returns from Vienna to his small hometown in Cornwall, where he is warmly received by his father Dr. Robert Blood (Hunter) and where he begins to court his father's nurse Linda (Court). Linda soon discovers that Peter is performing clandestine experiments on cadavers in the abandoned tin mines underneath a coastal castle, however. He injects people with the South American paralyzing poison curare, and then later removes the heart while the victim is still alive. By transplanting the living heart into a dead body he can return the corpse to life, thus hoping to revive great scientists and philosophers at the expense of useless commoners. Peter tries to impress Linda by resurrecting her husband Stephen (Stockman), several years dead—but Stephen only returns as a mindless zombie, attacking Linda and strangling Peter. The relentless action score tries to make the movie more exciting than it actually is. The neon hues of early color cinematography and some gorgeous coastal Cornish scenery help keep the production visually alluring, even as the characters conduct their clichéd adventure.

Stephen, the only revived corpse, is only on-screen for two minutes, at the movie's climax. He's horribly decomposed, with greenish, cracked skin, and some sort of unappetizing bright green moss growing all over his face in thin strips. Upon being revived he speaks the name "Linda," and thus seems to preserve his former identity, but when we next see him, standing around meditatively in the mine, he is entirely inscrutable. Linda objects that it's just the "physical shell" that Peter can revive, not the person, and indeed all Stephen does is attack the two indiscriminately. In the struggle, some chemicals are knocked over and a gas seeps out which deanimates him again. Though the dynamics of his mental faculties aren't really addressed, he is visually powerful—clearly new things are in the air for the screen zombie. Abandoned Cornish tin mines would again serve as the zombie setting in *The Plague of the Zombies* (1966).

Dr. Butcher, M.D.

(Orig. *La regina dei cannibali*). *Dir*: Marino Girolami. *Prod*: Gianfranco Couyoumdijan, Fabrizio de Angelis. *Screenplay*: Marino Girolami, Fabrizio de Angelis. *Cast*: Ian McCulloch, Alexandra Cole (Alexandra delli Colli), Sherry Buchanan, Peter O'Neal, Donald O'Brian. Flora Film/Fulvia Cinematografica/Gico Cinematografica (Italy), 1980.

Italian horror movies of the late '70s and early '80s are famous for zombies and cannibals; this shabby production offers an island populated by both. A rash of missing body parts and mutilated cadavers at various hospitals puts New York police on the track of ritual cannibalism. Police detective Peter Chandler (McCulloch, who also fought zombies in Fulci's *Zombie*) travels to a Southeast Asian archipelago in an ill-defined plan to investigate the suspected cult. There Chandler and friend Laurie (Colli) are welcomed by local mad scientist Dr. Abrero (O'Brian), stalked by savages, and spooked by the gruesome, disfigured zombies who stand about and wander aimlessly in the jungle. As with most Italian cannibal films, the savages are played by real natives, and presented with almost unpalatable realism. Some of the gore effects are quite good, but other than that the movie is a stock accumulation of familiar motifs. The North American release begins with a few minutes of added footage from an unrelated NYU project, and was immediately successful thanks to a vigorous advertising campaign.

The zombies are the by-products of Abrero's longevity experiments, the bodies left after he has removed the brains. They are sewn-up, patchwork rejects, who breathe like obscene phone callers and occasionally growl a little. Though mostly under the control of Abrero, they also exhibit faint flickers of internal impulse, which they act upon with evident difficulty. Though they never aspire to actions more complicated than grabbing at people, all in all even this is pretty impressive, considering their brains have been surgically removed. Three are deanimated during the course of the film: one is burned, another is hacked and eaten by the (undiscriminating) savages, and one has his head puréed by a portable outboard motor. The zombies' role in the movie is purely passive, since the cannibals are on hand to do all the killing.

Alternate titles: *The Island of the Last Zombies*, *Queen of the Cannibals*, *Zombi Holocaust*.

Dr. Jekyll's Mistress see ***Dr. Orloff's Monster***

Dr. Orloff's Monster

(Orig. *El secreto del Dr. Orloff*). *Dir*: Jesús Franco. *Screenplay*: Nick Frank, Jesús Franco. *Cast*: Agnes Spaak, Joseph Raven, Pearl Cristal, Patrick Long, Mike Arnold, Caniel Plumer, Hugo Blanco. Cooperativa Cinematográfica/Leo Films (Spain), 1964.

Though ostensibly a sequel to Franco's career-making *The Awful Dr. Orloff* (1962), this is actually a flavorless retelling with different actors. Suspicious Uncle Conrad and drunkard Aunt Ingrid welcome niece Melissa (Spaak) to their country estate, where she is surprised to find her long-dead father Andros (Blanco) going around killing local women. Conrad has raised him from the grave with ultrasonic waves, and kills women rather indirectly by giving them necklaces containing ultrasonic transmitters, which Andros then homes in on.

Brought back from the grave and controlled through sound waves, Andros is effectively Conrad's robot. He keeps a blank expression and has cracked, parchment-like skin. Despite the scientific rationale provided for the phenomenon (that his cells are merely animated in response to the ultrasonic impulses), he's not totally devoid of independent volition. He refuses to harm his daughter Melissa, for instance, and at one point he flees to the graveyard to ponder his own tomb with evident emotion. He exhibits superhuman strength, and is immune to bullets—except for one spot, the back of his head (and thus, curiously, he anticipates the head-vulnerability of Romero's zombies by several years). Otherwise, Andros is not particularly interesting, and certainly not frightening—especially in his turtleneck and evening jacket.

Franco's movies are generally either boring or deliberately offensive (blending violence and pornography), so at least this dreary feature is only boring.

Alternate titles: *Brides of Dr. Jekyll, Dr. Jekyll's Mistress, Mistresses of Dr. Jekyll, The Secret of Dr. Orloff.*

Dr. Satan vs. Black Magic

(Orig. *El Dr. Satán y la magia negra*). *Dir*: Rogelio A. González. *Cast*: Joaquín Cordero, Noe Murayama, Sonia Furio, Luz María Aguilar, Aurora Clavel. Bruckner (Mexico), 1967.

Virtually unknown in the States, this priceless camp thriller from Mexico comes complete with a vampire, rubber bats, zombie women in tight sweaters, and a cameo by a Doré–like Prince of Darkness. It's an epic battle between sorcerers. In one corner is Dr. Satan (Cordero), raised from oblivion by the devil to defeat a mortal enemy, with the promise of eternal rest if he's successful. In the other, East Asian Jay Lin (Murayama) is a vampire-sorcerer (hence "Black Magic"), who has stolen a formula to turn base metals into gold, which the devil also wants. Dr. Satan is the good guy—at least, more so than the insidious and inscrutable Jay Lin—but after numerous misadventures, the two nemeses destroy each other. The most delectable scenes are those in Dr. Satan's secret laboratory, where colored liquids bubble and smoke in assorted flasks, and cosmic vibraphone effects emanate from the electronic equipment. The weird sounds accompany not only mysterious events such as telekinesis, but even simple motions such as pushing buttons and mixing chemicals. Watch for mind-boggling script absurdities—such as the police sergeant opening a file, after the mysterious murder of a scientist, and finding in a report that Jay Lin was "due to rob" the scientist's formula.

Dr. Satan creates two zombie women by means of an injection, after which they obey his instructions unquestioningly. He keeps them in a pair of coffins, where they sleep with arms folded neatly across their chests. One works part-time as the receptionist in Dr. Satan's office. They don't look unusual, other than their lethargic manner and glassy stares, but they retain no memories from their lives. They do speak, however, calling Dr. Satan "my love" and politely asking him questions about his day. They suffer momentary shock from being stabbed in the back, but are basically invulnerable. The two walk together with steps in perfect sync. When Dr. Satan has no further need of them, they all tearfully say good-bye while violins play. They express affection and fear of being apart from him, but he assures them they will meet again in the land of shadows. Then they eat a pinch of dust he gives them, and vanish. Among the most primped zombies in the genre, the two zombettes wear colorful sweaters and perky torpedo bras—their miniskirts and sweaters even change from scene to scene. The best scene is vampire Jay Lin attempting to feed off the dormant zombies, but becoming instantly repulsed to find they are zombies after biting into their necks: "I'm going to be sick!"

El Dr. Satán y la magia negra see ***Dr. Satan vs. Black Magic***

Don't Go in the House

Dir: Joseph Ellison. *Prod*: Ellen Hammill. *Screenplay*: Joseph Ellison, Ellen Hammill, Joseph Masefield. *Story*: Joseph Masefield. *Cast*: Dan Grimaldi, Robert Osth, Ruth Dardick. Turbine Films, 1980.

Shy mama's boy Donny (Grimaldi) brings home unwitting women whom he strips and burns to death in a custom-made, aluminum-sided room. At last the charred corpses of his victims, which he keeps sitting around in chairs wearing pretty dresses, rise against him. Their blackened, hairless bodies form a grotesque contrast with the Ellie-Mae dresses they wear, as they walk slowly across the room toward him and gruffly utter pleasantries like "We hate you." They're only animated for a few moments before the house catches fire and they all fry.

Don't Open the Window see ***Let Sleeping Corpses Lie***

Dracula and the Seven Golden Vampires see ***The Legend of the Seven Golden Vampires***

Drums of the Jungle see ***Ouanga***

...E tu vivrai nel terrore! L'aldilà see ***The Beyond***

The Earth Dies Screaming

Dir: Terence Fisher. *Prod*: Robert Lippert, Jack Parsons. *Screenplay*: Henry Cross (Harry Spalding). *Cast*: Willard Parker, Virginia Field, Dennis Price, Thorley Walters, Vanda Godsell, David Spenser, Anna Palk. Lippert Films (England), 1964.

You can't tell from this spirited and mostly harmless apocalypse that director Fisher (better known for his work at Hammer Studios) reportedly hated science-fiction. Robots from outer space with potatoes in vacuum-tubes for heads use gas warfare to wipe out all human and animal life on earth, save only a handful of people who happen to have been in airtight shelters or oxygen masks at the time of invasion. The robots reanimate certain cadavers to help them track down the few remaining survivors, but the moseying marauders hardly present a threat to nimble, turtleneck-sporting protagonist Jeff Nolan (Parker) and his rag-tag, fugitive band of panicky halfwits. Finding that the robots are controlled by sonic waves, the heroes summarily defeat them by blowing up their poorly guarded broadcasting tower. The hour-long, fast-paced production rewards the viewer with scenes of darling Tudor cottages in rustic English villages, contrasted delightfully with the clunky, aluminum foil robots ambling through the streets like tourists. Along with *Invisible Invaders*, *The Birds*, and *The Last Man on Earth*, *The Earth Dies Screaming* is an obvious precursor of *Night of the Living Dead.*

The robot invaders' ability (or desire) to resurrect human cadavers as slavish minions is an odd touch never fully explained. A skeptical character surmises that the victims aren't really dead, but only suffer from suspended body functions (since they bleed and can be killed by gunfire). But by 1964 that's a little like saying "Ceci n'est pas une pipe": these fiends plod forward stiffly and most zombesquely, devoid of mind, intelligence, or emotional response; and there's no mistaking their cold, grey eyes lacking pupils or expression. Too bad they're no more effective assailants than their incompetent robotic overlords.

Erotic Nights of the Living Dead

(orig. *Le notti erotiche dei morti viventi*). *Dir*: Aristide Massaccesi. *Cast*: Laura Gemser, George Eastman, Dirce Funari, Mark Shannon. Stefano Film (Italy), 1979.

Sexploitation director Massaccesi weaves a tiresome tale of endless romantic escapades capped off with a fifteen-minute undead invasion in this questionable Spaghetti Zombie. Hotel surveyor John Wilson (Shannon) accompanies paid escort Fiona (Funari) and hired yacht pilot Larry O'Hara (Eastman) to the locally shunned Island of the Cat, where they confront a mysterious native couple and an army of hostile zombies. Massaccesi seems to confuse "eroticism" with abundant sex, and besides that, the entire concept of combining scenes of lovemaking with a zombie massacre presupposes a strange sort of mood to begin with. There are fleeting moments of talent, however, especially in the visual conceptualization of the zombies and the mesmerizing invasion sequence, which is sensuous in its own apocalyptic sort of way. Funniest scene: surrounded by the cannibal zombies who threaten to rend them to pieces and devour them at any moment, Larry warns Fiona to watch out because they probably carry all sorts of diseases.

The zombies were once the island's luckless inhabitants, all killed by an earthquake and an epidemic. Guarded by a strange native woman and a demon cat (whose connection with the zombies is never satisfactorily addressed), they now rise at night from their shallow, sandy graves. Intriguingly enough, these dusty natives, fully covered in long, loose robes, are dressed more like nomads of the Sahara than Caribbean islanders. Half-eaten from disease as well as decay, the cloaked undead noiselessly stalk their prey through the palms of the tropical sea-coast, to bite them in the jugular. But they are unimpressive assailants, easily dispatched by being impaled, decapitated, or burned; and they also turn away when confronted with a protective amulet. Especially effective are the shots of them standing motionless on the coast, their robes blowing in the wind along with the palm leaves and ferns, as well as the prolonged chase scene at the climax, in which they emerge from every direction (even rising out of the sea itself), accompanied by a hypnotic chorus and synthesizer score.

Alternate titles: *Island of the Zombies, Night of the Zombies, La notte dei zombi, La notte erotiche dei morti viventi, Sexy Nights of the Dead.*

El Espanto surge de la tumba see ***Horror Rises from the Tomb***

The Fall of the House of Usher see ***Zombie 5: Revenge of the House of Usher***

The Fear see ***The Gates of Hell***

Fear in the City of the Living Dead see ***The Gates of Hell***

The Fiend with the Atomic Brain see ***Blood of Ghastly Horror***

The Fiend with the Synthetic Brain see ***Blood of Ghastly Horror***

Fin de semana para los muertos see ***Let Sleeping Corpses Lie***

Flesheater

Dir: Bill Hinzman. *Prod*: Bill Hinzman. *Screenplay*: Bill Hinzman, Bill Randolph. *Story*: Bill Hinzman. *Cast*: Bill Hinzman, John Mowood, Leslie Ann Wick, Kevin Kindlin, James J. Rutan, Denise Morrone, Charis Kirkpatrick Acuff, Lisa Smith, Mark Strycula, Rik Billock. H & G Films/Hinzman Production, 1988.

Bill Hinzman, the unforgettable cemetery ghoul (and cinematographer) in the original *Night*, thinks that his one-time bit part qualifies him to make a zombie movie of his own. In this reworking of Romero's classic, a group of college kids in rural Pennsylvania head for the woods on a hayride one Halloween night for some good times. A nearby farmer accidentally unearths a coffin covered with rusting locks, a pentangle, and an inscription reading, "This evil which will take flesh and blood from thee and turn all ye unto evil" (baleful times are best foreboded by chillingly incomplete sentences, I gather). The ghoul "Flesheater" (Hinzman, appearing much as he did in *Night*) pops out of the coffin to spark off the inevitable zombie Armageddon. Zombies chase and idiots flee, until a barn is burned to the ground for the finale. While the even-tempo, nostalgic piano score by Erica Portnoy complements the mournful autumn landscape, it doesn't do much for escalating chase and attack scenes. Amateur, juvenile, and depressing, *Flesheater* is mostly a waste of a good barn. Aging Hinzman transparently casts himself groping naked women. Though there's no narrative tie-in with the events in *Night*, the ghouls here don't deviate substantially from Romero's conceptualization: they feed on the flesh of the living, can only be deanimated by being shot in the head, and transfer their necroanimate condition to their victims. Hinzman goes down for a few moments when bludgeoned with a large stick, but otherwise the ghouls show little response to damage. The zombies here are more keen on weapons than those in *Night*, though: they kill with a pitchfork and a hatchet, and one uses a hook to drag a woman scurrying up a ladder back down to him, by her calf. Ouch!

Alternate titles: *Revenge of the Living Zombies*, *Zombie Nosh*.

The Fog

Dir: John Carpenter. *Prod*: Debra Hill. *Screenplay*: John Carpenter, Debra Hill. *Cast*: Adrienne Barbeau, Jamie Lee Curtis, Janet Leigh, Tom Atkins, Hal Holbrook, John Houseman, Rob Bottin. Avco-Embassy Pictures, 1979.

Carpenter and Hill, who inaugurated an entire era of slasher films in 1978 with *Halloween*, downplay violence for suspense again in this mournful ghost story. Sleepy coastal California town Antonio Bay celebrates its hundredth anniversary, only to find itself menaced by a wind-defying fog that comes in from the sea and conceals a mysterious troupe of hook-wielding wraiths. It appears the town's forefathers treacherously engineered the wreck of a shipload of lepers to obtain their gold, and now the mangy mariners are back to exact revenge. The events are helplessly narrated from a lighthouse by a radio broadcaster (Barbeau), while a seaman (Atkins) and a drifter (Curtis) drive around in circles. The scenes of the ominous fog rolling into the desolate bay area are stunning, and the stark film refuses to cushion the grey, lonely atmosphere it creates, even at the end. Best line, from Jamie Lee Curtis: "Things seem to happen to me. I'm bad luck."

The sea wraiths are called "ghosts" in the credits, and exhibit some amorphous traits such as appearing and disappearing, but basically they're zombies: they have to besiege buildings from the outside, and must break into them through the doors and windows. Lepers to begin with, after dying horribly and then spending a century under water, the vengeful marauders don't half look ugly: they're claggy, mottled, and bulbous beyond recognition. Unspeaking, yet malign and knowing, the unwholesome visitors wield a variety of sharp and heinous dock implements. Awesome Blake (Bottin) steals the show as the silent, dark silhouette with glowing red eyes, still bent on taking his now useless gold back to his watery grave with him.

The Four Skulls of Jonathan Drake

Dir: Edward L. Cahn. *Prod*: Robert E. Kent. *Screenplay*: Orville H. Hampton. *Cast*: Eduard Franz, Valerie French, Grant Richards, Henry Daniell, Paul Wexler, Lumsden Hare, Howard Wendell, Paul Cavanaugh. Vogue Pictures/United Artists, 1959.

Like Ed Wood, Edward Cahn consistently buttresses his hackneyed plots with minute attention to the conceptual background and supporting mythology, which keeps his movies entertaining so long as you don't try to fit it all together too closely. Jonathan Drake (Franz) fears for his skull, which immortal mad scientist Emile Zurich (Daniell) covets for his Drake family skull collection. Police Lt. Rowan (Richards) pieces together the unspeakable truth: Zurich, who is actually the head of a white man sewn onto the body of a Jivaro Indian, has spent the last two centuries getting back at the Drakes for wiping out his tribe in the Amazon jungle. Zurich is thus an abomination who physically embodies the awkward blend of native Indian and European, while his undead Indian slave Zutai (Wexler), whose lips are sewn shut, is a walking parable of the silenced and subservient New World native.

Zurich may be a sort of Frankenstein monster composed of parts, but his assistant Zutai is more enigmatic and compelling. The sinister South American native has long, black hair and wears a tunic and sandals made of human skin. The reason his mouth is sewn shut is to show his contempt for food and air, and the long threads trail down several inches past his chin. His job is basically to extract and tote around skulls, for which purpose he carries a wicker basket and spends a lot of time hiding in bushes. Though fully sentient and emotive as far as we can tell, he doesn't exhibit any volition independently of Zurich's orders. Curiously, though, he does explode when kicked into a fire.

Frankenstein Island

Dir: Jerry Warren. *Prod*: Jerry Warren. *Screenplay*: Jaques LaCouter. *Cast*: Robert Clarke, Steve Brodie, Robert Christopher, Tain Bodkin, Patrick O'Neil, Andrew Duggan, Cameron Mitchell. Chriswar, 1981.

Warren's incredible remake of his own earlier *Teenage Zombies* is a ludicrous mishmash of random elements, lovingly stirred into a burgoo of cinematic insanity. OK, where to start ... Four men in a hot-air balloon are blown down to sea, finally drifting to an island in a life raft. There they are taken in by a friendly tribe of young Amazon women in leopard-skin bikinis, and run into Sheila Frankenstein (the famous doctor's great-granddaughter), who is keeping alive her 200-year-old husband Dr. Von Helsing by draining blood from an imprisoned sea captain who thinks he's Edgar Allan Poe. Oh, yeah—and it also turns out that the island was once the landing site for members of a superior alien species, and that the ghost of the real Dr. Frankenstein (superimposed clips of John Carradine) is still in touch with Sheila, from beyond. With an unwieldy Gatling gun, the heroes preposterously storm the laboratory, and its odd, drone-like seamen guards. The villains respond by unleashing the original Frankenstein monster, who (it also turns out) has been chained up in an underwater grotto on the island all these years and who doesn't seem terribly clear which side he's supposed to be on. The monster and the drones are all powered by a disembodied brain in a vat, and they fall to the ground lifelessly when the brain is knocked over. But there's a backup brain elsewhere that will kick in shortly (and I'm not making this up), during which pause the balloonists escape. It's all indescribably silly. Though apparently made in 1981, the film texture, coloring, and scripting seem more like the '60s.

The drone servants are the crewmen of a ship that crashed near the island, who have been reprogrammed by Sheila and Von Helsing to serve as sleepless guards and general lackeys. The stooping half-wits wear black shirts and dock-worker caps, and occasionally growl in a low voice. They have no blood stream, but run on pure "psychic energy," and consequently are impervious to bullets and bleeding-related injuries. They're said to be sensitive to light and thus have to wear dark glasses (as in *Shock Waves*, 1977), though nothing is ever done with this carefully stated vulnerability. Some are forebodingly said to be "less predictable" than others, but nothing is made of that either. The drones engage in boxing and karate matches in their spare time, but they'll need a lot more practice—in the final brawl, the dainty Amazon women and halfhearted protagonists take them on without any trouble.

From the Dead of Night

Dir: Paul Wendkos. *Teleplay*: William Bleich. *Original novel*: Gary Brandner. *Cast*: Lindsay Wagner, Bruce Boxleitner, Robin Thomas, Robert Prosky. Phoenix Entertainment Group, 1989.

Another variation on the *Carnival of Souls* theme, this drowsy made-for-TV commodity is slightly less interesting than the very similar *Sole Survivor* (1982). Fashion designer Joanna (Lindsay Wagner a.k.a. Jaime Sommers) has a near-death experience, encountering six shadowy figures on her spiritual journey through the obligatory light-drenched tunnel to the afterlife. Resuscitated moments later, she finds herself subsequently stalked by six "walkers"—corpses who come back to life in order to reclaim her. The continuous attention to Joanna's high-schoolish relationship troubles doesn't help the pace any, while the occasional shots in slow-motion keep you expecting the bionic creaking sound to kick in.

The six "walkers" are blanched, bloody, and bent on Joanna's destruction. Only her avuncular physician recognizes her and resists the urge to kill her when he returns as a zombie. The undead can be deanimated permanently so long as they are killed violently the second time (car crash, sucked into boat propeller, etc.). The actual appearances of the zombies only total a few minutes of screen time, however. Apparently disembodied spirits wear business suits.

Frozen Scream

Dir: Frank Roach. *Prod*: Renee Harmon. *Screenplay*: Doug Ferrin, Michael Soney, Celeste Hammond. *Story*: Renee Harmon, Doug Ferrin. *Cast*: Renee

Harmon, Lynne Kocol, Wolf Muser, Thomas Gowen, Wayne Liebman, Lee James, Sunny Bartholomew, Bill Oliver, Bob Rochelle. Clara, 1980.

This dismal and homely backyard effort features robotic acting, abrupt transitions, and annoying "Wonder Years"–like voice-over narration. Police Sgt. Kevin McGuire (Gowen) teams up with ex-fiancée Ann (Kocol) to investigate two evil doctors, whose experiments in immortality involve turning medical students into zombies. People run around a lot in poorly-lit hallways, while the movie embodies its primary theme of immortality by refusing to end.

The uninteresting mad doctors simulate immortality by reducing the patients' life functions to death or near-death levels, and then reviving them at a lower body temperature. However, the patients' personalities are altered in the process, such that they wind up "altered, diffused—almost soulless." They're kept in cold storage when not out on some killing errand. The zombies wear black hooded cloaks that associate them with a certain pre–Christian immortality cult and cheesy moustaches that associate them with the '70s.

Gamma 693

Dir: Joel M. Reed. *Prod*: Lorin E. Price. *Screenplay*: Joel M. Reed. *Cast*: Jamie Gillis, Ryan Hilliard, Samantha Grey, Ron Armstrong, Juni Kulis, Alphonse DeNoble. NMD Film Distribution, 1981.

The Nazi zombie (hitherto sighted in *Shock Waves* and *Zombie Lake*) finally evolves sufficiently to leave the water, taking to the snowy Alps in this confused and over-complicated zombie invasion detective movie. Tough CIA agent Nick Monroe (Gillis) teams up with geeky scientist Clarence (Hilliard) to locate some missing canisters of the experimental World War II gas Gamma 693. In the brisk Bavarian highlands, Nick finds both American and German zombie troops still fighting the war. Turned into immortal cannibals by their exposure to Gamma 693, the soldiers plan to spread their own kind across the globe while breeding mortals for fodder. Stock footage of German tanks plowing through a snowy landscape caps off the film. The low-budget monstrosity features bad sound and lighting and uneven pacing, and fails to generate sympathy for either protagonists or zombies.

The Nazi zombies appear as young, healthy men when they get their daily ration of Gamma 693, but if they miss it, they deteriorate into ghastly white spectres with dark eyes and nasty strips of wattle peeling from their faces. They silently stalk through the wintry nighttime mountains, rifles in hand, trying to stay inconspicuous but occasionally shooting the odd trespasser. Simply out of boredom, the undead soldiers spend their nights conducting military exercises, filling the skies with heavy artillery fire (so much for staying inconspicuous). They feed on human bodies, raw or cooked, and have even started a human stock farm with some captive villagers. On the whole, the zombie portrayals are sadly disappointing—their unaltered personalities make them little more than very ugly soldiers, and the exciting visual possibilities of the snow-covered mountain landscapes remain mostly unexploited.

Alternate titles: *Night of the Wehrmacht Zombies*, *Night of the Zombies*, *Night of the Zombies II.*

Garden of the Dead

Dir: John Hayes. *Prod*: H.A. Milton. *Screenplay*: John Jones. *Cast*: Phil Remmealy, Duncan McLoud, John Dullaghan, John Dennis, Marland Proctor, Lee Frost. Clover, 1972.

This scruffy low-budget production anticipates the pointless and depressing amateur zombie movies of the early '90s by almost twenty years. Prisoners who are forced to labor at the Camp Hoover low-security formaldehyde processing camp make their toils seem less wearisome by sniffing the formaldehyde vapors. A handful of them are shot during an attempted prison break, and come back to life plenty ugly and nine kinds of mad after formaldehyde soaks into the ground of their shallow, unmarked graves. They run around the prison compound killing at random until resourceful Sgt. Dublonsky at last traps them using a woman as decoy. Backed by an anachronistic '60s jazz score, the spartan feature is lonely and humorless.

The revived chain gang cons have dark, sunken eyes and wear the camp standard issue, blue shirt and jeans. They're a little starchy when first emerging from the ground, but quickly regain their speed and agility—thus they run, sneak, dodge, and hide as they besiege the prison compound. In fact, their favorite attack is a rather complicated sprint and pick-axe swing technique. They go around growling in low voices, only speaking a few brief phrases with difficulty. Braddock, the leader of these makeshift Hogan's Heroes of the Dead, summarily announces, "We will destroy the living!" They're fairly resistant to bullets, but go down when blasted with a shotgun at close range.

More interestingly, they're also destroyed by light: one collapses, instantly dessicates, and froths at the mouth from having a spotlight trained on him. There's no indication that any of this is tongue-in-cheek, but it's awfully hard to take the undead inmates seriously as they go around growling like bad pirate impersonators the whole time.

Alternate title: *Tomb of the Undead.*

The Gates of Hell

(Orig. *Paura nella città dei morti viventi*). *Dir*: Lucio Fulci. *Prod*: Giovanni Massini. *Screenplay*: Lucio Fulci, Dardano Sacchetti. *Cast*: Christopher George, Katherine MacColl, Carlo DeMejo, Antonella Interlenghi, John Morghen, Daniela Doria. Dania Film/Medusa/International Cinematografica (Italy), 1980.

The second of Fulci's zombie cycle, this is less of a coherent zombie-invasion story than a loose collection of gratuitous shocks and sensationalistic horror images. By hanging himself, a priest unlocks a portal to hell in the New England town of Dunwich, built on the site of the "original" town of Salem. During a séance the danger is revealed to Mary (MacColl), who sets out for Dunwich from New York City accompanied by a reporter (George). They have until All Saints' Day to destroy the priest's body, Mary believes, or else all the dead will rise and rain destruction upon humankind. In the meantime, those that have already risen go ahead and warm up, murdering at random and capriciously terrorizing the locals. There are some memorable shocks and creative stylistic touches, but in terms of zombie consistency and development, this is the least satisfying of Fulci's zombie repertoire.

The movements and motives of the living dead aren't really explained, other than that they wish to spread evil generally. They are unleashed by the power of the ancient *Book of Enoch*, an early Jewish apocalyptic text that doesn't actually provide instructions for raising the dead or sparking Armaggedon in most modern editions. These zombies (actually more like ghosts) can teleport, which they often do for no apparent reason. They seem to be cannibalistic—a zombie is certainly chewing on a victim's corpse at one point—but this isn't consistently sustained. One zombie is deanimated by being stabbed through the stomach with a metal pole; the others combust spontaneously when the priest is killed. But the zombies represent only one of the numerous evil manifestations accompanying the Enochian curse, another of which is the sudden bursting open of the windows followed by a swarm of grubs pouring into the room, covering the four protagonists and carpeting the floor. Fulci notes in an interview: "It was not easy; actors would not quite accept all those worms stuck on their faces—we used thousands of them, over twenty pounds!"

Alternate titles: *City of the Dead*, *City of the Living Dead*, *The Fear*, *Fear in the City of the Living Dead*, *Twilight of the Dead*.

The Ghost Breakers

Dir: George Marshall. *Prod*: Arthur Hornblow Jr. *Screenplay*: Walter DeLeon. *Original Play*: Paul Dickey, Charles Goddard. *Cast*: Bob Hope, Paulette Goddard, Richard Carlson, Paul Lukas, Willie Best, Pedro De Cordoba, Virginia Brissac, Noble Johnson. Paramount Pictures, 1940.

This is considered to be among Bob Hope's finest pictures, and the direction is smooth and the lines delivered flawlessly, but black actor Willie Best's jokes about fried chicken are no longer funny, and smarmy Hope isn't funny to begin with. Radio personality Larry (Hope) and his valet Alex (Best) accompany recent acquaintance Mary Carter (Goddard) to visit her newly-inherited haunted castle on Black Island off the coast of Cuba. A motley assortment of secondary characters provides suspects for the ghostly happenings at the castle; someone is obviously trying to scare them away from what turns out to be a silver mine underneath the castle. The ghost of long-dead slavelord Don Sebastian, a native zombie, and other spooks keep the heroes shaking until cowardly Alex accidentally takes out the villain by pushing the wrong button and springing a trap. All right gang, back to the Mystery Machine for some rooby-racks. *The Ghost Breakers* was the first attempt to integrate the zombie into a comic rather than straight horror script, thus setting the general tone for the wartime zombie movies to follow. The movie was remade in 1953 with Dean Martin and Jerry Lewis as *Scared Stiff*.

Silent screen star Noble Johnson plays the bald and slightly disfigured zombie who guards the ancient castle from intruders. A local Havana man explains, "A zombie has no will of his own. You see them sometimes, walking around blindly, with dead eyes—following orders, not knowing what they do, not caring." But this zombie has to make all sorts of decisions: he hears others coming while

Silent screen star Noble Johnson, two years before the end of his career, plays a pensive African-Cuban zombie opposite Bob Hope in *The Ghost Breakers* (1940). A pioneer in the early film industry, Johnson formed the first all-black motion picture company in 1916, which consistently portrayed African-Americans as competent and intelligent (a vision completely subverted in *The Ghost Breakers*).

he's chasing Mary, and opts to climb into a suit of plate armor rather than continue following her. Then he's (regrettably) interrupted from braining Hope with a huge mace by the sight of Mary dressed to the nines. Not only is the zombie able to weigh factors and deliberate, then, but this is even his downfall: he spends too long just standing around, giving Larry and Alex enough time to stuff him in a closet. Though the zombie scene is brief and tangential, it's easily the most memorable of the film.

Ghost Brigade see ***The Lost Brigade***

The Ghost Galleon see ***Horror of the Zombies***

Ghost Ship of the Blind Dead see ***Horror of the Zombies***

Ginseng King

Dir: Rotar Ru-Tar. (Thailand), 1989.

In this obscure and psychotic East Asian fairy tale, a Nazi zombie (called a "hopping corpse") comes to life when a whisker from the thousand-year-old Ginseng King, the ancestor of all the impish ginseng roots that frolic in the forest, falls on his grave. The raging, blood-sucking zombie bumps into trees and other objects, continuously raising his arm in salute and addressing the inanimate obstacles with a hearty "Heil Hitler!" The fanged menace becomes supercharged after drinking ginseng broth, until he is momentarily stopped by the sight of a swastika on a Buddhist's sidebag, and is finally destroyed by being lured into a minefield. A very strange zombie in a very strange movie.

The Gore-met Zombie Chef from Hell

Dir: Don Swan. *Prod*: Don Swan. *Screenplay*: Don Swan, Jeff Baughn, William Highsmith. *Cast*: Theo Depuay, Kelley Kunicki, C.W. Casey, Michael O'Neill, Jeff Baughn. Swanfilms, 1986.

Too low-budget to appear in most reference works, this sketchy camp feature runs on fumes the entire time with the possible exception of a few good lines. In 1386, Goza (Depuay), a priest of the Holy Order of Righteous Brothers, is convicted of high treason by his brethren and cursed with eternal life. The curse is that he cannot die, but must consume human flesh daily to keep from decaying horribly.

Six hundred years later, Goza is still an evil and powerful warlock, but now he runs a seedy bar and grill called "Goza's Deli and Beach Club." With the aid of his assistant Blozor (O'Neill), another immortal refugee from the Holy Order, Goza dismembers customers with power tools and serves his leftovers to other customers. At last the incarnation of a long-prophesied High Priestess arrives to combat the ghoulish entrepreneur. She exclaims, "Goza—you have lost that loving feeling," as she fires off a nail gun repeatedly into the soles of his feet. The film insists on a great deal of metaphysical trimming embarrassingly at odds with its amateur production values. Meanwhile Goza tries to play his role like Lugosi, but it's hard to take him seriously in his wide array of Hawaiian shirts.

Goza despises human flesh, but is driven to eat it—this is his twofold curse. He gnaws directly at body parts, or else prepares them in a variety of dishes, such as slicing them in his deli-slicer to make a cold-cut sandwich. The capable and conversant chef is not really a "zombie," except that when he doesn't get his daily human flesh, he develops open sores and takes on a zombie-like appearance (apprehensive customer: "Are you sure you should be serving food with that skin condition?"). Some designation such as "ancient immortal cannibal demon sorcerer" would technically be more accurate than "zombie," but understandably the title was getting too long as it was.

Grave Misdemeanors see ***Night Life***

The Grave of the Living Dead see ***Oasis of the Zombies***

Grey Knight see ***The Lost Brigade***

The Hanging Woman see ***Return of the Zombies***

Hard Rock Zombies

Dir: Krishna Shah. *Prod*: Krishna Shah. *Screenplay*: Krishna Shah, David Ball. *Cast*: E.J. Curcio, Geno Andrews, Sam Mann, Mick Manz, Jennifer Coe, Ted Wells. Patel/Shah Film Company, 1984.

A cheesy KISS-impersonating band led by Jesse (Curcio) receives a poor welcome in prudish Grand Guignol, California. To begin with, an Addams–ish family kills them off for sport, but Jesse's admirer Cassie (Coe) brings them back to life by playing a tape of occult medieval riffs Jesse has been experimenting with. The zombie rockers seek vengeance on their killers (who turn out to be Hitler, Eva

Braun, and several other Nazis) and faithfully play their scheduled gig before returning to their graves. Nazi zombies are fairly common, but this is the only movie to present Hitler himself as one. The plot is slight and the thrills driven by adolescent concerns, but the variations on the usual zombie motifs are more innovative than in most of the camp zombie flicks to follow over the next decade. Strange moments abound, such as a zombie dwarf who, through the course of the movie, devours himself entirely to nothingness.

An old tome explains that zombies "feed on living flesh" and that "They rip off your skin while the blood is still flowing in your veins." It goes on to state that "Certain ghouls don't eat heads ... ghouls hate heads the way Satan hates the church.... Ghouls are the antithesis of intellectual existence, which centers within the head. In the ghoul, the brain dissolves to become their venom." After reading this, the enterprising townspeople attempt to drive the ghouls away by carrying around large posters displaying oversized heads (of Elvis, Marilyn Monroe, John Wayne, etc.) This only works for a few minutes before the zombies scarf the lot.

The undead condition is highly contagious: as an ancient guru in the town unintelligibly puts it, "Ghouls begetting ghouls—evil begetting evil—epidemic. One bite from ghoul's mouth—venom making you to be dying." Apart from the band playing their instruments, evidence of zombie tool use is limited to a salt shaker and a jar of mustard. The four character zombies—the rock band, whose deathly pallor makes them resemble KISS all the more—don't seek the flesh of the living or follow the bidding of Satan, but are driven only by the pathetic desire to keep on rocking.

Heavy Metal

Dir: Gerald Potterton. *Prod*: Ivan Reltman. *Screenplay*: Dan Goldberg, Len Blum. *Voices* ("B-17"): George Toglistos, Don Francks, Zal Yanovsky. Columbia (Canada), 1981.

I'm not systematically covering zombies in animated features, but this book would be glaringly incomplete without a mention of the "B-17" episode from this early '80s animation anthology. A small green orb representing the sum of all evil winds its way through a series of stories, set throughout time and across the cosmos. Around the middle of the film it lands aboard a badly-hit World War II bomber shortly after a dog fight, turning all the corpses aboard into demonic skeleton zombies. A pilot parachutes out in time, only to find the tropical island below equally infested with undead. The horrific zombies wear navigator caps and flying jackets, clawing their way from the shattered cockpits and ball-turrets of the wrecked bombers. The episode's effectiveness arises not only from the superb undead themselves, but also from the well-focused—almost single-minded—narrative momentum: the entire story is simply zombies pursuing a victim, closing in on him increasingly. Based on a story by Dan O'Bannon (who would soon change the course of zombie history with *Return of the Living Dead*), this vignette is the shortest of the film's episodes, and the only straight horror piece.

Hell of the Living Dead see ***Night of the Zombies***

Hell of the Living Death see ***Night of the Zombies***

Hellgate

Dir: William A. Levey. *Prod*: Anant Singh. *Screenplay*: Michael O'Rourke. *Cast*: Ron Palillo, Abigail Wolcott, Carel Trichardt, Petrea Curran, Evan Klisser, Joanne Ward, Frank Noyard. Ghosttown Film Management, Distant Horizon/Anant Singh (South Africa), 1989.

A special effects artist (*Hellraiser*, *Hellbound*) directs an unthinkably stupid debacle about ghosts harassing a group of young funseekers in an abandoned mining town. In one very brief and entirely gratuitous scene, all the town's dead rise and stalk them en masse, but then quickly disappear again. Apparently even zombies find it boring.

Homecoming Night see ***Night of the Creeps***

Horror Express

(Orig. *Pánico en el transiberiano*). *Dir*: Eugenio Martin. *Prod*: Eugenio Martin, Bernard Gordon. *Screenplay*: Arnaud d'Usseau, Julian Halevy, Eugenio Martin. *Cast*: Christopher Lee, Peter Cushing, Alberto de Mendoza, Silvia Tortosa, Julio Peña, Angel del Pozo, Helga Liné, Telly Savalas. Granade Films/Benmar Production (Spain, England), 1972.

A prehistoric ape-creature hosting a parasitic alien life form is thawed from the frozen Chinese highlands, subsequently coming to life on the trans–Siberian railway. After slaughtering a troop of Cossacks led by Telly Savalas, the creature revives their bodies and sends them against the other passengers. Though very brief, the scene in which the blind zombies with their blank, white eyes stumble through the train toward the rear car is highly effective.

Alternate title: *Panic in the Trans-Siberian Train.*

The Horror of Party Beach

Dir: Del Tenney. *Prod*: Del Tenney. *Screenplay*: Richard Hilliard. *Cast*: John Scott, Alice Lyon, Allan Laurel, Eulabelle Moore, Marilyn Clarke. Inzom, 1963.

Del Tenney's incomparable relic, a '50s beach movie and monster flick rolled into one, is all the more hilarious for being played seriously. Radioactive waste dumped into the sea causes skeletons in a shipwreck on the ocean floor to grow flesh and rise as reptilian fishmen with googly eyes. Their assaults bring a welcome halt to the tireless twisting and shaking of the teens on the fun-filled Connecticut beach, and they proceed to slaughter a slumber party of bubbly teen girls and to attack anyone else out after dark. Dr. Gavin (Laurel) discovers that they are in fact giant protozoan colonies and so have sea anemone instead of human tissue. Never mind that protozoa and sea anemones aren't even in the same kingdom—the upshot is that they're like big jellyfish and can't be killed by shooting them or even cutting them up. Since protozoa are mostly water, sodium (which reacts violently with water) turns out to be the requisite miracle weapon. The protagonists are preposterous, the beach bands are bouncy, while the humanoid fish-creatures look like they're just trying to get back to a school play. Director Tenney's kids later used the masks left over from the movie for Halloween costumes.

So what does any of this have to do with zombies? It's beyond me, but the shooting title was *Invasion of the Zombies* and the script insists on calling the mutated fish-men "zombies" at every turn. A radio newscaster refers to them as "sea zombies," and Dr. Gavin's black maid Eulabelle (Moore) even makes a voodoo doll for protection against the alleged living dead. During a discussion on whether a person whose human tissue has been entirely replaced by protozoa is alive or dead, Elaine, influenced by Eulabelle's superstitions, ominously concedes that maybe the creatures are "the living dead—zombies" after all. Dr. Gavin rightly points out, however, that the question of whether a creature is plant or animal has nothing to do with whether it's alive or dead. But none of this prevents the perky teens from dancing the "Zombie Stomp" on the beach to the sassy stylings of the Del-Aires: the partners approach each other slowly and stiffly with straight arms outstretched until their bodies collide. By all accounts, then, the filmmakers really do know what zombies are, and only by the most unrestrained lexical or taxonomical presumption have they appropriated the term for their humanoid sea anemones.

Horror of the Zombies

(Orig. *El buque maldito*). *Dir*: Amando de Ossorio. *Prod*: J.L. Bermúdez de Castro. *Screenplay*: Amando de Ossorio. *Cast*: María Perschy, Jack Taylor, Bárbara Rey, Carlos Lemos, Manuel de Blas, Blanca Estrada. Ancla Century/ Belen Films (Spain), 1974.

The boys are back in de Ossorio's third entry of the Blind Dead series, this time taking to the high seas in an atmospheric sixteenth-century galleon with rotted timbers and ragged sails. When two models who lose themselves at sea in a small boat as part of a publicity stunt fall prey to the seafaring undead, sporting goods magnate Howard Tucker (Taylor) comes to look for them with another boatload of zombie fodder. Finding themselves trapped on board the galleon with the menacing zombie brethren, the characters notice that the monks must return to their coffins in the ship's hold during daylight hours, and so they throw all the coffins overboard before the sun goes down. The ship bursts into flames, however, while the zombies climb out of the sea on a nearby coast. Although the essential ingredients of de Ossorio's tried recipe are present (most unhurried zombie monks, eerie groaning chants, and a moody galleon as a worthy substitute for the monastic ruins), here they aren't as well exploited as in the first two movies. The chanting only starts after the zombies appear, for instance, thus undermining its taut, foreboding chilliness. Worst of all, the model boat used for long-range shots is laughably unconvincing—most unfortunately, since the ship is ostensibly the film's major innovation. The sets for action on-board are passably atmospheric, though, as are the shots of the cloaked marauders emerging from the blue waves at the end. Some reference works cite the movie's original title as *El buqué maldito*, but actually that would have our fearsome antagonists terrorizing a "cursed bouquet."

The zombies adhere closely to their established visual and behavioral norms, adapting well to their new nautical lifestyle. De Ossorio varies the mythological background for the zombie monks even more drastically this time: they aren't explicitly identified as the Templars, for instance, and they don't really seem to be blind anymore. *Horror* pays as much attention to the greater forces of evil guiding the monks as it does to the monks themselves—the coffins open themselves, the ship navigates itself in a mysterious fog, and a horned skull representing Satan burns the ship down after the zombies have left. Professor Gruber (Lemos) combats these forces with Catholic ritual: "Spirits of evil, united to the devil, rejoin your master, leave us. Gaze—gaze on the fiery cross, and return to the darkness of your cold tombs." The monks recoil before the holy words, holding up their withered arms across their faces, and retreat into the hold. Though they lack the creative spark that instilled them with solemn grace in the first movie and with initiative in the second, the monks never prove themselves more doggedly persistent than they do here, lumbering up to dry land from the bottom of the ocean.

Alternate titles: *The Ghost Galleon, Ghost Ship of the Blind Dead, La noche del buque maldito, Ship of Zombies.*

Horror Rises from the Tomb

(Orig. *El espanto surge de la tumba*). *Dir*: Carlos Aured. *Prod*: Ricardo Muñez Suay, José Antonio Pérez Giner. *Screenplay*: Jacinto Molina (Paul Naschy). *Cast*: Paul Naschy, Emma Cohen, Vic Winner, Helga Line. Profilmes/Avco Embassy (Spain), 1972.

The spirit of the fifteenth-century sorcerer Alaric de Marnac (Naschy) terrorizes his descendents in modern France while a ponderous organ score repeats itself incessantly. In a certain *Night*–inspired scene two-thirds of the way through the film, Alaric raises the characters killed up to this point, who crawl from a nearby lake and attack the house. The rasping, moaning, white-eyed zombies are at last driven back with torches, and are found deanimated in the lake again the next day. Former Spanish weightlifting champion Paul Naschy (Jacinto Molina) appeared in at least three movies with zombies in 1972.

The House by the Cemetery

(Orig. *Quella villa accanto al cimitero*). *Dir*: Lucio Fulci. *Prod*: Fabrizio de Angelis. *Screenplay*: Dardano Sacchetti, Giorgio Marluzza, Lucio Fulci. *Story*: Elisa Livia Briganti. *Cast*: Katherine MacColl, Paolo Malco, Ania Pieroni,

Giovanni Frezza, Silvia Collatina, Dagmar Lassander, Giovanni de Nava. Fulvia Film (Italy), 1981.

A nice family moves into a nice house on the outskirts of Boston, only to be greeted by the hideous zombie in the basement, nineteenth-century surgeon Dr. Freudstein (de Nava), with knives, skewers, and other sharp instruments of welcome. Freudstein is tall and wears an old-fashioned suit, but hardly looks respectable with his clammy, discolored features and misshapen insect head.

Alternate title: *The House Outside the Cemetery.*

The House of Seven Corpses

Dir: Paul Harrison. *Prod*: Paul Lewis, Paul Harrison. *Screenplay*: Paul Harrison, Thomas J. Kelly. *Cast*: John Ireland, Faith Domergue, John Carradine, Carol Wells, Jerry Strickler, Charles Macaulay, Wells Bond. Television Corporation of America/International Amusement, 1973.

Routine but capably handled, this fourth-quarter shocker was filmed in the old governor's mansion in Salt Lake City. Edgar Price (Carradine), the caretaker of the old ninteenth-century Beale estate house, which has a history riddled with murders, welcomes a film crew looking for a good set to shoot their horror movie. Crotchety director Eric (Ireland) snaps at the cast, while Price keeps out of the way. Middle-aged actress Gayle (Domergue), playing a Satan worshipper, reads from a copy of the *Tibetan Book of the Dead* that is lying around the house, as the cameras roll: "Exsurgent mortui et ad me veniunt" ("may the dead rise and come to me"; apparently the scriptwriters believe the *Tibetan Book of the Dead* is in Latin). As the actor zombie rises, so also a real zombie (Bond) gropes its way out of the ground outside in the Beale cemetery. It kills Price first and then makes a pass through the house, while other zombies begin to emerge from the cemetery. Though there's an abundance of potential victims in the movie, they don't start dying until after an hour and ten minutes—at which point they all go down in a single sweep. The deaths of the crew and cast are meant to recreate the murders and suicides of the actual Beale family, but the connections aren't well explained.

There's only one main zombie who does most of the killing—a black, muddy form, who breathes raspily but otherwise makes no sound as he walks, slowly undulating as he struggles with each step. With bedraggled hair and clothes, his face is powdery white, and his eyes too sunken to see. He kills by strangling, flinging heavy objects from three stories up, and other suitably dramatic means. The zombies only target those in the manor, and there's no hint of a larger zombie invasion. A graceful if humble zombie massacre awaits those who make it through the tedious first two–thirds of the film.

House of Terror see ***Return of the Zombies***

The House on Skull Mountain

Dir: Ron Honthaner. *Prod*: Ray Storey. *Screenplay*: Mildred Pares. *Cast*: Victor French, Janee Michelle, Jean Durand, Mike Evans, Xernona Clayton, Mary J. Todd McKenzie. Chocolate Chip and Pinto/20th Century–Fox, 1974.

In this altitudinous, Atlanta–shot snorefest, estranged relatives gather at a spooky old mansion to hear the requisite reading of matriarch Pauline Christophe's will. The voodoo priest/butler Thomas (Durand), the last descendent of the Pétions, wishes to wipe out the last of the Christophes, and thus resolve a political feud from the ruling factions of early nineteenth-century Haiti. After terrorizing the family with snakes, Thomas at last summons old lady Pauline (McKenzie) herself from the grave, but she doesn't so much follow his bidding as kill him. Oops.

Pauline appears as a zombie only in the closing scene, climbing from her leafy grave and dragging herself back into the ancestral house. With her long, white burial robe and spazzed-out hair, she comes across as a sort of zombie Miss Havisham. By hearing the name of the goddess Erzule, she regains sufficient power and autonomy to cast a spell against Thomas. Though pretty useless as a zombie, Pauline at least shows some taste: she leaves after seeing a minute or two of the crusty acting and hokey dialogue.

The House Outside the Cemetery see ***The House by the Cemetery***

El Hundimiento de la Casa Usher see ***Zombie 5: Revenge of the House of Usher***

I Eat Your Skin

Dir: Del Tenney. *Prod*: Del Tenney. *Screenplay*: Del Tenney. *Cast*: William Joyce, Heather Hewitt, Walter Coy, Dan Stapleton, Betty Hyatt Linton. Del Tenney Productions, 1964.

Never mind the title—this is as mild as horror gets, and nobody eats any skin. Tenney's unreleased film (*Voodoo Blood Bath*) was shelved for seven years, until Jerry Gross blew the dust off it in 1971 and renamed it to make a double-feature with his own *I Drink Your Blood*. Hard-boiled sleazeball Tom Harris (Joyce) is a best-selling writer whose publisher drags him to "Voodoo Island" in the hope of inspiring him with material for his next novel. Voodoo and live sacrifices run rampant on the Caribbean island, inhabited by cliché-ridden natives who speak schoolroom Spanish and conduct interminable rituals. Harris stops the island's overseer Charles Bentley (Coy) and his resident mad scientist from taking over the world with an army of zombies. As the heroes speed away in a boat, the laboratory explodes and the island, at last revealed to be a tiny model, bursts into tiny flames. All aspects of writing, staging, and dialogue are hopelessly contrived.

Although Bentley wishes to create an army of the undead to conquer the world, he only seems to have about half a dozen so far. A substance distilled from poisonous snake venom, once injected into the subject, instantly causes the face to deteriorate into a mottled, stucco-like texture, and robs the victim of independent will. The make-up effect consists of a coating of plaster over the face and neck (which apparently doesn't reflect decomposition, since it appears so quickly). O'Neill aptly calls them "bug-eyed, crud-faced zombies." Harris stumbles into the hut where they're kept in between sinister errands, and there's something ominous in the way the zombies just stand around open-eyed, not responding in any way to his intrusion.

They generally keep a slow, steady gait, but can also swing a mean machete. In an anomalously creative scene, a zombie blows up the protagonists' plane by casually walking into the propeller while holding a box of explosives—a zombie suicide bomber. Harris keeps trying to shoot them throughout the movie, not figuring out that they are unharmed by bullets. Though momentarily thwarted by a good pummel or a torch to the face, none are actually deanimated. They never speak or express any facial sentiment (after all, their faces are covered with plaster), but once or twice they issue a low guttural noise. Though highly cheesy, these zombies are definitely game, continuously providing amusement in the midst of a chafingly vapid island adventure sorely in need of it.

Alternate titles: *Voodoo Blood Bath*, *Zombie*, *Zombies*.

The Incredible Doktor Markesan

(Episode, *Thriller*). *Dir*: Robert Florey. *Prod*: William Frye. *Teleplay*: Donald Sanford. *Story*: August Derleth and Mark Schorer. *Cast*: Boris Karloff, Dick York, Carolyn Kearney, Richard Hale, Henry Hunter, Basil Howes, Billy Beck. Hubbell Robinson Productions, 1962.

Thriller was a short-lived TV series hosted by Boris Karloff, who also stars in this particularly memorable episode. Down on their luck and broke, Fred (Dick York—yes, Darren from *Bewitched*) and wife Molly (Kearney) travel to the estate of Fred's estranged uncle and former scientist Doktor Konrad Markesan (Karloff) for a place to stay. He receives them coldly, and they slowly discover why: he's actually dead, and each night he resurrects three former colleagues (Hale, Howes, Beck) who got him fired from Penrose College by testifying against him at a hearing. All night he forces the tortured, unwilling, dead professors to rehearse and amend their testimony over and over again. Markesan eventually catches Molly and turns her into one of his creepy, marble-faced undead also—poor Dick York never can get it together with his wives.

The living dead plead with Markesan that they be allowed to rest in peace, but since he's the most recently dead and therefore the most limber of the lot, Markesan is clearly in control. The bodies are hooked up to some sort of I.V. unit as they lie in their coffins, where they remain dormant until Markesan comes to rouse them each night. The most noteworthy scene is when the four silently close in on Molly with arms outstretched, stiff and cadaverous, with dark, sunken eyes and little colonies of funk growing on their heads. So gruesome was this early instance of visible decay that censors cut out the close-ups before the show could air in England. The four of them are rational, deliberative, and articulate—in fact, far too much so. All four are academics, and the scenario here imagined—an eternal faculty meeting with professors pontificating interminably and correcting each other on minor points—is truly a poignant vision of hell.

Incredibly Mixed-Up Zombie see ***The Incredibly Strange Creatures Who Stopped Living and Became Mixed-Up Zombies***

The Incredibly Strange Creatures Who Stopped Living and Became Mixed-Up Zombies

Dir: Ray Dennis Steckler. *Producer*: Ray Dennis Steckler. *Screenplay*: Gene Pollock, Robert Silliphant. *Cast*: Cash Flagg [Ray Steckler], Sharon Walsh, Brett O'Hara, Atlas King, Erina Enyo, Carolyn Brandt. Morgan/Steckler Productions, 1964.

Steckler reportedly came up with the idea for this notorious "monster musical" when he acquired the leftover costumes from a Vegas–style dance revue. Thus the film features a number of protracted song and dance numbers decidedly at odds with the build-up of any suspense or horror. Jerry (Flagg), Angela (Walsh), and friends encounter embittered fortune-teller Madame Estrella (O'Hara) on a visit to the local amusement park. The malefic mystic hypnotizes Jerry using a revolving hypno-spiral and sends him to commit various murders. When she discovers that he remembers too much in his waking state, Estrella decides to add him to her menagerie of "pets"—that is, she throws acid on his face and leads him to an improbable side-room where she keeps three or four disfigured former lovers caged like animals. The fiends escape when she opens the door, however, and go on the requisite killing rampage. If there is entertainment to be gleaned from the movie, it's more likely to come from the surreal dialogue and period hair than from the halfhearted choreography or ketchup-and-scream murders. As a promotional gimmick, actors in make-up leapt at the audience from behind the screen at first-run showings.

Though Jerry is under Estrella's hypnotic control, and the acid-maimed fiends in the side-room are stooped, raving killers with tattered clothes, long hair, and monstrous faces, none of these actually "stop living" in any way. The fiends manically go around strangling people indiscriminately in their brief rampage, until the police gun them down. However monstrous, the fiends at least have taste: zombie Jerry, dressed like a jogger, steps on-stage in a packed night club and knifes a wearisome pair of dancers to death; while the whole crew of disfigured brutes storm a cheesy South-Pacific dance number in progress and strangle everyone.

Alternate titles: *Diabolical Dr. Voodoo*, *Incredibly Mixed-up Zombie*, *Teenage Psycho Meets Bloody Mary*.

Incubo sulla città contaminata see ***City of the Walking Dead***

Inferno dei morti viventi see *Night of the Zombies*

La Invasión de los muertos see *Invasion of the Dead*

La Invasión de los zombies atómicos see *City of the Walking Dead*

Invasion of the Atomic Zombies see *City of the Walking Dead*

Invasion of the Dead

(Orig. *La invasión de los muertos*). *Dir*: Rene Cardona Sr. *Prod*: Rene Cardona Jr., Enrique Rosas. *Cast*: Zovek, Blue Demon, Christa Linder, Raul Ramirez, Carlos Cardan, Polo Ortin. Productora Filmica/Producciones Nova (Mexico), 1972.

Cardona proves that Mexicans can do industry-standard, post–*Night* zombies too, and with only a minimum of wrestling. A big, smoking bowling ball from outer space causes the dead to rise and go on a killing spree. Short, pudgy, out of shape, masked wrestling hero Blue Demon puzzles over mysterious happenings from his boiler room crime lab, while glittery nightclub escape artist "Professor" Zovek heads out to the desert to examine some strange pictographs. The two heroes bravely grapple the escalating numbers of revived corpses who are gathering in the barren wastes and a couple of wolfmen who show up randomly, too. Mexican zombies are always outrageous, and it's a pity more of these movies don't make it to the States.

There's no real explanation for the unhappy catastrophe afflicting the Mexican countryside—just a lot of talk of the mysteries of the cosmos and shots of a starry sky. Whatever's to blame, the dead return from their moldy coffins with blank stares and a thirst for murder. Congregating in large groups, they choke and maul their victims and then tip over the furniture for good measure. There's no question of cannibalism, though, in a mainstream Mexican feature of the period. Their victims also reanimate, apparently as a result of some sort of radiation emitted by a dry ice machine near the spherical meteorite. Most interestingly, these zombies have an unprecedented fetish for vehicles: they hover around a bulldozer, and make off with any car or truck the keys have been left in. One even hijacks a helicopter, leading to a very bizarre moment that crosses *Night of the Living Dead* with the crop-duster scene from *North by Northwest*. A zombie is blown up by having a two-way radio tossed at him (however that works, exactly) and the rest burst into flames when the bowling ball is destroyed. I can never tell when Mexican B–movies are trying to be funny or serious, but watching wrestlers pummel unresponsive zombies in the face repeatedly is certainly more entertaining than Paul Naschy's gothic undead period pieces of the same time.

Invasion of the Zombies

(Orig. *El Santo contra los zombies*). *Dir*: Benito Alazraki. *Prod*: Alberto López. *Story*: Antonio Orellana, Fernando Osés. *Adaptation*: Benito Alazraki, Antonio Orellana. *Cast*: Rudolfo Huerta, Armando Sylvestre, Lorena Velázquez. Azteca/Panamericana (Mexico), 1961.

Mexico's answer to Batman is El Santo ("the Saint"), an indefatigable professional wrestler complete with tights, a sleek whole-head mask, and a glittery cape, who solves crimes in his spare time. Controlled by a mad, black-masked villain from his underground lair, zombies begin a crime wave, and baffled police call in Santo to help them. He drives around in his sporty convertible, combatting zombie wrestlers in and out of the ring, pursuing them wherever they threaten law-abiding citizens. He at last infiltrates the villain's secret cave and destroys the main computer, cutting off all the power to the fiendish undead. There are some odd touches never quite explained—such as how Santo is able to observe so much on a video screen in his computerized crime lab, including the villain himself, before he even knows who or where this villain is. The adventure movie with its comic-book plot, hero, and villain is fun to watch in an MST-3K spirit, right down to the closing scene in which Santo leaves in a ray of beatific light while admirers ponder his identity and wonder at his magnanimity. It's fun, that is, as long as the prolonged wrestling sequences (including the first full ten minutes of the movie) aren't too off-putting. Santo was a real Mexican wrestler (Rudolfo Guzmán Huerta, 1919–1984), who won a championship title in 1942 and retired undefeated in the late '50s. He went on to star in forty or so movies, of which *El Santo contra los zombies* was among the first. In them he grapples with vampires, witches, wolfmen, mummies, Martians, other wrestlers, and more zombies (*The Land of the Dead*, 1969; *The Mummies of Guanajuato*, 1970; *Santo vs. Black Magic*, 1972).

The zombies are mostly revived killers and thugs, whom the police recognize as having died horribly long ago. Although their deaths involved mutilation and even burning, their bodies don't have any visible defects or scars (thus the zombification surgery apparently involves reconstructive cosmetics as well). In tunics, belts, and tights, they look like overgrown elves. They walk and even turn their heads in sync with one another, and when not being used by the villain for his diabolical schemes, simply stand around in his cave. There are maybe a dozen or so that we see, but the villain calls them by numbers that go up at least into the twenties. They receive their instructions from him by remote control, or else over their car radio. Their basic weapon is a steel rod like a crowbar that they hold upright in front of them as they walk.

The Keebler zombies wear electronic belts that are the source of their power. The belts also have other uses—in one scene, two zombies out-wrestled by Santo turn a knob on their belts and thereby disappear into thin air. They don't return to the villain, since he wonders what became of them too, so this probably represents some sort of self-destruct mechanism. The zombies aren't fazed by bullets, but they can be deanimated by removing or disabling the electronic belts (which sometimes just means bumping up against them too hard). A couple are even short-circuited when Santo tosses a flashlight battery at them. They're all reduced to smoldering piles when the main computer is destroyed at the end. Though providing endless moments of paramount absurdity, these low-budget fiends are basically bad actors in tights, and ugly ones at that; the filmmakers obviously expended all of their creativity on the intricate plot and thoughtful dialogue instead.

Alternate title: *Santo vs. the Zombies.*

Invisible Invaders

Dir: Edward L. Cahn. *Prod*: Robert E. Kent. *Screenplay*: Samuel Newman. *Cast*: Philip Tonge, John Agar, Jean Byron, Robert Hutton, John Carradine. United Artists/Premium Pictures, 1959.

Though clearly a product of its own time and a low-budget, *Invisible Invaders* is engaging and fast-paced, riddled with genuinely inspired twists alongside breathtaking implausibilities. Invisible aliens inhabiting human corpses attempt to conquer Earth. They claim that they never bothered with Earth so long as we remained primitive—but with nuclear science and the dawn of the space age, humankind has now become a threat. Unless we surrender completely, the invaders will occupy corpses all over the planet, and "The dead will

Dapper cadavers overrun '50s America in Edward Cahn's provocative *Invisible Invaders* (1959).

kill the living, and the people of Earth will cease to exist." Scientist Adam Penner (Tonge), Major Bruce Jay (Agar), and some others lock themselves in a bomb shelter/laboratory to look for an answer (as in *Day of the Dead*), while civilization collapses and the living dead pound at their very doors. Ultrasonic waves save the day. This '50s science-fiction fossil represents the first genuine zombie apocalypse of the big screen, though its importance ultimately lies more in its influence on the Romero trilogy (especially *Night*) than in its intrinsic merits.

The invisible aliens can enter or depart from the cadavers at will. When inhabited, the ambulant corpses have a pale, ashen pallor and drawn features, and if not quite rotting yet, they're certainly teetering at their expiration date. They show no vestiges of their former minds or personalities; the body is simply a vehicle for the invaders. The most memorable scenes are of a dozen or so zombies coming over a rocky ridge toward the bunker, arms out stiffly in front of them, ambling down slowly but unstoppably. Dressed impeccably in suits and ties, they look very conservative and unhappy. These respectable-citizen Eisenhower zombies are, ironically, the perfect embodiments of the perverse '50s America the protagonists are struggling to protect. (A shot from this scene appears on the cover of the 1984 The Fiends album, "We've Come for Your Beer.") These scenes, along with those of the corpses soaking up gunfire as they advance, bear the most striking resemblance to their later, more compelling counterparts in *Night.*

La Isla de los muertos see ***The Snake People***

The Island of the Last Zombies see ***Dr. Butcher, M.D.***

Island of the Living Dead see ***Zombie***

Island of the Snake People see ***The Snake People***

Island of the Zombies see ***Erotic Nights of the Living Dead***

Isle of the Snake People see ***The Snake People***

I Walked with a Zombie

Dir: Jacques Tourneur. *Prod*: Val Lewton. *Screenplay*: Curt Siodmak, Ardel Wray. *Cast*: James Ellison, Frances Dee, Tom Conway, Edith Barrett, James Bell, Christine Gordon, Teresa Harris, Sir Lancelot, Darby Jones. RKO Radio Pictures, 1943.

Lewton shot this lyric ode to sadness and entropy—among his finest films—just after his classic *Cat People.* RKO assigned Lewton the exploitation title, for which he and his company, hoping to adapt *Jane Eyre* to the West Indies (a half century before Jean Rhys' *Wide*

Statuesque zombie "Carrefour" (Darby Jones), the keeper of the crossroads, allows mindless Christine Gordon (left) and her caretaker Frances Dee (center) to pass in Val Lewton's classic *I Walked with a Zombie* (1943).

Sargasso Sea), created an atmospheric and intelligent vision unparalleled in zombie film. Nurse Betsy Connell (Dee) leaves blustery Ottawa for a position in St. Sebastian in the West Indies to care for zombie-like madwoman Jessica Holland (Gordon). There she finds herself caught in the middle of a war between two half-brothers, gloomy Paul Holland (Conway) and alcoholic Wes Rand (Ellison), and is increasingly drawn into the frightening yet ultimately knowing rituals of the natives. Fate's inexorable hand weighs heavily on the spent Europeans, while the natives are presented with an appreciation and sensitivity refreshingly at odds with Hollywood standards of the day. The stately plantation house and the sublime fields and beach are all permeated by a suffocating sense of degeneration, leaving an overall impression of the inseparability of beauty and sadness, in nature no less than in love.

There are two zombies in the movie, white Jessica and native "Carrefour" (Jones)—though it's carefully left ambiguous whether Jessica is actually undead or simply insane. The doctor explains that she had a severe tropical fever, in which portions of her spinal cord were "burnt out." She is thus "a woman without any willpower, unable to speak, or even act by herself—though she will obey simple commands." She occasionally walks about the plantation restlessly, without purpose. Gaunt and eerie Carrefour is of a different mold, his hard, stony expression contrasting with Jessica's listless sullenness. When at the climax he pursues Jessica, whose lifeless body Wes has carried to a watery grave, he stops at the shoreline, the surf washing about his feet. What's most interesting about Carrefour is that he seems not so much an unholy monster as a natural part of the cane fields and sandy shore, themselves dark and mysterious—he is, as it were, an embodiment of the will of the natives and of the land itself, a will expressing disapproval of the moral trespasses of the decadent colonialists.

I Was a Teenage Zombie

Dir: John Elias Michalakis. *Prod*: Richard Hirsh, John E. Michalakis. *Screenplay*: James Martin. *Cast*: Michael Ruben, Steve McCoy, George Seminara, Robert Sabin, Cassie Madden, Peter Bush, Allen Rickman, Kevin Nagle, Ray Stough. Periclean Motion Pictures, 1986.

Star-crossed zombie love blossoms in this irreverent amateur parody of high school romance films in the *Sixteen Candles* tradition. Bored teens have a run-in with sleazy pusher Mussolini (McCoy), who becomes a ferocious zombie after his body is thrown in an irradiated river. He kills Dan (Ruben), whom the boys then also throw into the river to create a zombie ally against their undead opponent. But all Dan winds up doing is moping in the basement of their favorite soda shop, trying to build up the nerve to ask Cindy (Madden) to the Spring Dance. Though Cindy tries to love him, bless her heart, she can barely stand to be near him, what with his stony complexion and gaping sores (she's not as open-minded as Missy in *My Boyfriend's Back*). She eventually dies also, and zombie Dan carries her body into the radioactive river, so they can be together forever. Though a successful spoof of movies that beg for it, this small-scale production suffers from drywall acting and sound/lighting limitations, and includes a distasteful rape scene. *Deadly Friend* and *I Was a Teenage Zombie* spark off the zombie romantic comedy trend of the late '80s and early '90s.

Not only do the two zombies keep their former personalities, but Dan even has to be told that he's a zombie. Zombie Mussolini, who seems to spend his time in or near the river, eats the tongue of one of his victims, and chews on a live eel when emerging from the river, but this could be an expression of rage rather than hunger. Though zombies, their physical powers are heightened by the "pure kinetic energy" that has reanimated their bodies, so they're both strong and dexterous. Ostensibly the film's major attraction, the zombies still aren't very interesting; but there are some amusing scenes, such as the one in which the kindly soda shop owner tries to convince love-struck Dan that Cindy isn't going to want to go to the dance with him because he's a zombie.

I Was a Zombie for the F.B.I.

Dir: Marius Penczner. *Prod*: Marius Penczner, Nancy Donelson. *Screenplay*: Marius Penczner, John Gillick. *Cast*: James Rasberry, Larry Raspberry, Christina Wellford, John Gillick, Laurence Hall, Anthony Isbell, Rick Crowe, Alan Zellner. Penczner Productions, 1984.

A light-hearted tribute to classic '40s detective thrillers, this over-long, black-and-white university project from Memphis comes out as a cross between *Dragnet* and *Halloween III: Season of the Witch*. Aliens take over the Health Cola plant in tiny Pleasantville, and turn the local population into subservient zombies while plotting world conquest. Hard-boiled special agents Rex Armstrong (Rasberry) and Ace Evans (Raspberry) must surmount a variety of criminals, aliens, and a clay-mation monster from outer space as they penetrate the cola plant to uncover the evil scheme and rescue Armstrong's love interest Penny (Wellford). The scripting and acting are surprisingly clean for such a small scale production, but the clichés come a little too thickly and the Zombie Noir experiment pushes the limits between satirizing the old movies and just making another one of them. Despite the flashy title, the F.B.I. agents and the zombies are entirely distinct.

More in the tradition of *Invasion of the Body Snatchers* than *Night of the Living Dead*, these zombies aren't resurrected dead but simply hypnotized living. Around Pleasantville they sit motionless, or perform only basic activities, such as listlessly pushing a rotary lawn-mower along a paved sidewalk. Doctor Kaufman's (Zellner) examinations reveal that, "subjects are still able to maneuver quite easily, relying on a primitive sensory perception. Heartbeat continues at an inordinately low rate of forty beats per minute, due to what I believe is a reduction of impulses from the sino-acrial node.... This reduction in blood flow through much of the subject's peripheral muscle tissue—particularly in the facial region—results in an ashen appearance." Entirely mechanical and expressionless, they perform their tasks around the plant (moving boxes, etc.) with the necessary coordination, though occasionally bumping into a chair. They don't seem to eat anything, but they do take regular breaks to drink the cola which keeps them mindless. Purely subordinate to their alien masters, the zombies themselves are innocuous background trimming.

I, Zombie: The Chronicles of Pain

Dir: Andrew Parkinson. *Prod*: Andrew Parkinson. *Screenplay*: Andrew Parkinson. *Cast*: Giles Aspen, Ellen Softley, Dean Sipling, Claire Griffin. Lost Films (England), 1998.

The amateur zombie movie wave of the '90s contagiously spreads to England for one of the last zombie movies of the twentieth century. Collecting moss samples on a field trip, grad student Mark (Aspen) is bitten by a spastic zombie in an abandoned house and gradually becomes a monstrous, flesh-eating fiend himself. He has to eat someone every few days or else go into wild convulsions (and even with eating people, he still has a fit once in a while), and he decomposes slowly. As the months turn to years, he narrates his deteriorating condition into a dictaphone while yearning for his understandably estranged partner Sarah (Softley). The prolonged scenes of Mark moping and motionlessly contemplating his plight don't help the pace any, but with contoured, sympathetic characters, *I, Zombie* is more competent and compelling than most of its small-scale yankee predecessors.

Though Mark analyzes his condition scientifically, the movie is more concerned with his meandering inner world than his symptoms. There's never any explanation for the phenomenon (and who needs one, by now?), and no indication of how many others out there might be suffering from the same affliction. The movie is a little short on laughs, but memorable moments include Mark applying a dainty antibacterial pomade to his gaping lesions, and later screwing metal splints onto his own festering leg using a power drill. Mark is as manly a gut-chomping ghoul as the best of them, though he does touch himself down below more often than most zombies tend to.

It Fell from the Sky see ***The Alien Dead***

Kill and Go Hide see ***The Child***

Killing Birds see *Raptors*

The Killing Box see *The Lost Brigade.*

Killing Spree

Dir: Tim Ritter, Vincent Miranda. *Prod*: Al Nicolosi. *Screenplay*: Tim Ritter. *Cast*: Asbestos Felt, Courtney Lercara, Raymond Carbone, Bruce Paquette, Joel Wynkoop. Twisted Illusions, 1987.

People with too much time on their hands in Palm Beach throw together an uninteresting backyard slasher movie with a zombie twist. Tom Russo (Felt) mistakes his wife's (Lercara) steamy fantasy stories for an actual diary, and slaughters everyone she comes into contact with in fits of frothing, jealous insanity. They all come back at the end in states of gruesome disrepair (depending on how they were killed), and argue among themselves who gets to kill him. The only creative scenes, the murders themselves, total maybe four minutes of screen time.

King of the Zombies

Dir: Jean Yarbrough. *Prod*: Lindsley Parsons. *Screenplay*: Edmond Kelso. *Cast*: Dick Purcell, Mantan Moreland, John Archer, Joan Woodbury, Henry Victor, Marguerite Whitten, Patricia Stacey, Leigh Whipper, Madame Sul-Te-Wan, Guy Usher, Jimmy Davis. Monogram, 1941.

Monogram's answer to RKO's hit of the previous year, *The Ghost Breakers*, was this utterly absurd and delightful thriller featuring a veritable smorgasbord of alternative consciousness—hypnotism, zombification, and transmigration of souls. Even-keeled Bill Summers (Archer), irascible James McCarthy (Purcell), and Bill's energetic valet Jefferson (Moreland) crash-land on a mysterious island somewhere between Cuba and Puerto Rico. There they are welcomed by courteous yet sinister Dr. Sangre (Victor), a Nazi spy who's been trying to extract military information from an abducted admiral (Usher) by transferring the admiral's soul to another body for questioning, through voodoo rituals. The only really spooky scene (Archer and Moreland finding a desiccated mummy) didn't make it into the final movie except for a brief glimpse, and neither did Bela Lugosi, originally up for the part of Dr. Sangre. To cap off the list of near-misses, the film's unremarkable music score (by Edward Kay) actually went up against that of *Citizen Kane* for the 1941 Academy Award. But Moreland's running commentary on the undead keeps the dialogue lively, and this is easily the funniest of the zombie comedy-horrors of the 1940s.

Except for McCarthy, the zombies are all large native men with stern faces, but generally look too wasted and empty to seem especially menacing. Moreland refers to them as "dead folks what's too lazy to lay down," and later hypothesizes of a suspected zombie, "Supposin' he's dead and don't know it." They stand straight and tall, their heads never tilted down—even when they eat soup. Sangre insists that zombies don't eat meat, but the servants pointedly tell African-American Jackson that the "haints" prefer *dark* meat. Sangre hypnotizes Jackson into believing he's a zombie, but Samantha (Whitten) snaps him out of it again by making him eat salt (salt causes true zombies to shrivel up and "get dead again"). She also mentions that zombies can't talk and don't cast a reflection in a mirror. In the original script, they were not only supposed to talk, but actually to sing a number called "The Grave Digger's Song." Despite Moreland's Shaggy–like fear of the zombies, they never really wind up hurting anyone. As Tom Weaver observes, "The impression the film gives is that all they ever do is wander around outside the kitchen waiting to be fed."

Kiss Daddy Goodbye see ***Revenge of the Zombie***

Kung Fu Zombie

Dir: Hwa I Hung. *Prod*: Pal Ming. *Cast*: Billy Chong, Chan Lau, Chang Tao, Cheng Ka Ying, Kwon Young Moon, Pak Sha Lik, Shum Yan Chi. (Hong Kong), 1982.

In the opening scene, a Mau-Sham priest demonstrates his powers to a potential customer by reanimating three sprightly leaping zombies, nimble and lightning-quick, who literally fly out of their coffins. They all fight for a few moments before being sent back to their graves; then the rest of the movie is about a pair of demon vampires instead. The speeded-up cinematography of martial arts action sequences always gives zombies in East Asian cinema a novel, charismatic twist.

La Cage aux Zombies

Dir: Kelly Hughes. *Screenplay*: Kelly Hughes. *Cast*: Cathy Roubal, Eric Gladsjo, J.R. Clarke, William Love, Betty Marshall, Beautiful Barb. Lucky Charm Studio, 1995.

Not everyone likes their undead in G–strings and long lashes, but never say the zombie isn't versatile. Upset to discover that her irritable husband (Clarke) is an international drug lord rather than a publisher, Norma (Roubal) tries to run off to Vegas with a bag of his money. Her plans are sidetracked when her boyfriend Brent (Gladsjo) dies and becomes a zombie of equivocal sexuality, while an army of drag-ghouls forms in the streets. It seems a team of muscular football players who went down in a plane wreck (and were forced to eat each other) have risen again by means of "strange voodoo" and unleash their uniquely risqué brand of evil upon Seattle. Those who are bitten strip down to bulging jockstraps and kill with tomahawks and powder puffs. Look not for subtlety in this ultra-camp zombie marathon, but it's certainly less predictable than the average '90s undead home movie. An aristocratic Nazi lady goes around spurting blood at people from her empty arm socket the entire movie, for instance, and in one scene a transvestite zombie standing around in a bathroom pats himself on the stomach for maybe two full minutes while a woman (well, could be a woman) watches from a wheelchair. Still, this sort of forced weirdness gets old after a while. The cameraperson half-heartedly mutters "k-pow" to represent gunshots.

Le Labyrinthe see ***A Virgin Among the Living Dead***

Le Lac des morts vivants see ***Zombie Lake***

El Lago de los muertos vivientes see ***Zombie Lake***

The Lake of the Living Dead see ***Zombie Lake***

The Land of the Dead

(Orig. *El mundo de los muertos*). Dir: Gilberto Martínez Solares. *Prod:* Jesús Sotomayor Martínez. *Story:* Rafael García Travesí, Jesús Sotomayor Martínez. *Cast:* Santo, Blue Demon, Pilar Pellicer, Carlos León, Antonio Raxel, Guillermo Bianchi, Carlos Suárez. Sotomayor (Mexico), 1969.

El Santo continues his fight for truth and justice, this time saving fiancée Alicia (Pellicer) from a vengeful 300-year-old witch. The antiquated sorceress sends three reanimated corpses against Santo, who fight him in his home, in the wrestling ring, and in some nearby fields. In a terrific sequence, fearless Santo even travels to the fire-choked pits of hell (shown in red-tint and dubbed over with the wailing of the damned), where he wrestles some more. The most ambrosial part of it all, though, are the savory glimpses we get into Santo's private life: with cardigan and slacks he goes on a group tour in a museum, with suit and tie he attends a party, and with night shirt he reads in bed—the whole time wearing his ludicrous whole-head wrestling mask.

The undead are shown rising from their tombs in the seventeenth century, and later more cadavers emerge from steaming red tombs in hell itself (say, what does it mean to be dead in hell, anyway?). The fiendish grapplers follow the bidding of the Satan-worshipping witch, and are themselves driven by infernal powers. Thus they can teleport at will, even appearing in the ring while Santo is trying to fight. They're immune to all regular attacks, but they can be driven away temporarily by a cross, the first rays of dawn, or a good wrestle.

Alternate titles: *Santo and Blue Demon in the Land of the Dead*, *El Santo en el mundo de los muertos*.

The Last Man on Earth

Dir: Sidney Salkow. *Prod*: Robert L. Lippert. *Screenplay*: Logan Swanson, William Leicester. *Cast*: Vincent Price, Franca Bettoia, Emma Danieli, Giacomo Rossi-Stuart. AIP/Alta Vista Productions, 1964.

Richard Matheson's novel *I Am Legend*, the ultimate inspiration for George Romero's screenplay for *Night*, enjoys a fairly close screen adaptation with a strong lead from Vincent Price. Price is Robert Morgan, the last living human being after an all-encompassing plague has devastated the earth and transformed the human race into vampires. By day Morgan systematically scours the city trying to locate and kill them; by night he tries to stay sane in his barricaded house as the plague-ridden undead incessantly pound at his door and call out his name. At last Morgan stumbles across a woman who reveals to him an underground society of survivors who are only partially infected, whom he has been unwittingly killing along with the vampires. The ending is more upbeat than that of Matheson's novel, but this doesn't detract from the grim and potent statement on modern society implied in the macabre parody of daily routine. *The Omega Man* with Charleton Heston is a much freer and more sensationalistic adaptation of the same story.

Elegant interior decorator Vincent Price calls out over the empty airways to ascertain whether he is really *The Last Man on Earth* (1964).

The undead vestiges of the former human race represent a seamless blend of vampire and zombie elements. Superimposed on what is (to all appearances) a zombie are the Hollywood trimmings of a vampire: they can't bear to see their reflection or to smell garlic, they can't stand sunlight, and they can be killed by driving a stake through the heart. But I know a zombie when I see one: these mindless hulks lumber around in tattered and soiled clothes, devoid of emotion and humanity, repetitively droning a few simple phrases. Though they seem to remember a few simple things and can identify Morgan by name, their mental faculties are all but erased. It takes zombie Cortman three years, for instance, to figure out how to knock the mirror off of Morgan's door—simply by approaching it from the side. The undead wield sticks or whatever else they pick up, using them to pound half-heartedly at Morgan's door and walls. They are utterly ineffective in their manipulation of these tools, however; Cortman probably hits himself as often as he does the barricaded door. Overall the relentless zombies are quite chilling, forming a solid bridge between those of *Invisible Invaders* and *Night*. One scene in which they scrounge for implements and begin assaulting the house to the sound of a grand choral arrangement is particularly grandiose and artistic.

The Laughing Dead

Dir: S.P. Somtow. *Prod*: Lex Nakashima. *Screenplay*: S.P. Somtow. *Cast*: Tim Sullivan, Wendy Webb, S.P. Somtow, Premika Eaton, Patrick Roskowick, Larry Kagan, Krista Keim, Ryan Effner. Archaeopteryx/Tercel, 1989.

Kindly but world-weary priest Ezekiel O'Sullivan (Sullivan) takes a group of high school kids for an archaeology field trip to Oaxaca, Mexico, during the Festival of the Laughing Dead. There, the evil Dr. Umtzec (Somtow) targets them as sacrifices for a ritual he's planning, to prevent an astrological harmonic convergence. O'Sullivan becomes possessed by a demon during a backfiring exorcism, while the rest of the group attempt to marshal the aid of benevolent god Quetzalcouatl through New-Age crystal power. Sucked into an alternate world through a rune-marked portal, the group confronts Umtzec and his army of zombies. Following ancient Aztec traditions (sort of), the humans play the zombies in "the Ball Game of Death" (actually just basketball), that the humans easily win for obvious reasons. Light-hearted even at its most climactic moments, the horror spoof yields some fairly funny scenes for those who can sit through the arduous character development.

In the subterranean caverns of the alternate world, the decayed, long-haired zombies wander around carrying long, pointed sticks, awaiting Umtzec's bidding. They are stiff-jointed and slow, still wearing their torn and bloodstained white sacrificial robes. (There's even a glimpse of a zombie wearing sports socks in the basketball scene.) They only appear briefly, to champion the cause of evil in the ceremonial ball game. Bless their bodies, the plodding undead do manage some rudimentary attempts at dribbling, faking, passing, and shooting, though they're no match for opponents of normal human dexterity. Discouraged, they take to assaulting the human team instead. The zombies don't get much screen time and are only used as comic foils, but the basketball scene is truly one of the great moments in zombie cinema.

The Legend of the Seven Golden Vampires

Dir: Roy Ward Baker. *Prod*: Don Houghton, Vee King Shaw. *Screenplay*: Don Houghton. *Cast*: Peter Cushing, David Chiang, Julie Ege, Robin Stewart, Shih Szu, John Forbes-Robertson, Chan Shen. Hammer/Shaw (England, Hong Kong), 1973.

Hammer Studios, known for atmospheric period horror, and the Shaw Brothers, a martial arts company, collaborate to create a high body-count kung fu–vampire hybrid. This colorful mongrel filmed in Hong Kong is definitely not the usual Hammer fare. Professor Van Helsing (Cushing), having just completed his famous adventures in Transylvania, accompanies Hsi Ching (Chiang) and his seven siblings—all masters of martial arts, and each specializing in a particular weapon—across the forbidding Chinese wilderness to subdue seven vampires. In a final kung fu bloodbath, the vampires and their undead army besiege the brothers and other villagers in the walled town of Ping Kwei. Intoxicating and continually varied, this resituates gothic Hammer themes and production values (already past their prime in 1973) in a fresh setting, injecting them with the frenetic energy of martial arts movies.

The Seven Golden Vampires are withered, crusty-skinned demons with long fangs. They reside with Dracula in a pagoda temple, calling on the "demons of hell" to preserve them, and summoning their former victims from the graveyard by chiming on a large gong. The first scene in which the dead rise is very powerful—mostly reduced to mere skeletons, these zombies ascend fluidly from their misty graves (in slow motion, following de Ossorio) and converge to form a sizable army. They wear tattered robes with sashes, their long black hair flowing around their grey skull-faces. No hoes or farming implements for this undead army—they sport tridents, spears, and a formidable arsenal of other impolite hooked, pointed, and edged weapons. The awesome and unhurried ceremony of the first zombie sequence isn't sustained, though: in the final siege, the zombies trot along at a brisk pace behind their mounted vampire masters. Furthermore, the zombies exhibit a strange habit of running in place even when not actually advancing, giving them an air of edgy restlessness. Nonetheless, the undead army of *Seven Golden Vampires*, formally decked out in battle gear, is one of the most visually spectacular in zombie cinema. The more recent undead siege in *Army of Darkness* (1992) is undermined by camp silliness and slapstick comedy.

Alternate titles: *Dracula and the Seven Golden Vampires*, *The Seven Brothers Meet Dracula*.

Let Sleeping Corpses Lie

(Orig. *No profanar el sueño de los muertos*). Dir: Jorge Grau. *Producer:* Edmondo Amati. *Screenplay:* Sandro Continenza, Marcello Coscia. *Cast:* Ray Lovelock, Christine Galbo, Arthur Kennedy, Jeannine Mestre, José Ruiz Lifante, Fernando Hilbeck. Star Films/Flaminia Productions (Spain, Italy), 1974.

Screen zombies are international if they're anything: Catalonian director Grau shot his surprisingly effective English-language, Spanish-Italian co-production on location in the green, bucolic splendor of northern England. Hapless Edna (Galbo) and vitriolic George (Lovelock) meet by accident and are quickly plunged into a series of bizarre happenings in the Lakes District highlands—Edna is attacked by a man known to be dead for a week (Hilbeck), and both out-of-towners are suspected by the local no-nonsense police sergeant (Kennedy) for the strange murders suddenly plaguing the area. Really to blame are the ultrasonic radiation rays put out by a device from the Department of Agriculture meant to destroy farm insects and parasites. The rays, which only affect more primitive nervous systems, are supposed to drive the insects mad so that they attack one another—but the experimental rays also affect newborn babies, and as it happens, the recently dead. A successful *Night of the Living Dead* remake and adaptation, this offers numerous edge-of-your-seat scenes with a minimum of the embarrassing lines and filler material characteristic of the genre. Clean direction and tolerable acting give the film a far more professional feel than most zombie gut-flicks of the period, and there is something poignantly jarring in setting the zombies against peaceful, pastoral hills and dales in full daylight.

These undead are sturdier and stronger than the easily-repelled zombies of *Night*, and certainly more intelligent. Not simply mindless killers, they flee from superior numbers and are not above lurking in shadows to bide their time. They kill by strangling, crushing bones, stabbing and hacking with sharp objects, and in one scene, they hurl a large tombstone as a projectile. They even employ the tombstone as a battering ram in a two-zombie coordinated effort, though that's the extent of their technological and strategic sophistication. The ghouls respond negatively to bright light and recoil from fire, but display no other pain responses or emotional behaviors. They unflinchingly suffer being impaled, chopped, shot, and smacked upside the head with a rock, and are never the worse for wear. Burning seems to be the only way to stop them.

Although only recently dead corpses are directly revived by the radiation, older ones can also be raised through an odd ritual. In a moment of unusual clarity and purpose, one zombie lightly dabs the eyes of several other corpses with fresh blood, causing them to rise as zombies. The anomalous rite is unnecessarily mystical and religious in a movie otherwise content to treat the phenomenon as a nervous disorder. The zombies' main motivation seems to be pure hostility, but they also feast on their victims, either from a secondary hunger impulse, or simply as an extension of their aggression. Sober English landscape notwithstanding, they also share the propensity of many Spanish-Italian ghouls for tearing blouses and generally fixating on breasts. Otherwise, though, they are restraintful and captivating, perhaps the best zombies in a year of very good zombies.

Alternate titles: *Breakfast at the Manchester Morgue*, *Don't Open the Window*, *Fin de semana para los muertos*, *Living Dead at the Manchester Morgue*, *Non sì deve profanare il sonno dei morti*, *Zombi 3: Da dove vieni?*

Linnea Quigley's Horror Work-Out

Dir: Hal Kennedy. *Prod*: Fred Kennamer. *Screenplay*: Hal Kennedy. *Cast*: Linnea Quigley, and zombies: Jeffrey Bowser, Patricia Harras, Randall Harvey, Erica Horn, Brent Jasmer, Prince Jones, Heather Jean McKenzie, Cyndi Newton, Kathi Obrecht, Rico Telles, Clayton Woolley. KDRQ Productions, 1989.

Overrated B–horror scream-queen Quigley (famous for her tombstone dance in *Return of the Living Dead*) dishes out self-serving nonsense for video distribution, featuring clips from her movies and Linnea making simple-minded jokes as she does calisthenics in a metal-studded bra and fishnet stockings. The middle segment finds her jogging innocently through a graveyard, when a gaggle of zombies inexplicably rise from their graves and pursue her. They're supposed to be crawling from their tombs, but are obviously just standing up from lying around in the grass. They finally overtake her at a swimming pool (rather implausibly, since they are stumbling along slowly and she is jogging), where she confronts them with being out of shape: "Just because you're dead do you think you can let yourselves go?" Then they all begin a coordinated exercise routine. They manage all right with "the jerk" and "the swim," but the dead are especially bad with knee-lifts. Though the exercise routines are just tedious enough to suggest an off-beat work-out video, the camera angles and jokes presuppose more of an adolescent male couch audience.

Living a Zombie Dream

Dir: Todd Reynolds. *Prod*: Todd Reynolds. *Screenplay*: Todd Reynolds. *Cast*: Amon Elsey, Michelle White, Mike Smith, Frank Alexander. Borderline, 1996.

How do you stretch forty or fifty minutes of iffy footage into a feature-length film? Possibly by repeating scenes over and over in different combinations, and marketing the disjointed mosaic as stream-of-consciousness. Here our troubled, unnamed protagonist (Elsey) can't patch up a failing relationship with his significant other (White), in part because of his increasing cannibalism and zombiedom. His zombie brother (Smith) and a zombie psychopath (Alexander) appear to him in dreams and follow him around, drawing him deeper into their Donner–like diet. In the absence of even the most rudimentary details of the protagonist's life (background, profession, etc.), though, it's a little hard to connect the themes of alienation and cannibalism-as-empowerment with specific anxieties. Fractured splices of the individual scenes, which are surreal and virtually devoid of dialogue to begin with, are oddly juxtaposed with one another, over and over. The shoestring odyssey is hardly a Lucasfilm production; the few names in the cast credits are re-shuffled to form the technical credits.

The psychopath (credited as the "Zombie Lord") kills the protagonist's brother and drinks his blood. The brother comes back as a mangy zombie with hamburger complexion, gnawing on human skin and intestines whenever he finds a donor. When he complains that what he eats only falls out of his open abdominal cavity, the fraternal protagonist obligingly sews him shut again. A voice-over periodically explains what it feels like to be dead, offering insights such as "Flies have laid eggs in my skull." The narrator at last resolves a running tension between whether he should eat the flesh of the living or the dead: apparently, one should eat the flesh of the dead, and drink the blood of the living. But then, there's more talk than stalk, and the zombies don't kill any more victims than the living characters do, so the whole question is academic.

Living Dead at the Manchester Morgue see ***Let Sleeping Corpses Lie***

Living Dead in Tokyo Bay

Dir: (Gaira) Kazuo Komizu. *Prod*: (Gaira) Kazuo Komizu. *Screenplay*: Kei Dai. *Cast*: Cutei Suzuki, Kera, Heiko Hayase, Kenzi Ohtsuki. (Japan), 1992.

As if Tokyo hasn't been terrorized by enough monsters, Romero-esque zombies now add to their ranks in a comic-book action-adventure feature. A meteor crashes off the coast of Japan, releasing a gaseous cloud that kills everyone and then reanimates them as ghoulish undead. Since the plague spreads like wildfire, the army is forced to section off the entire city, killing anything that tries to leave the perimeter. Resourceful heroine Keiko (Suzuki), armed with huge guns, clever gadgets, and ninja-like prowess, is the Snake Plissken of this Japanese *Escape from New York*. She teams up with a handful of renegades to combat a corrupt military general as well as the zombies. East Asian action movies always have lively choreography, but low-budget effects and goofy costumes are devastating for a science-fiction apocalypse feature such as this one.

All corpses in the Tokyo area rise as cannibal zombies, due to radiation from the meteor (the "DNA–charged atmosphere"). They range from fairly normal-looking (freshly dead) to greenish, wrinkled goblins (vintage). They weave and sway with difficulty, arms outstretched, rasping deeply and dryly. Only in a few scenes are the zombies really the central interest, since the major battles are between Keiko and human opponents. There's nothing especially interesting about these undead, except maybe that post-apocalyptic Tokyo offers a slight change of background scenery.

Loonies on Broadway see ***Zombies on Broadway***

The Lost Brigade

Dir: George Hickenlooper. *Prod*: Brad Krevoy, Steve Stabler. *Screenplay*: Matt Greenberg. *Cast*: Corbin Bernsen, Adrian Pasdar, Ray Wise, Cynda Williams, Roger Wilson, Martin Sheen. Motion Picture Corporation of America, 1992.

In this slick Civil War period piece with name stars, a high budget, and lofty aspirations, a Union tracker (Pasdar) and a Confederate POW (Bernsen) must team up to find the mysterious Alabama 51st, a supposedly extinct regiment causing much undue mayhem on the Kentucky-Tennessee border. With the assistance of a mute but telepathic runaway slave (Williams), they learn that the massacred platoon was revived by certain "Makers," dark forces unleashed in Africa and brought to the New World by slave traders. The Makers dwell in subterranean tunnels, feeding off the weak and "making" the strong—that is, reviving them as undead cannibals. These beings roam the earth at night, indiscriminately killing people from either side of the Mason-Dixon, slowly raising an undead army. After much careful build-up and creative mythology, they are disappointingly eradicated with old B–horror staples such as running water and silver bullets. The movie features strong conceptual underpinnings, though it's a little dragged down by tritely over-demonized foes.

The undead Confederates are like zombies in some ways, like vampires in other ways, and like crude backwoods yokels in most ways. Though said to be soulless, they retain their memory and personality, with the additional knowledge and power of primal supernatural forces. They feed on humans and small woodland animals, and those bitten also become infected (well, the humans, anyway). The film poses an interesting ideological paradox in conflating the racist Southerners with black African spirits: the Rebels advance to the beat of a marching drum juxtaposed with an African drum, and they even decorate themselves with tribal war paint while wearing CSA uniforms. All in all, though, the careful conceptual framework behind the undead soldiers is wasted on the foul-mouthed, brutish riff-raff they turn out to be. Surely primordial evil is something more than concentrated redneck energy.

Alternate titles: *Ghost Brigade*, *Grey Knight*, *The Killing Box*.

The Love Wanga see ***Ouanga***

The Man with the Synthetic Brain see ***Blood of Ghastly Horror***

La Mansión de los muertos vivientes see ***Mansion of the Living Dead***

Mansion of the Living Dead

(Orig. *La mansión de los muertos vivientes*). Dir: Jesús Franco. *Novel*: D. Khunne. *Cast*: Candy Coster, Robert Foster, Mabel Escaño, Eva León, Albino

Grazián, Mamie Kaplan, Jasmina Bell. Golden Films Internacional (Spain), 1982.

Jess Franco, notorious for movies on women in prison, sex crimes of the SS, and other tasteful fare, cashes in on de Ossorio's success with his own sordid *Tombs of the Blind Dead* rip-off filmed in the Canary Islands. The spirits of the Spanish Inquisition live on in an 18th-century monastery at an isolated tourist beach region, where they offer human sacrifices, when available, to the devil. Four nymphomanic waitresses come to unwind but instead fall prey to the monkish zombies. The unhelpful hotel manager, who keeps his starving wife chained to a wall and who is also one of the undead monks, becomes convinced that one of the four women is the incarnation of a certain princess whom the monks have long awaited to release them from their curse. Certain features of the movie are unusual—for instance, nothing takes place at night (the monastery is at least as brightly lit as the hotel), and the monastery is clean and well-kept rather than dusty and crumbling. The film is marked throughout, however, by a disturbing hostility toward women: they are sexual objects from start to finish, and the voyeuristic impulse would seem less offensive if it weren't accompanied by unashamed misogynistic violence. Jess Franco, who plays jazz and speaks six languages, annoyed his family of eminent writers by giving up his studies in law and philosophy to crank out formula sexploitation movies by the score. He is by far the most prolific of the European sex-horror directors, with around 150 full-length features.

The zombie Inquisitors vary in their physical appearance—some wear goofy skull masks, while others simply have what looks like mayonnaise smeared on their faces. In their white cowls and hoods, standing around the room, the monks force sinners (i.e., women) to their knees and make them stand trial for their crimes. They are invariably found guilty, gang-raped by the grotesque zombies, and then stabbed to death. The monks say they are guided by a "Satanic decalogue," and openly pay homage to "our father who is in hell." The hotel manager refers to their continued existence as a curse, and in fact the cheerless monks seem more resigned than libidinous as they ritually rape the accused (they even keep mumbling prayers the whole time). Depraved, unlikable, and artless, Franco's inquisitorial zombies are among the ideological and aesthetic low-points of the species.

Messiah of Evil

Dir: Willard Huyck. *Prod*: Gloria Katz. *Screenplay*: Willard Huyck, Gloria Katz. *Cast*: Michael Greer, Mariana Hill, Joy Bang, Anitra Ford, Royal Dano, Elisha Cook Jr., Charles Dierkop. V/M Production, 1972.

The makers of *American Graffiti* (1973) warm up with a dream-like tale of descent into madness and monstrosity. Unsuspecting Arletty (Hill) travels to a small coastal town in California to track down her estranged father, but finds that somehow things aren't quite right: he's missing, and the locals are all mutant cannibals. With the help of a suave travelling playboy (Greer), she penetrates the conspiracy of secrecy and uncovers the town's dark past. It seems that a century before, a certain "dark stranger," who crossed the mountains with the Donner party and partook of human flesh, placed a curse on Point Dune and threatened to return after a hundred years. Now the entire population of soulless cannibals holds rituals and lights bonfires on the beach, awaiting his return. Arletty relates all this from an insane asylum, indicating at the end that the stranger has in fact returned, and that the evil will now spread from the town and slowly make its way inland. The heavy, lugubrious atmosphere is fraught throughout with disjointed images and an unshakable sense of the uncanny. There are certain logic and continuity problems, but the movie's two main protagonist deaths (in a supermarket and a movie theater) are superbly executed, and the theme song is unusually haunting.

Just about everyone in the quiet town has succumbed to the ancient evil that is slowly manifesting itself. They have become mere shells of their former selves, moving as if in slow motion and always giving the impression that they're up to something. Actually, the two main things they're up to are eating flesh (preferably human, but they're not too picky) and preparing for the return of the dark stranger. The process of becoming one of these zombies involves bleeding from the eyes and becoming insensitive to pain. Bodies must be burned to prevent them from returning. Memorable moments include an elvin, inbred villager snacking on a crunchy mouse, and a group of the peckish townspeople tearing into the meat section at a supermarket like pigs at a trough.

Alternate titles: *Dead People*, *Return of the Living Dead*, *Revenge of the Screaming Dead*, *The Second Coming*.

The Midnight Hour

Dir: Jack Bender. *Prod*: Ervin Zavada. *Screenplay*: Bill Bleich. *Cast*: Lee Montgomery, Jonna Lee, Shari Belafonte-Harper, LeVar Burton, Peter DeLuise, Kevin McCarthy, Dedee Pfeiffer, Dick Van Patten. American Broadcasting Companies, 1985.

Even zombie completists will have a hard time stomaching this lame made-for-TV drivel, which unapologetically attempts to cash in on the success of Michael Jackson's "Thriller" video. Bored high schoolers in Pitchford Cove, a small New England town with roots in the days of witchcraft and Wolfman Jack for a DJ, read an ancient scroll of summoning in the graveyard on Halloween night for a lark. The spell commands the demons of hell to appear and the dead to rise: "Life to the dead, death to the living." As in *Children Shouldn't Play With Dead Things*, the joke spell actually works, and a bizarre range of fiends present themselves: the rotting dead crawl from their graves, an ancient witch returns as a vampire, a werewolf or two come out of nowhere, and most frightening of all, a perky '50s cheerleader shows up to flirt with geeky protagonist Phil (Montgomery). These fiends begin to visit slaughter upon the town, until Phil dispels them all with a counter-ritual. The movie comes across largely as a string of parody and homage elements from B–horror and other movies, right down to Sandy from *Grease*. "Eight is Enough" dad Dick Van Patten is a vampire dentist.

The Midnight Hour focuses somewhat more on the vampires, who represent the serious threat, than on the zombies, who are mostly the butt of jokes and parody. These parodies aren't especially subtle or sophisticated, either. At a teen kegger, an ugly dwarf zombie puts on sunglasses and drinks straight out of the punch bowl; another ill-mannered stiff stuffs his face with popcorn and gruffly mutters, "Popcorn!"; and a zombie couple make out on the couch, the decomposing man trying to grope the decayed woman while she swats his hand away. No Swiftian satire here. The party culminates in a synchronized undead dancing scene à la Michael. Lead actress Belafonte-Harper sings the song, "Get Dead," which was clearly intended to be abstracted as a music video for MTV—but I never saw it. Only at the end are the creatures employed briefly for serious effect, when the zombie army slowly advances against Phil and Sandy. There's also an operatic pageant of zombies in one offbeat scene scored with a classical aria, featuring bride and groom zombies, undead revolutionary soldiers, and a discontented dead milkman pouring out his milk.

Mistresses of Dr. Jekyll see *Dr. Orloff's Monster*

Las Momias de Guanajuato see *The Mummies of Guanajuato*

Monster High

Dir: Rüdiger Poe. *Prod*: Eric Bernt. *Screenplay*: Roy Langsdon, John Platt. *Cast*: Dean Iandoli, Diana Frank, David Marriott, Robert Lind, Sean Haines, David Fuhrer, David Bloch. Catapult Productions/Lightyear Entertainment, 1989.

Space criminal Armageddon (Marriott), who plans to destroy the earth as soon as he's done harassing some high school kids, kills a prep (Bloch) by suffocating him with an enormous condom, and then revives him as a cannibal zombie. The zombie is the subject of several juvenile gags (e.g., when someone recoils from him in horror, he sniffs at his armpits), until Candice (Frank) impales his head with a flagpole. Another student (Fuhrer) bitten by him also rises, but Candice deanimates this one as well, by beating his head repeatedly with a book. Indeed.

Monster Hunter see *Zombie 6: Monster Hunter*

Monstrosity

Dir: Joseph Mascelli. *Prod*: Jack Pollexfen, Dean Dillman Jr. *Screenplay*: Vy Russell, Sue Dwiggins, Dean Dillman Jr. *Cast*: Marjorie Eaton, Erika Peters, Frank Gerstle, Frank Fowler, Judy Bamber, Lisa Lang. Emerson Films, 1963.

The cinematographer of Steckler's *Incredibly Strange Creatures who Stopped Living and Became Mixed-Up Zombies* directs a deservedly infamous biomedical horror. Three women are imprisoned by cranky old Heddy March (Eaton), who seeks a nubile young body into which she hopes to transplant her brain with the help of her disgruntled, basement-dwelling mad scientist Dr. Frank (Gerstle). One woman is given a cat's brain, while a wolf-man prowls about the estate from a dog-brain implant that went awry. This riotous potpourri of horror motifs features surprising cruelty to the protagonists, but crusty Mrs. March steals the show as she makes the young women try on clothes and prods about them with her cane, coldly inspecting the body she soon plans to inhabit.

She must reject subjects who aren't absolutely fresh, since "brain deterioration is too extensive for thought processes" (this is the earliest explicit statement that brain decay accounts for the zombie's diminished intelligence, which Romero will later render canonical). One woman Frank brings back from the dead must not have been too fresh, then: retaining only basic motor functions, the "walking, breathing, zombie-like creature" wanders around the cellar laboratory in her white robe and bare feet with a blank stare. She soon meanders out a door accidentally left open and is torn to pieces by the dog-brained wolf-man. Good stuff.

Alternate title: *The Atomic Brain.*

La Muerte viviente see ***The Snake People***

The Mummies of Guanajuato

(Orig. *Las momias de Guanajuato*). *Dir*: Federico Curiel. *Prod*: Luis Quintanilla Rico. *Screenplay*: Rogelio Agrasánchez. *Cast*: Blue Demon, Mil Máscaras, Santo, Elsa Cárdenas, Juan Gallardo, Jorge Pingüino. Películas Latinoamericanas (Mexico), 1970.

Mexico is in a unique position to capitalize on the Hollywood zombie and assimilate it with its own indigenous culture, because of certain remarkably preserved cadavers in a town north of Mexico City. The "mummies" of Guanajuato (not wrapped in bandages like Egyptian mummies) are a famous tourist attraction, featuring naturally embalmed bodies that have been preserved as gaunt, gruesome figures twisted into contorted positions through the chemical properties of the soil in which they were buried. This would be a beautiful opportunity to create a zombie movie with anthropological and historical resonance, but—no big surprise—actually it turns out to be little more than the backdrop for another wrestling marathon. Among the preserved bodies is a certain "Satan," an antiquated grappler in tattered red wrestling tights, who was cheated of the world championship title a hundred years ago by the ancestor of El Santo, and who now returns from death for a grudge match. A small platoon of zombies reanimate along with him to spook locals. Blue Demon, Mil Máscaras ("Thousand Masks"), and Santo pummel away unsuccessfully at the indestructible zombies for a while, until figuring out that they're highly flammable. The victorious athletes then run off to Denny's or something for a bite to eat.

The zombies aren't half bad—wretched, grisly forms with deformed features and patches of long, straggling hair on their bald heads. Apparently due to some chemical loophole, though, their bodies from the neck down are perfectly preserved, still pink, smooth, healthy, and highly un-zombielike. However ferocious they look, the fiends are pathetic fighters, swatting feebly at the masked protagonists while off-screen foley artists clap sticks together to produce striking sounds of monotonous regularity. Why it takes an entire triad of wrestling heroes to defeat these dura-flame zombies is anybody's guess.

El Mundo de los muertos see ***The Land of the Dead***

Muñecos infernales see ***The Curse of the Doll People***

Mutant

Dir: John "Bud" Cardos. *Prod*: Igo Kantor. *Screenplay*: Peter Orton, Michael Jones, John Kruize. *Story*: Michael Jones, John Kruize. *Cast*: Wings Hauser, Bo Hopkins, Jody Medford, Lee Montgomery, Marc Clement, Jennifer Warren, Cary Guffey. Laurelwood Productions, 1984.

This fairly humorless and uncomplicated zombie invasion exercise, though less bothersome than half a dozen others of its kind, is still derivative and unnecessary. City boys Josh (Hauser) and Mike (Montgomery) roll through a small Southern town on vacation, but quickly irk local rednecks and zombies. Josh joins up with schoolteacher Holly (Medford) to expose the evil goings on at a certain "New Era" chemical waste plant on the outskirts of town, which is responsible for the town's entire population becoming either mutant zombies or food for the mutant zombies. Production values are just solid enough to keep the last half of the movie (the zombie invasion itself) vigorous, though the shocks and general story line are more than familiar.

After contact with the toxic waste, the victims become ill and then finally transform all at once into pullulating blue meanies. Surlier than the average zombie, these growling brutes steal blood by the pint from the local medical clinic when no victims are available. Their touch is corrosive, even eating through glass (though this motif isn't really sustained consistently). The zombies feel pain and can be killed with gunfire, though they're pretty tough and can swallow a few shots first. They're also highly sensitive to light, and can be driven back with car headlights. Otherwise they correspond to standard notions of zombie behavior and appearance in most respects, grasping mindlessly through windows, with hands and fingers waving around like cilia. The closing sequence presents a well-executed zombie onslaught fraught with tension, unburdened by comic relief or facile one-liners.

My Boyfriend's Back

Dir: Bob Balaban. *Prod*: Sean S. Cunningham. *Screenplay*: Dean Lorey. *Cast*: Andrew Lowery, Traci Lind, Danny Zorn, Matthew Fox, Paul Dooley, Austin Pendleton, Bob Dishy. Touchstone, 1993.

Touchstone's light-hearted zombie-nerd-winds-up-with-homecoming-queen romantic comedy is creative and playful—in fact, it's so innocuous you'd hardly guess it was produced by Sean Cunningham (*Friday the 13th*). In a convenience store hold-up, Johnny Dingle (Lowery) takes a bullet meant for his childhood crush Missy McLoud (Lind). After the funeral he crawls from his grave as a zombie and tries to reintegrate himself with the community. Missy falls for zombie Johnny despite herself, as he struggles to overcome prejudice against the undead and tries his hardest not to eat too many people. Johnny is plagued by two main worries—decaying and being a cannibal—both of which threaten to render him even more of a social outcast at school than when he was alive. He has to eat human flesh to keep from rotting, but really he only wants to remain fresh long enough to take Missy to the prom. Like Paul in *My Zombie Lover*, Johnny is torn between caring for Missy and hungering for her flesh (cannibalism as a thinly veiled metaphor for sexual desire). *My Boyfriend's Back* is unquestionably wittier and smoother than the other zombie romantic comedies of the late '80s and early '90s, and it also makes explicit all the adolescent anxiety metaphors only suggested in them (e.g., decay as acne and zombie as outsider). The dialogue remains pleasantly challenging and surreal ("It's not her fault—she was taken in by his wily decaying ways"), but the movie becomes decidedly syrupy.

In a sequence set in heaven, we learn that Johnny was allowed to return as a zombie because someone messed up in the heavenly bureaucracy, and in such cases the victim of the blunder is allowed a second chance at life, as a zombie. The entire pearly-gates episode is presented in an antiseptic, pastel heaven of the George Burns variety, and the zombie concept is reduced to a cheesy "second chance to do

Traci Lind overcomes local prejudice, agreeing to go to the prom with Andrew Lowery despite his recent death. *My Boyfriend's Back* (1993) is the best of the inexplicably popular zombie romantic comedies of the late '80s and early '90s.

good" theme familiar from other saccharine family comedies such as *Heaven Can Wait*. Is this what the zombie has become?

My Zombie Lover

(Episode, *Monsters*). *Dir*: David Misch. *Prod*: Bill Siegler. *Teleplay*: David Misch. *Story*: Bill Burnett, David Misch. *Cast*: Tempestt Bledsoe, Steve Harper, Ed Wheeler, Marcella Lowery, Eugene Byrd. Laurel Production, 1988.

This comic episode of the light-hearted cable series "Monsters" relates a budding living-dead high school romance between "Vanessa" from *The Cosby Show* and a disfigured zombie. The opening scene shows Mr. Lamesh routinely boarding up the doors and windows as he prepares to go out shooting zombies on the "Night of the Dead," the one night of the year when the dead rise from their graves to feast on the flesh of the living. No one knows, apparently, whether the phenomenon is due to a gypsy curse, nuclear testing, or shoddy embalming techniques. The entire family goes zombie hunting except for introverted bookworm Dottie (Bledsoe), home from her first semester in college. Shy, stiff-limbed Paul Nichols—who was killed in a car accident and is now a grotesque zombie with a bedraggled Wesleyan sweatshirt—comes to call on her with a bouquet of flowers and a big smile. Immediately she calls the "zombie hotline," and a recorded message tells her, "If a zombie's approaching your house, press 1. If a zombie's in your house, press 2. If a zombie's eating your body, press 3."Lonely and dissatisfied with her own social life, though, open-minded Dottie eventually lets him in and consents to a kiss, and soon they're chatting away in each other's arms. After they come home, Dottie's parents have trouble accepting the mixed relationship until Dottie dies and becomes a zombie also. The zombie lovers fall into each other's arms, even if sort of stiffly.

Netherworld

Dir: David Schmoeller. *Prod*: Thomas Bradford. *Screenplay*: Billy Chicago. *Story*: Billy Chicago, Charles Band. *Cast*: Michael Bendetti, Denise Gentile, Anjenette Comer, Holly Floria, Robert Sampson, Robert Burr. Full Moon Entertainment, 1991.

A few sporadic zombie elements grace an unremarkable Dixieland shocker from dubious Full Moon studios. Corey (Bendetti) crosses over from a Louisiana cathouse into another dimension to reconcile himself with his dead father Noah (Sampson), only to find his father an evil zombie who intends to trade Corey's soul for his own ("Christ died for his daddy—what are you complaining about?"). Back in this dimension, Noah winds up a zombie parrot with half its face missing. Polly want some brains?

Neurosis see ***Zombie 5: Revenge of the House of Usher***

Nevrose see ***Zombie 5: Revenge of the House of Usher***

The Night Andy Came Home see ***Dead of Night***

A Night in the Crypt see ***One Dark Night***

Night Life

Dir: David Acomba. *Prod*: Charles Lippincott. *Screenplay*: Keith Critchlow. *Cast*: Scott Grimes, Cheryl Pollak, Anthony Geary, Alan Blumenfeld, John Astin, Phil Proctor. Creative Movie Marketing, 1989.

Cretins chase each other around for ninety minutes in a routine and laborious living-dead exercise. Unpopular Archie Melville (Grimes) hopes to leave his one-horse town by working for his Uncle Verlin (Astin), the crotchety town mortician. A carload of high school bullies die in a wreck and return to life because of a chemical spill or because the mortuary is hit by lightning or something. The revived teens immediately take to killing at random, primarily targetting Archie and his friend Charly (Pollak). Though tolerably well acted and directed, the script is spiritless and the movie leaves no lasting impression.

The four zombie high school in-crowders are speedy and dexterous, but their mental capacities are a little hard to determine. They display general cognitive competence and can play tapes and drive vehicles, but they don't speak, and (other than having sex with each other in one brief scene) they exhibit no impulse other than pure homicidal aggression. The cadavers are unfazed by gunshots and minor bodily damage, but can be deanimated by complete physical trauma: explosion, head split open with axe, or being run through a wood chipper, for instance. The banal movie devotes almost no attention to the zombies themselves, preferring to focus on the meandering dreams of starry-eyed teens instead.

Alternate title: *Grave Misdemeanors*.

Night of Anubis see ***Night of the Living Dead*** (1968)

Night of the Blind Dead see ***Tombs of the Blind Dead***

Night of the Blood Cult see ***Night of the Seagulls***

Night of the Creeps

Dir: Fred Dekker. *Prod*: Charles Gordon. *Screenplay*: Fred Dekker. *Cast*: Jason Lively, Steve Marshall, Jill Whitlow, Tom Atkins, Allan Kayser, Wally Taylor, Bruce Solomon. Tri-Star Pictures, 1986.

Prom-bound Jill Whitlow and Jason Lively stop off to combat zombies and alien slugs with a blowtorch (*Night of the Creeps*, 1986).

Clever and lighthearted, the vaguely titled *Night of the Creeps* updates the old '50s-style "monster-amok-on-campus" movies with a colorful array of fiends and plot twists. Christopher (Lively) and J.C. (Marshall) accidentally release an alien slug parasite from a man kept in cryogenic suspension; the mutant slug's offspring spawn in people's brains and turn them into zombies until their heads explode, sending out dozens of new slugs. Chris teams up with new love Cynthia (Whitlow) and troubled police detective Ray Cameron (Atkins) to combat the growing menace. The slugs inhabit the mangled bodies of a crashed busload of fraternity members on their way to a formal, and the entire troop—decked out in blood-soaked tuxes and cummerbunds—besiege the nearby sorority house. Classic motifs from such movies as *Plan Nine from Outer Space* and *The Blob* blend with more recent ones from *The Wrath of Khan* and *Dawn of the Dead*, while nerds triumph over jocks and a whiskey-soaked cop faces up to his past. To boot, possessed dogs cough up alien slugs into people's faces. Zesty.

The zombies are merely breeding grounds for the slug eggs incubating in their brains. When a slug enters a living host, biological functions such as the heartbeat cease, but the subject remains sentient for at least a little while longer. Thus J.C. leaves a brief account of his own deteriorating condition on tape, shortly before his head explodes: "I can feel it ... it's in my brain." Most of the reanimated corpses don't seem so much hostile as confused, but the fraternity zombies at the end pretty clearly have murder on the mind. The make-up is convincing throughout, and the operative allegory of campus Greeks as zombies, if a little obvious, is far more capably handled than in the following year's *Zombie High*.

Alternate titles: *Creeps*, *Homecoming Night*.

Night of the Day of the Dawn of the Son of the Bride of the Return of the Revenge of the Terror of the Attack of the Evil Mutant Hellbound Flesh-Eating Subhumanoid Living Dead, Part II

Filmmaker: Lowell Mason [pseud]. Jyvass Productions, 1992.

Like Woody Allen's *What's Up Tiger Lily?*, this bizarre amateur spoof of *Night* was made by keeping the film itself intact while dubbing it over with entirely new sound and dialogue. Revelling in its own sacrilege, the film rethinks scenes and relationships, with occasional touches of ingenuity. The scene in which Harry first goes down to the basement to rejoin wife Helen and daughter Karen, for instance, is classic: here it's redone as though they're only meeting for the first time, and Harry tries to pick her up while he starts going through her purse. Upstairs, Ben breaks out rapping periodically, while Tom is convincingly recast as a surfer dude. The tense in-fighting becomes a running debate about who's going out for pizza and cannolis. Ben's most heartfelt monologue in the original *Night*, in which he describes what's happened to him so far while dismantling furniture, here becomes a none-too-subtle pick-up spiel as he tries to hit on Barbara. With an intent look on his face he woos her feelingly: "I want to lay your naked ass out on the floor and just ... just sail into you like a caboose, mama [gestures with hand].... But a gentle caboose—a gentle one." Though certain scenes are redone creatively, however, the film generally loses momentum as it goes on, and the rhythm is periodically broken by random interludes (gratuitous dancing scenes and lame jokes). The scatological humor requires a certain mood, the Howard Stern–like racial humor may not be funny to all, and the light-hearted treatment of rape is offensive. In fact, the script is marked throughout by a violent undercurrent that doesn't always come across as tongue-in-cheek. Presented in "Shocking 2-D."

The zombies are simply the over-worked and underpaid—they are the work force of America, the 7-Eleven clerks and executives and gas station attendants. A psychiatrist on TV explains that ninety-nine percent of the work force is on the verge of becoming over-worked zombies, and only the smallest snap is enough to push them over the edge. The zombies mill about, muttering about having to be up early in the morning, not getting a raise, needing a vacation, etc. Grasping after the pickup truck, they ask for a quarter or a lift to the bowling alley. In other words, the metaphor implicit in the original *Night* (and in all zombie invasions) is spelled out in black and white, for the benefit of those who haven't caught on.

Night of the Death Cult see *Night of the Seagulls*

Night of the Flesh Eaters see *Night of the Living Dead* (1968)

Night of the Living Bread

Dir: Kevin S. O'Brien. *Cast*: Vince Ware, Katie Harris, Robert J. Saunders, Gina Saunders, Wolfgang S. Saunders, Stephen R. Newell, Steve Herminghausen. Films from Hell, 1990.

It probably took ten dollars and all of forty-five minutes for Ohio University students to grind out this unfunny spoof of *Night*. Johnny (Herminghausen) and Barbra (Harris) pull into a cemetery, where a slice of white bread lying on the ground kills Johnny by flying up and adhering itself to his face. Barbra flees to an abandoned house and meets up with some others, who secure the house by taping sandwich bags over the windows, and who ward off the menacing slices of bread that lie scattered across the lawn with a toaster and toaster oven. Eventually all the characters succumb to the inexplicably lethal baked goods. The uncomplicated title pun should scarcely have elicited a laugh, much less an eight-minute parody film.

Night of the Living Dead

Dir: George A. Romero. *Prod*: Russell Streiner, Karl Hardman. *Screenplay*: John Russo, George Romero. *Cast*: Duane Jones, Judith O'Dea, Karl Hardman, Marilyn Eastman, Keith Wayne, Judith Ridley, Kyra Schon, Charles Craig, Bill Hinzman. Image Ten, 1968.

Romero is the Shakespeare of zombie film, and this is his *Hamlet*. One of the few horror movies to make a lasting contribution outside of the genre (apart from Hitchcock), *Night* is deservedly revered by critics and popular audiences alike. Pursued by a strange assailant (Hinzman—who went on to make his own zombie movie, *Flesheater*), Barbara (O'Dea) locks herself in an abandoned farmhouse in rural Pennsylvania. There she's joined by Ben (Jones) and a few other scared survivors, who board up the doors and windows against growing numbers of mindless attackers. The quarrelling group holds out desperately until at last succumbing to the ghouls, redneck posses, and to their own in-fighting. The tension is relentless: there are no romantic sub-plots or humorous interludes, only a growing sense of helplessness and claustrophobia. The domestic space is explored in detail from an entirely instrumental point of view—almost every household object is scrutinized, and exposed as either immediately useful (and not for the use originally intended), or rejected as altogether meaningless. Finally, the crisp, stark minimalism of the dialogue, creatures, and staging provides disarmingly austere subjects for the Hitchcockian cinematography. The low budget comes out in many aspects of production, but what stands out more is the tight control of pacing and suspense, and the unashamed abandonment of generic conventions (boy meets girl, teens can't convince authorities, protagonists discover monster's weakness, etc). The distributors wouldn't release the film until the crew tagged on some sort of explanation for the phenomenon, however—hence the references to an explorer satellite sent to Venus bringing back mysterious, high-level radiation. *Night* gained a steadily increasing cult following in drive-in and midnight movie circuits, and was soon featured at a special series at the Museum of Modern Art. Most of what you're holding directly imitates or responds to *Night* in some way.

The word "zombie" never appears in the film—"ghoul" is the preferred term, occasionally varied with "flesh-eating ghoul." Their clothes are slightly scruffed and torn, and a few are a little mangy in the face, but on the whole the fiends appear as normal people. They're

After George Romero's landmark *Night of the Living Dead* (1968), the zombies are no longer African-Caribbean natives or alien invaders: they're everyday people—they're us.

afraid of open flame, and when caught on fire, try to beat it out with their hands—thus some self-preservation instinct remains. They perform other simple instinctual reflexes also, such as brushing a low-hanging branch or clothes line out of their way as they stumble along. They never run, but occasionally stagger briskly. The ghouls consume flesh (human or animal—one chewy-faced woman scarfs a gross bug she finds on a tree), and they can only be deanimated by destroying the brain. From their appearance here, these conventions would become staples of zombie lore.

The ghouls preserve some basic memories and understanding, such as when the Hinzman ghoul tries to open a car with the handle. Beyond that he uses a brick to smash in the car-door window, and others use rocks to smash the headlights on Ben's car. At last, after building up sufficient nerve, the ghoul horde launches a concerted attack on the farmhouse, pounding at the door with clubs and breaking the windows with rocks. Thus the vestiges of a functioning human psyche are intact, with some rudimentary intelligence, learning capacity, and emotion. Though they're slow and unable to think strategically as individuals, their sheer numbers and indefatigability make them formidable as a group. *Night*'s zombies are unforgettable—tireless, clawing, and almost pathetic in their simplicity of needs and abilities.

Alternate titles: *Night of Anubis*, *Night of the Flesh Eaters*.

Night of the Living Dead

Dir: Tom Savini. *Prod*: John A. Russo, Russ Streiner. *Screenplay*: George A. Romero. *Cast*: Tony Todd, Patricia Tallman, Tom Towles, McKee Anderson, William Butler, Kate Finneran, Bill Mosley, Heather Mazur. Twenty-First Century Productions, 1990.

Tom Savini, famous for his make-up work in *Dawn* and *Day*, directs this color remake of the classic, rewritten by Romero himself. The same story is essentially retold, though packed with in-jokes to the first, and subtly incorporating societal changes from the last twenty years (thus, trying to barricade the house, Ben is disgusted to find only cheap plywood doors). Probably the most significant difference is the rethinking of gender roles: Barbara (Tallman) is no longer a passive vegetable, but proves to be the most multidimensional character and ultimately the most capable of survival. Meanwhile the squabbling between Ben (Todd) and Cooper (Towles) is intensified, and their aggression is explicitly linked with male territoriality. Overall the careful build-up of suspense is gone, however: this movie is a desperate race the whole way through. Instead of maddening waiting and slowly mounting interpersonal tensions, this version comes across mostly as a lot of noise, shooting, and screaming. The gore is surprisingly subdued, considering the director. Finally, though, after almost 60 years and more than 130 zombie movies, someone (Barbara) at last notices: "They're so slow—we could just walk right past them."

Night of the Seagulls

(Orig. *La noche de los gaviotas*). *Dir*: Amando de Ossorio. *Prod*: José Angel Santos. *Screenplay*: Amando de Ossorio. *Cast*: Víctor Petit, Maria Kosti, Sandra Mozarowsky, Julie James. Profilmes/Ancla Century (Spain), 1975.

The fourth and last of de Ossorio's Blind Dead chronicles resituates the monks in a castle near an ancient coastal village with crumbling stone houses. For six centuries the terrified villagers have paid a burdensome toll: every seven years, they pay a tribute of seven women to the zombie monks, who sacrifice them to a sea-god. An obnoxious young doctor and his whiny wife move to the village and stop the curse by toppling the helpless fish-god idol from its pedestal. The seagulls who circle in the sky and cry excitedly are the damned souls of past sacrifice victims. The bright, sun-drenched closing frame, though still accompanied by the plodding and desolate Abril music, implies the zombie menace is over permanently. The film competently delivers the usual atmospheric settings, well-composed shots, and glacier-slow zombies, though overall it's probably the least interesting of the tetralogy. The horde of slimy crabs that scamper out to devour the victims' bodies after the monks have finished with them is a nice touch. De Ossorio eventually retired from his prolific filmmaking career to paint the Templar monks and other weird subjects.

Though the coastal atmosphere and pagan fish-god imagery is new, the zombie monks themselves appear and behave much as in the other films. They exhibit a minimum of tool use, recoil from open flame, and ride their ghost stallions. Here, unlike the middle two installments, they seem genuinely blind again: at one point, a zombie turns his head from side to side, waiting to hear a sound from the nearby victim (she promptly complies). One monk is burned to ashes, and the rest crumble to dust when their idol is destroyed. Although the zombies of the second film were defeated at the end also, here not just the zombies but also the blasphemous powers behind them are confronted and conquered, signaling more permanent closure for the Templar saga. Probably for the best.

Alternate titles: *Bloodfeast of the Blind Dead*, *Night of the Blood Cult*, *Night of the Death Cult*, *Terror Beach*.

The Night of the Sorcerers

(Orig. *La noche de los brujos*). *Dir*: Amando de Ossorio. *Prod*: José Antonio Pérez Giner, Luis Laso Moreno. *Screenplay*: Amando de Ossorio. *Cast*: Simón Andreu, Kali Hansa, María Kosti, Lorena Tower, Joseph Thelman, Bárbara King, Jack Taylor. Profilmes/Hesperia (Spain), 1973.

Blind Dead–maestro de Ossorio's unfortunate female vampire feature embodies all that's worst in the Euro-vamp movies of the period. A team of wildlife researchers arrives in Bumbasa, Africa, sixty years after a platoon of armed white men wiped out an entire gathering of native voodoo practitioners. A hokey vampire scantily clad in leopard skin and her zombie cohorts still conduct bizarre sacrificial ghost-rituals. The women of the research team are summarily killed, only to return as more cheesy vampires, all bearing their fangs and prancing around in slow-motion. Fake animal masks passed off as leopards peep out of the foliage while occasional stock wildlife footage fills in the gaps. Insulting at any of a number of aesthetic and ideological levels, the movie lacks any of the situational humor or atmospheric effectiveness of the Blind Dead series (the second of which also came out in 1973).

The mindless zombies are black–African natives, entirely subservient to the cunning European vampire women who lead the dark rituals. The zombies wear tooth necklaces, animal skins, and frightful tribal masks, anticipating the dubious "National Geographic zombies" of early–'80s Italian cinema (e.g., *Night of the Zombies* and *Dr. Butcher, M.D.*). They appear at night when the ghost rituals begin, slowly crawling from the stone cairns covering their bodies. Their movements are deliciously slow, as one expects of de Ossorio—so slow, in fact, that there is a curious scene in which Carter (Andreu) runs over them in his Jeep, driving back and forth to take out a few more, before proceeding on his way. (Though there's no reason to think it's deliberate, the way the native zombies stand still as statues in their impractically oversized ceremonial masks, simply watching Carter run over them, presents a shrewd parable for colonialism.) Their ashen, stony faces are mostly hidden by masks, while their quasi-ghostly habit of appearing and disappearing without a trace leaves an impression of facile scriptwriting rather than occult mystery. While the zombies are merely passive spectators who only procure and bind victims for the vampires, they at least maintain a certain dignity completely lacking in their sultry feline mistresses.

Alternate title: *Night of the Witches.*

Night of the Wehrmacht Zombies see ***Gamma 693***

Night of the Witches see ***The Night of the Sorcerers***

Night of the Zombies see ***Erotic Nights of the Living Dead***

Night of the Zombies see ***Gamma 693***

Night of the Zombies

(Orig. *Inferno dei morti viventi*). Dir: Bruno Mattei. Prod: Sergio Cortona. Story and Screenplay: Claudio Fragasso, J.M. Cunilles. Cast: Margit Evelyn

Newton, Frank Garfield (Franco Giraldi), Selan Karay, Robert O'Neil, Gaby Renom, Luis Fonoll. Beatrice Film/Films Dara (Italy, Spain), 1981.

Similar though inferior to Fulci's *Zombie 2* released the previous year, this Spanish-Italian movie traces a small but well-armed band through a zombie-infested jungle. Experiments on overpopulation ("Operation Sweet Death") in New Guinea go horribly wrong; the resulting chemical vapors bring the dead back to life throughout the island. The first victim is a plant worker who gets eaten by a crazed zombie rat that crawls into his anti-contamination suit, and so the best scene is over within the first two minutes. A SWAT team of idiots sent to investigate the crisis meets up with reporters Lia Rousseau (Newton) and Max; together they scurry from site to site evading the spreading ghoul menace. The movie is largely a quilt of random footage from various mismatched jungle and savanna settings, spliced into but wholly unconnected with the main story line. Though the movie takes an explicitly anti-colonial stance, it consists entirely of European heroes gleefully gunning down natives. Like Jess Franco, Mattei is notorious for Nazi-sex and nunsploitation movies.

The reason the problem is spreading so quickly is that the natives refuse to bury or burn the dead. The stiff-limbed New Guinea zombies gasp and wheeze as they trudge along languidly. Most have powdery white and bluish faces; some have a dry, peeling stucco look, while others have black and slimy faces that contrast starkly with their white eyes and teeth. They eat flesh, deanimate when shot in the head, spread the disease by contagion, etc. They recoil from fire, and pause or even back up a little to avoid blows. Otherwise they show no intelligence or deliberation, and not even rudimentary tool use. In one or two shots, the zombies simply stand in place motionlessly, though there are victims in sight. This could be a sign of dormant or non-appetitive behavior, though probably someone just turned the camera on before the director yelled "action." The zombie make-up effects and blocking are overall decent, though wasted on such a lifeless script and hopeless cast of characters.

Alternate titles: *Apocalipsis canibal*, *Cannibal Virus*, *Hell of the Living Dead*, *Hell of the Living Death*, *Virus*, *Virus cannibale*, *Virus—L'inferno dei morti viventi*, *Zombie Creeping Flesh*, *Zombie Inferno*, *Zombie of the Savanna*.

Nightmare **see** ***City of the Walking Dead***

Nightmare City **see** ***City of the Walking Dead***

Night of the Zombies II see *Gamma 693*

Night Star—Goddess of Electra see *War of the Zombies*

Night Walk see *Dead of Night*

No profanar el sueño de los muertos see *Let Sleeping Corpses Lie*

La Noche de la muerta ciega see *Tombs of the Blind Dead*

La Noche de los brujos see *The Night of the Sorcerers*

La Noche de los gaviotas see *Night of the Seagulls*

La Noche del buque maldito see *Horror of the Zombies*

La Noche del terror ciego see *Tombs of the Blind Dead*

Non sì deve profanare il sonno dei morti see *Let Sleeping Corpses Lie*

La Notte dei zombi see *Erotic Nights of the Living Dead*

Le Notti del terrore see *Burial Ground*

Le Notti erotiche dei morte viventi see *Erotic Nights of the Living Dead*

Nudist Colony of the Dead

Dir: Mark Pirro. *Prod*: Mark Headley. *Screenplay*: Mark Pirro. *Cast*: Deborah Stern, Tony Cicchetti, Rachel Latt, Braddon Mendelson, Jim Bruce, Barbara Dow, Heather McPherson, Peter Napoles, Steve Wilcox, Juan Tanamera, Forrest J Ackerman, Dave Robinson. Artistic License, 1991.

One of the few zombie musicals, this amateur summer-camp slasher spoof isn't as wacky as it thinks it is. When Judge Rhinehole (Ackerman) of Pristine County rules in favor of the Bible-thumping moral majority and closes Sunnybuttocks Nudist Camp, the nudists commit mass suicide and vow to seek vengeance even in death. The land becomes a Bible retreat spot, Camp Cutchaguzzout, where the dead rise from their graves to off the pious campers in various ways. The musical numbers in this lame production vary from catchy to stupid (mostly leaning toward the latter), while the dialogue is permeated with simplistic ethnic humor. Best line (priest addressing congregation): "Remember—your children can't praise the Lord if they've got genitals in their mouths."

The title song proclaims, "They'll kill and hurt and chop and maim, / Exposing gonads with no shame," and in a hip-hop number the park ranger adds, "They be nudists of the past—and now they're back to kick some ass." In fact, though they're supposed to be naked, the zombie nudists' naughty bits are all strategically covered with large, flapping sections of skin. The unclothed undead are fully rational, and sufficiently intelligent to cut the phone line to the ranger's cabin and even remove the engine from a van (heck, I don't think I could do that). They also run people over cartoonishly with an industrial steam roller. Other methods of slaughter include using a wire to cut a victim in two, force-feeding a person cement, and stuffing a Bible all the way into a camper's mouth. The zombies themselves sing and dance in the closing number ("Kill, kill, kill all the zealots"), and are still crooning as they return to their graves to await the next season of campers. I think that about covers it; now you don't have to see it (you owe me one).

La Nuit des étoiles filantes see ***A Virgin Among the Living Dead***

Oasis of the Zombies

(Orig. *La tumba de los muertos vivientes*). *Dir*: Jesús Franco. *Screenplay*: A.L. Mariaux, Jesús Franco. *Cast*: Manuel Gelin, France Jordan, Jeff Montgomery, Myriam Landson, Eric Saint-Just, Caroline Audret, Henry Lambert. Eurociné (Spain, France), 1982.

Nobody has much good to say about this admittedly slow-paced Spanish-French co-production, but I've always been strangely fascinated by it. A group of students from London travel to the North African desert seeking a fortune lost during World War II, where a German special task force transporting treasure was slaughtered in an Allied ambush. Natives avoid the cursed oasis where the Nazi soldiers still guard their treasure, but the students must go in to see for themselves. Massacre ensues. The movie's technical flaws are numerous and obvious, including sloppy make-up effects and the unlikely opening scene in which two scantily-clad women happen to be sightseeing three hundred miles out in the middle of the desert. Yet *Oasis* presents a simple, unhurried, and unpretending appreciation of zombies and their habitat, a fresh and provocative desert landscape. There are some striking silhouettes, with their dark forms on sand dunes against dusky pink and orange skies, or blending in with dark foliage; the bright sunlight vs. dark shadow contrasts within the oasis itself are also visually effective. The zooms become tiresome, but the cheesy synthesized music, consisting mostly of odd successions of single notes or chords, somehow matches the barrenness of the landscape and lends the zombie attacks a hypnotizing ambience. Some reference works question the attribution of this movie to Franco (Daniel Lesoeur also uses the pseudonym A.M. Frank on occasion).

Clad in khaki army uniforms, the pasty, purulent Nazi zombies haven't fared well in the harsh desert climate. They are utterly silent, although their approach is invariably accompanied by a certain groaning, grating sound, like a creaky door opening or a stick being dragged along a washboard. It's never clear what this represents, but it's not simply mood sound—the characters in the film hear it too (possibly the *Blair Witch Project* crew stalking around, playing with their heads?). The zombies are painfully slow and stiff, crawling from the sandy dunes anew at the beginning of each new attack scene (apparently the desert covers them up again in between scenes). They generally bite directly into their prey, but one zombie, who has no teeth because of his advanced stage of decay, has to strangle his victim. Several are ignited with a torch, but they're smart enough (if not always quick enough) to recoil from the torches and to stay outside a ring of fire ignited to keep them at bay. They only come out at night, but either the zombies or the filmmakers have a loose definition of nighttime, since they're obviously standing in broad daylight in most of their appearances. The condition is supposed to be contagious, according to the natives, but none of the characters killed by the undead Nazis actually come back. The zombies themselves are amateurish and somewhat inconsistent, but are more than redeemed by the incomparable desert landscape and by some creative camera work and shot composition.

Alternate titles: *Bloodsucking Nazi Zombies, El desierto de los zombies, The Grave of the Living Dead, The Treasure of the Living Dead.*

One Dark Night

Dir: Thomas McLoughlin. *Prod*: Michael Schroeder. *Screenplay*: Thomas McLoughlin, Michael Hawes. *Cast*: Meg Tilly, Melissa Newman, Robin Evans, Leslie Speights, Donald Hotton, David Mason Daniels, Elizabeth Daily, Adam West. The Picture Company, 1982.

In this low-budget yet quirky suspense piece, Julie (Tilly) agrees to spend the night with a sleeping bag and flashlight in a vast mausoleum as part of her initiation into a snobby high school clique.

Recently interred in the mausoleum is mad Russian psychic Raymar, who exerts his evil influence even from beyond the grave. A "psychic vampire," Raymar feeds on people's "bioenergy" and uses it to menace Julie and her friends by causing coffins to break open and animating the corpses. Though nothing really happens for the first hour, the unique zombie invasion sequence in the closing scene is highly eccentric. Adam West of *Batman* fame is depressing as Olivia's irritable and patronizing husband, but a zombie does him in later in *Zombie Nightmare* (1987).

Some of the bodies Raymar telekinetically animates are fresh, while others are virtually reduced to skeletons. There is no question of sentience or will; the corpses are merely moved around like marionettes on strings. Most interestingly, the movie refuses to follow the well-entrenched paradigms of zombie behavior so prevalent in the early '80s. The corpses don't walk, but glide along smoothly in the air several inches off the ground, their feet dragging along the floor behind them. They exert no autonomous bodily motion whatsoever, which inevitably affects their mode of attack: they don't reach out with limbs, or try to bite, but simply collide with the victim—Raymar causes the bodies to slam into people and pile upon them until they smother. In other words, he uses the cadavers as simple bludgeoning instruments and weights, purely physical instruments with no moving parts. Thus, in the end, there is a certain ultra-zombieness about these creatures: they are quintessentially material hulks, without the faintest glimmer of autonomous animation. If zombie movies parody normal human behavior by unceremoniously reducing it to its bare essentials, this movie parodies even normal zombie behavior.

Alternate titles: *A Night in the Crypt, Rest in Peace.*

La Orgía de los muertos see ***Return of the Zombies***

La Orgia dei morti see ***Return of the Zombies***

Gli Orrori del castello di Norimberga see ***Baron Blood***

Ouanga

Dir: George Terwilliger. *Prod*: George Terwilliger. *Screenplay*: George Terwilliger. *Cast*: Fredi Washington, Philip Brandon, Marie Paxton, Sheldon Leonard, Winifred Harris, Sid Easton, Babe Joyce. Real Life Dramas, 1935.

"Wanga" is a more palatable spelling for the voodoo charm that gives this early zombie snoozer its title. Haitian banana magnate

Voodoo priestess Fredi Washington dons a protective amulet in the uneven zombie adventure *Ouanga* (1935). The mulatto actress eventually left her promising Hollywood career to take up with a black acting company in Washington, D.C., after the motion picture industry began casting her in increasingly stereotyped roles.

Adam (Brandon) is about to marry Eve (Paxton) but neighboring plantation owner Clelie (Washington) loves him so deeply that she'll stop at nothing to prevent the wedding. Her skin is white but her heart is black—and since she's also the local voodoo high priestess, she has no problem summoning dark powers to aid her. She raises two zombies from the grave to abduct Eve, but Adam's mulatto foreman (Leonard), who desires Clelie as madly and vindictively as she desires Adam, confronts her, and the two dark and tormented souls destroy each other. The awkward feature boasts some provocative symbolism (specifically, there are curious twists on black vs. white imagery, both moral and racial), but ultimately its unquestioning equation of black with evil sits uncomfortably in the midst of a largely black supporting cast. The movie was shot shortly after *White Zombie*, but not released until 1935 (in England) and even later in the U.S. Terwilliger started to film in Haiti, but was forced to move the shoot to Jamaica when resentful natives, ironically enough, left the crew a real ouanga.

Ouanga's two zombies rise from their open coffins in broad daylight, as Clelie makes pulling motions with her hands (as though lifting marionettes). The native men are clean and kempt and wear nothing but pants, standing with their hands at their sides and staring straight ahead as Clelie addresses them. The zombie phenomenon here comes across more as hypnotism: "You are powerless to talk or respond to any directions," she tells them, "save those I give you." (But in fact, they follow Adam's directions in a later scene, when he threatens them with a whip). One of the two undead blinks in most unzombie-like fashion while abducting Eve, who is too busy making the worst attempt on record at acting frightened to flee their leisurely approach. They are finally sent back to their graves after being sprinkled with salt; otherwise, it's said, they can only be killed with a silver bullet (oh please!). Their presence at all is purely gratuitous, since they don't do anything any two thugs wouldn't have done for a few coins.

Alternate titles: *Crime of Voodoo*, *Drums of the Jungle*, *The Love Wanga*.

Panic in the Trans-Siberian Train see ***Horror Express***

Pánico en el transiberiano see ***Horror Express***

Paura nella città dei morti viventi see ***The Gates of Hell***

Pet Sematary

Dir: Mary Lambert. *Prod*: Richard P. Rubinstein. *Story and Screenplay*: Stephen King. *Cast*: Dale Midkiff, Fred Gwynne, Denise Crosby, Blaze Berdahl, Brad Greenquist, Miko Hughes, Peter Stader. Paramount Pictures, 1989.

A Micmac Indian graveyard reanimates those buried in it as flesh-eating demons with glowing eyes (not a very effective graveyard, all in all). In a "Monkey's Paw"–like flashback story, Timmy Baterman (Stader), killed in World War II and raised by the native burial site, returns as a blithering ghoul, bloodied and animalistic, throwing his father around the house and gasping, "love dead ... hate living." Zombies are, if nothing else, focused and goal-oriented.

Pink Eye

(Episode, *South Park*). *Creator/Producer*: Trey Parker, Matt Stone. *Screenplay*: Trey Parker, Matt Stone, Philip Stark. *Animation*: Eric Stouch. Comedy Central, 1997.

The psychotic animated hit show that put Comedy Central on the network map devotes its first Halloween episode to a zombie invasion. Hapless Kenney dies earlier than usual, when the Russian space station Mir crashes into his head. At the South Park Morgue, Worcestershire sauce spills into the embalming fluid, turning him into a cannibal zombie. As the epidemic spreads, smooth-talking Chef leads grade-schoolers Stan, Kyle, and Cartman in a moist chainsaw assault against the hordes of undead. Numerous motifs recall *Return of the Living Dead*, such as doctors puzzling over patients whose temperature is room temperature, and the protagonists calling a 1-800 number on the side of the Worcestershire sauce bottle. *South Park*'s creative graphic presentation is at least as entertaining as the irreverent themes or attempted parody—there's something deliciously incongruous about the very idea of casting a zombie invasion in construction paper cutout animation.

Kenney is exquisitely cool and detached as the harbinger of the zombie plague. The undead are spotty, maimed, and have exposed bones and brains, and by the end of the episode, both of Kenney's arms have dropped off. (This still doesn't prevent him from crunching into people's skulls with breakfast-cereal chomping sounds, though.) Despite the fourth-grade art class animation, the kids' chainsaw rampage against the zombies is raw and brutal. Dismemberment is the only way to deanimate the zombies, but by calling the Worcestershire sauce company, Kyle learns that all the zombies will revert to their normal human state when the original zombie is himself killed. Thus he promptly saws Kenney down the middle from head to toe, saving South Park and freeing Kenney to die a third time in an aborted return-from-the-grave shock ending. Choice.

The Plague of the Zombies

Dir: John Gilling. *Prod*: Anthony Nelson-Keys. *Screenplay*: Peter Bryan. *Cast*: Andre Morell, Diane Clare, Brook Williams, Jacqueline Pearce, John Carson,

Alex Davion, Marcus Hammond, Roy Royston. Seven Arts/Hammer (England), 1966.

This well-acted and capably-produced movie from Hammer Studios is more important in the evolution of the screen zombie than is generally recognized. In the nineteenth century, eminent physician Sir James Forbes (Morell) and his daughter travel to a small Cornish village in response to a mysterious letter from James' former pupil Peter (Williams). Soon the visitors fall afoul of Squire Clive Hamilton (Carson), an aloof aristocrat who spent many years in Haiti, and who is bringing the corpses back from the graves in the village cemetery to work as slaves in his tin mines. This is a robust and visually appealing movie from Gilling, who also directed the much-admired *The Reptile* at the same time, using the same sets.

A menacing Cornish zombie evicts Jacqueline Pearce from his tin mine in the moody British *Plague of the Zombies* (1966).

During a dream sequence in *Plague of the Zombies* (1966), an antiquated corpse crawls from the grave, apparently to direct traffic or throw a long pass.

Screen zombies were in transition in the late '60s, and *Plague* is at the threshold—it relies on the old codes of zombie behavior, but pioneers the appearance of the zombies to come. They are still the subservient, mostly passive, non-cannibal drones of early zombie film, but unlike previous zombies, these are decayed, blotchy cadavers, staggering around clumsily rather than walking in perfect, mechanical rhythm. The film is best known for a stunning dream sequence in which the dead all rise from the earth in a cemetery. Seventeenth–century corpses with flakes of grey skin peeling off like scorched paint slowly claw their way up from loose, damp clods of soil, wearing cowls and looking a little like an army of Friar Tuck zombies. The motif of zombies clawing their way directly out of the ground went on to become a staple of zombie movies, largely on the strength of this dream scene (the dead never crawl out of the ground in Romero's trilogy).

The real zombies differ only from those in the dream sequence in that they have no pupils, and these white, featureless eyes are decidedly unsettling. The undead in the tin mines wear drab brown cloaks, laboring in chains and suffering under the whips of Hamilton's overseers. They shrink from the whips, and try to hide themselves from the overseers to avoid work, so they are clearly able to feel pain and are conceptualized as sentient in some sense. Ironically, the overseers expend more effort whipping than the zombies do mining tin. They'd get rich quicker just mining it themselves. There is a disarmingly funny scene, in fact, in which one zombie listlessly holds a spike while another taps it lethargically with a sledgehammer—at this rate, they're not going to mine the ore a whole lot faster than natural erosion would.

The zombies only exist so long as the voodoo effigies of them remain in coffins upstairs in Hamilton's manor. When the coffins are set on fire, the zombies down in the mines begin to smoke and burn; they try to pat out the flames (and thus exhibit instincts of self-preservation), albeit halfheartedly. The bleak mine setting provides the perfect environment for these memorable zombies, who represent the screen's first troop of moldy zombies, even if the mood is ultimately defused by the safe and comfortable atmosphere of Hammer's glossy, polished production values and conservative insistence on order and rationality.

Alternate titles: *The Zombie*, *The Zombies*.

Plan Nine from Outer Space

Dir: Edward Wood Jr. *Prod*: Edward Wood Jr. *Screenplay*: Edward Wood Jr. *Cast*: Gregory Walcott, Mona McKinnon, Duke Moore, Tom Keene, Carl Anthony, Tor Johnson, Dudley Manlove, Joanna Lee, Bela Lugosi, Vampira, Criswell. Reynolds Pictures, 1958.

Ed Wood's chintz masterpiece, narrated as usual by bad-haired, droning, cue-card reading Criswell, well deserves its notoriety. Budget actors who refer to themselves as "space soldiers" land in flying hubcaps and implement "plan nine"—mounting an army here on Earth by resurrecting our own dead. The three reanimated bodies they have so far wander around a graveyard in San Fernando, where protagonists easily locate the spacecraft by following the trail of bodies that were somehow meant to throw them off the track. Hot-headed pilot Jeff Trent (Walcott) and local cop Lt. Harper (Moore) are welcomed aboard the suspect vessel by aliens Eros (Manlove) and Tanna (Lee). With the help of a translating "dictarobotary," Eros explains that humankind must be stopped, since it has developed weapon technology far in advance of its own maturity. He insists we are on the verge of discovering the dreaded "Solanarite Bomb," which threatens to destroy the entire universe. Eros succinctly concludes, "All you of Earth are idiots." As immortalized in the film *Ed Wood* with Johnny Depp, Wood talked a church group into funding the picture. The group required not only that Wood change the title from the original *Grave Robbers from Outer Space*, but moreover that the whole crew and cast be baptized.

The aliens resurrect bodies using "long-distance electrodes shot in the pineal and pituitary glands," which they fire from the electrode-pistols they carry in hip holsters. Eros insists the dead are resurrected in body alone, and can't think or feel. Two of the reanimated bodies—ugly Tor Johnson and a chiropractor pretending to be Lugosi by holding a cape over his face—attack by striking with two-handed karate chops. The third is Morticia Addams–like Vampira, whose victims are badly mutilated, as if attacked by a bobcat (though disappointingly, none of these assaults are ever shown on-screen). On the whole the reanimated bodies don't do much but lurk around the cemetery, but then, the true entertainment comes from watching the incredible background sets and trying to make sense out of the script. At one point Eros muses, "It's an interesting thing when you consider the earth people who can think are so frightened by those who cannot—the dead." Actually it's not very interesting, but it sounds profound if you don't think about it too much—like most of the script, starting with Criswell's opening statement: "Greetings, my friend. We are all interested in the future, for that is where you and I are going to spend the rest of our lives."

Queen of the Cannibals see ***Dr. Butcher, M.D.***

Quella villa accanto al cimitero see ***The House by the Cemetery***

Raiders of the Living Dead

Dir: Samuel M. Sherman. *Prod*: Dan Q. Kennis. *Screenplay*: Samuel M. Sherman, Brett Piper. *Cast*: Robert Deveau, Donna Asali, Scott Schwartz, Bob Allen, Zita Johann, Bob Sacchetti, Leonard Corman. Independent International, 1985.

Tame humans clash mildly with tepid zombies in this pointless PG undead rubbish. Investigative newspaper reporter Morgan Randall (Deveau) teams up with generic love interest Shelly (Asali) to uncover the corpse-raising activities of a defrocked prison warden. The non-adventure leads them to Rockmoor Island, where a correctional institute closed down many years prior for experimental research on patients still houses the restless dead. The evil warden calls them to his service by ringing a bell, but plucky pre-pubescent Jonathan (Schwartz) comes to save the day with a homemade laser gun improvised from discarded VCR parts. The sluggish story line consists of continuous talking without much intonation or expression. A couple of "Three Stooges" clips incorporated into the movie are the least exasperating parts.

The zombies are mostly the former inmates of the prison, although what the warden plans to do with them is never really clarified. They do kill a minor character (the scriptwriters apparently going out on a limb), but don't seem to eat him. Making a mid–'80s zombie movie without violence or gore is rather infelicitous, especially as 1985 is also the year of three pivotal, high-impact films: *Day of the Dead*, *Re-Animator*, and *Return of the Living Dead*.

Raptors

Dir: Claudio Lattanzi. *Screenplay*: Daniel Ross (Daniele Stroppa). *Story*: Claude Milliken (Claudio Lattanzi), Sheila Goldberg. *Cast*: Lara Wendel, Robert Vaughn, Timothy Watt, Leslie Cummins, James Villemaire, Sal Maggiore Jr., James Sutterfield, Lin Gathright. Filmirage/Flora Film (Italy), 1988.

Italian zombie movies are shot abroad as often as in Italy, and Lattanzi adorns this formula stalker with rich Louisiana swampland scenery and abundant footage of birds. A group of college students from Loyola head down to the bayou to find traces of the near-extinct ivory-billed woodpecker. There they meet blind ornithologist Frederick Brown (Vaughn), who, many years prior, killed off his family upon returning from Vietnam and then had his eyes plucked out by birds. The students stop for the night in the abandoned house where the massacre occurred, only to be picked off themselves by freak accidents and isolated zombie attacks. Brown explains that it's him they're really after, and after the departure of the two remaining students, Steve (Watt) and Anne (Wendel), he at last succumbs to the vengeful fowl. The atmospheric film is heavy on images but light on explanations. Though very slow getting in gear, it picks up decisively for the last half-hour when the zombies begin a concerted attack. Since the zombies are few, only appear sporadically, and never appear for longer than a moment or two, the suspense is generated almost entirely from dark corners and narrow passageways rather than actual danger.

Certain random shocks and haunted house happenings give the impression that immaterial ghosts or spirits of some sort are responsible for the pervasive evil, but there's nothing ephemeral about the zombies once they begin to stir. There's not really more than a couple of them (they are presumably Brown's old victims, who numbered four), but these few are more than up to the task of slaughtering the co-ed fodder. They are brackish, cloddy cadavers, with heads like big raisins. Though very slow (they only advance with one foot, using the other just to catch up), they're uncommonly strong—once they get a firm grip on a victim, no matter how many people pull from the other end, they don't let go until something comes off. We never see from where the mysterious swamp zombies emerge, learn next to nothing about their connection with the ominous, knowing birds who observe the film's events from a distance, and can't follow their independent motions or activities. Perhaps they have none: Brown says, "They feed on fear—it animates them, it gives them strength," which would explain why the zombie invasion has such a slow and erratic start, and only gains momentum as the group becomes increasingly terrified. Thus the film exhibits a certain leisurely patience that's bought at the price of only seeing about five minutes of zombies in a ninety-minute film. Bayou zombies enjoy a modest but noteworthy heritage, including *Revenge of the Zombies* (1943) and *The Beyond* (1981, another Italian film made in Louisiana, in which the stylish imagism and restraintful zombie employment is an obvious inspiration for *Raptors*).

Alternate titles: *Dark Eyes of the Zombie*, *Killing Birds*.

Re-Animator

Dir: Stuart Gordon. *Prod*: Brian Yuzna. *Screenplay*: Dennis Paoli, William J. Norris, Stuart Gordon. *Cast*: Jeffrey Combs, Bruce Abbott, Barbara

Crampton, David Gale, Robert Sampson, Gerry Black, Peter Kent. Empire/ Re-Animator Productions, 1985.

Stuart Gordon resituates the zombie menace in the sleek, sterile atmosphere of Miskatonic Medical School in this fast-paced and intelligent splatter fiesta. Jeffrey Combs steals the show as genius Herbert West, a likably brash and indignant medical student who has discovered a compound to restore the dead to life. Reluctantly, nice guy Dan Cain (Abbott) becomes increasingly entangled in West's clandestine experiments, while West contends against nemesis Dr. Hill (Gale) who threatens to steal his invention. Very loosely based on a Lovecraft story, the movie remains visceral yet funny, enjoys tight direction and a suspenseful score, and succeeds in creating a sense of seething depravity lightly concealed under the veneer of clinical professionalism.

West's green, glow-in-the-dark serum reanimates any dead tissue, even disembodied parts (as in the same year's *Return of the Living Dead*). The reanimated organism or tissue, however, flies into a spastically violent frenzy; West himself even takes tiny doses of the serum once in a while as a stimulant. The longer the corpse has been dead, the less memory or consciousness is restored, but power-hungry Hill gains control over a small platoon of the mindless, reanimated cadavers through a special surgical process. Hill's evil head remains sentient even after being removed from his body, leading to one of the most daring moments of '80s horror: having captured Megan (Crampton) and strapped her down to a table, Hill's pulpy, severed head (held by the rest of his body) runs its bloody tongue over her naked body while she screams hysterically. Not for the giddy. The final scene is a veritable bursting piñata of limbs and organs, which Linda Badley has aptly dubbed "Gordon's Guernica." The institutional setting of *Re-Animator*, conceptually supported by a steady stream of medical jargon, gives these zombies a very different feel from the rotting shambles dominating the zombie movie landscape of the '70s and early '80s. Here there are no religious overtones, no tombstone or graveyard trimmings, no need to look for horror or monstrosity anywhere but in the scientifically analyzed human body itself, laid out under septic bright lights.

Re-Animator II see ***Bride of Re-Animator***

La Rebelión de las muertas see ***Vengeance of the Zombies***

Rebellion of the Dead Women see ***Vengeance of the Zombies***

Redneck Zombies

Dir: Pericles Lewnes. *Prod*: Edward Bishop, George Scott, Pericles Lewnes. *Screenplay*: Fester Smellman. *Story*: Zoofeet, P. Floyd Piranha. *Cast*: Lisa DeHaven, William Benson, James Housely, Anthony Burlington-Smith, Martin Wolfman, Boo Teasedale, Darla Deans. Full Moon Pictures, 1987.

As expected from the Troma Team (who brought us *The Toxic Avenger* and *The Class of Nuke 'Em High*), the standards of gore are high and those of taste are low in this backwoods shambles. When Pa, Junior, Jethro, and Billy Bob find a lost barrel of experimental nuclear waste, they immediately convert it into a still. Needless to say, all those who imbibe the resulting sickly, greenish moonshine become crazed cannibal hooligans. Hapless Bob (Burlington-Smith), one of the group of campers who serve as victims, regrets having dropped acid right before the zombie invasion began. Cartoon-style antics and hillbilly stereotypes blend to produce a down-home mess not even fit for slopping hogs. The country folk colorfully threaten to give each other "what fer" and deliver lines I'm still not quite sure what to do with: "You quit your sassin', boy—I pulled you outta your mother, and I'll shove you right back in."

The white-faced, dribble-mouthed zombies, covered with generous portions of scum of all hues and consistencies, scamper around the county in their overalls and John Deere caps, feasting on the flesh of humans and farm animals alike. On the whole they don't seem to display much intelligence, but then again neither do any of the living characters. In a final bucoliphobic twist, it turns out that the only thing that can kill them is deodorant.

La Regina dei cannibali see ***Dr. Butcher, M.D.***

Rest in Peace see ***One Dark Night***

Return of the Blind Dead see ***Return of the Evil Dead***

Return of the Evil Dead

(Orig. *El ataque de los muertos sin ojos*). *Dir*: Amando de Ossorio. *Prod*: Ramón Plana. *Screenplay*: Amando de Ossorio. *Cast*: Tony Kendall (Luciano Stella), Esther Ray (Esperanza Roy), Fernando Sancho, Lone Fleming, Frank Blake (Frank Braña), Loretta Tovar, José Canalejas. Ancla Century Films (Spain), 1973.

De Ossorio follows his successful zombie debut (*Tombs of the Blind Dead*, 1971) not with a sequel but more of a retelling—the events in this capable feature are unrelated to and even incompatible with those of the first movie. Here it isn't crows that pluck out the Templar monks' eyes in the Middle Ages, but angry villagers who burn them out (shown as a flashback). Now, the village holds a festival commemorating the 500th anniversary of the execution of the Templars, which the monks themselves also decide to attend. When the vengeful dead gallop into the main plaza and begin slaughtering merrymakers, pyrotechnician Jack Marlowe (Stella) and fawning Vivian (Roy) lock themselves in the cathedral with the corrupt mayor, the village idiot, and other expendables. Though *Return* lacks the charming simplicity of the first Blind Dead film, it does sustain a gradual building of tension more successfully than *Tombs* (which only presented periodic attacks in isolation from each other). In fact, this second film is more obviously patterned after *Night of the Living Dead* than after *Tombs*. However, *Return* is hampered by dated characterization, the male players apparently competing among themselves for the Oscar in bad hair, wide lapels, and machismo alpha-male behavior.

The blackened, skeletal zombies are largely unchanged from *Tombs* (why tamper with perfection?), but this time the characters manage to deanimate some with fireworks and torches—in fact, so flammable are these zombies, one wonders why the protagonists don't just burn them all and have done with it. Still, however many are destroyed, more quickly appear, and there is a vague sense of unlimited numbers of them lurking behind every corner. In the end, nothing the characters do hinders their onslaught in the least; only the light of the rising sun brings the apocalypse to an end. *Return* also comes with a bonus zombie horse (somebody finally looks under one of the horse's hoods). De Ossorio continues his Blind Dead saga with *Horror of the Zombies* (1974).

Alternate titles: *Attack of the Blind Dead*, *Attack of the Eyeless Dead*, *Return of the Blind Dead*, *Revenge of the Evil Dead*.

Return of the Living Dead see ***Messiah of Evil***

Return of the Living Dead

Dir: Dan O'Bannon. *Prod*: Tom Fox. *Screenplay*: Dan O'Bannon. *Cast*: Clu Gulager, James Karen, Thom Mathews, Don Calfa, Beverly Randolph, Miguel Nuñez, Brian Peck, Linnea Quigley. Hemdale/Fox/Orion, 1985.

This highly popular and influential sequel to and reworking of

Night by O'Bannon (writer of *Alien*) successfully combines light-hearted fun with fast action and some of the orneriest zombies to hit the screen. Medical supplier Frank (Karen) explains to new employee Freddy (Mathews) that the basic story behind *Night of the Living Dead* was true, and that army cannisters containing the infectious zombies were mistakenly delivered to their warehouse. The two Einsteins accidentally release the 245-Trioxin gas from the cannisters into the nearby cemetery, promptly causing the dead to sprout from the ground and rampage indiscriminately. Joined by warehouse owner Burt (Gulager), mortician Ernie (Calfa), and Freddy's motley assortment of punk friends, they barricade themselves in the Resurrection Funeral Home against the swelling numbers of the hungry dead. When at last the military learns of the catastrophe, it responds by nuking the entire city (Louisville, Kentucky). Clean cinematography and editing, spirited writing, a lively metal score, and charismatic acting (especially from Ernie and Burt) give this pop-cult cash-in intrinsic merit. It brims with in-jokes to *Night* and never takes itself too seriously. *Return* was originally meant to represent John Russo's sequel to *Night*, but the finished product supposedly bears little resemblance to his initial conception.

The sleek, shambling zombies of *Return* are nothing like Romero's. For one thing, these ghouls aren't slow, but run as fast as their mucky legs can carry them. At one point the protagonists subdue and interrogate the top half of a specimen, an ancient (almost mummified) zombie whose brackish, protruding spine wags thoughtlessly like a tail as she answers their questions. She says she craves brains because eating them stops "the pain ... the pain of being dead." The eating of brains specifically is a new twist on the flesh-eating theme (Romero's zombies prefer entrails), one that was to stick in the minds of the public and become a permanent feature of zombie lore. Zombie Freddy, stalking his girlfriend, even says he can smell her brains.

Although fully articulate, the zombies rarely aspire to utterances beyond "Brains!" At one point, however, having already devoured one leather-clad punk, the zombie who originally emerged from the army cannister turns to the other punks menacingly and elaborates, "*More* brains!"

Romero's principle that zombies can be killed by destroying the brain is also forsaken ("You mean the movie lied?!" gasps Freddy). As Burt learns, "You can chop them up into pieces and the pieces still come after you." Moreover, these zombies are intelligent and capable of using tools—one rigs up a pulley and chain to pry open a locker door, and another uses a C.B. to call for more paramedics after having eaten those already dispatched. Admittedly, though, they don't really make use of this intelligence, and mainly just hover about in crazed packs. Nonetheless—spoof elements notwithstanding—from their speed, dexterity, and immunity to virtually all forms of attack, these are uncommonly dire undead.

Return of the Living Dead Part II

Dir: Ken Wiederhorn. *Prod*: Tom Fox. *Screenplay*: Ken Wiederhorn. *Cast*: Michael Kenworthy, Marsha Dietlein, Dana Ashbrook, Philip Bruns, James Karen, Thom Mathews, Suzanne Snyder. Lorimar, 1987.

The middle episode of the glossy, tongue-in-cheek *Return* trilogy, though tightly-wrought and well-acted, fails to recapture the fun, frenetic energy of O'Bannon's original. Bored kids break into a lost cannister left over from the first invasion, releasing a sickly green cloud that soaks into the ground of a nearby cemetery. The protagonists flee from the resulting undead onslaught through an unfinished housing development to a deserted hospital and at last to a power plant, where resourceful cableguy Tom (Ashbrook) contrives to electrocute them en masse. The horror-comedy keeps a fast pace but offers nothing that the first movie didn't already do better. Wiederhorn also directed the much superior *Shock Waves* (1977).

As in the first *Return*, the zombies are fully rational and articulate. They crave brains (and monosyllabically make mention of the fact frequently)—of any creature, human or non-human. In a classic scene, they plunder a pet store, emerging with cute poodles and budgies dangling from their mouths. They keep all knowledge from their former lives; thus they use tools, and even drive a car for a short distance. They shuffle along unevenly and never quite break into a run, but otherwise most of their motor functions seem to operate at the usual speed.

When a gravedigger and his assistant breathe the noxious green gas and slowly die, Mathews comments on this all being a bit familiar (he and Karen went through this before in the first *Return*). As a zombie, he corners his girlfriend in a church, telling her he craves her brains because they're "rich and spicy."

Return of the Living Dead Part III

Dir: Brian Yuzna. *Prod*: Gary Schmoeller, Brian Yuzna. *Screenplay*: John Penney. *Cast*: J. Trevor Edmond, Mindy Clarke, Kent McCord, Basil Wallace, Sarah Douglas, Pia Reyes. Trimark Pictures, 1993.

A departure from the zombie-invasion mania of the first two, the third *Return* is rather a sappy tale of ill-fated teen love. The military continues its experiments with 245-Trioxin, attempting to harness the undead as a new branch of bio-warfare. Angry young Curt (Edmond), the son of the officer in charge of the experiments (McCord), surreptitiously uses his father's lab to revive his punk girlfriend Julie (Clarke) after she dies in a motorcycle accident. As Julie gradually deteriorates into a brain-eating zombie, the pair flee through the sewers to avoid a group of hostile street thugs as well as the military containment unit. The film focuses on mutations and conglomerate mosaics of misshapen body parts (as in Clive Barker's *Nightbreed*), and there is a teeth-grating scene in which Julie pierces her body all over in cenobite-like fashion, tapping into the punk-gone-mainstream body piercing craze of the early '90s. The helplessness and desperation of the two earlier movies, as well as their creativity in finding variations on the zombie phenomenon, are entirely missing. Here there's never a sense that things are out of control; the half dozen or so zombies remain contained and away from the general populace the entire time. Though the "star-crossed lovers" theme is sometimes successfully updated and parodied in zombie romances (*I Was a Teenage Zombie*, *My Boyfriend's Back*, *My Zombie Lover*), here it flounders from being played far too seriously.

We learn that the reason zombies specifically crave brains is that they feed on electricity from the neurons, but this is the only addition to the received lore. Julie, who remains in a transitional state between living and undead throughout, doesn't adhere to expected zombie characteristics, leading to unsatisfying inconsistencies. The very fact that she doesn't arise immediately as a crazed zombie upon being infected with the Trioxin directly contradicts the nature of the infection in all three movies. Furthermore, she refuses to eat Curt's brain, which, the movie explains, is due to the strength of their emotional attachment. So are we supposed to imagine that the zombies who turn on their lovers and family members in the first two movies never had any emotional attachments to them? Julie becomes increasingly self-destructive, because, she explains, "The pain helps. The pain makes the hunger go away." She's never happy, torn between conflicting human and zombie desires, and so the featured zombie spends most of the film whining.

Return of the Zombies

(Orig. *La orgía de los muertos*). *Dir*: José Luis Merino. *Prod*: Ramón Plana. *Screenplay*: José Luis Merino, Enrico Colombo. *Cast*: Stanley Cooper (Stelvio Rosi), Dianik Zurakowska, Paul Naschy (Jacinto Molina), Gerard Tichy, María Pía Conté, Charles Quincey. Petruka/Prodimex (Spain, Italy), 1972.

Scenic ninteenth-century Sköpje forms the eerie and beautiful background for this grab bag of twisted motifs, suspect ideology, and gruesome zombies. Fearless but sleazy Serge Checkov (Cooper) visits a rustic mountain community to inherit his uncle's estate, but becomes drawn increasingly into the web of bizarre happenings and unexplained murders plaguing the village. It seems Leon (Tichy), the mad scientist in the basement, is animating the dead for no particular reason, and sending them to strangle anyone who threatens to uncover his illicit experiments. Though we're apparently meant to sympathize with Aryan protagonist Serge, he blackmails a frightened, crying woman into stripping before him, after he's beaten and fired the butler to rid the house of competition. Meanwhile, village idiot Igor (Naschy) keeps a harem of dead, decaying women (and not reanimated ones, either) for his personal enjoyment. Requires a particular mood, to say the least.

Leon raises corpses by exciting their nervous systems with electric charges. He then controls them by means of a capsule he has implanted in their brains to receive his thought patterns, or something like that. Thus they do his bidding up until the climax, when they inexplicably turn on him. Certain motor functions can be reanimated, but not the vocal or visual senses. Thus the revived corpses are blind—but like de Ossorio's blind zombies, they normally find their way around without bumping into things or tripping. There are only three or four zombies, and they only appear at the very end, but they're convincing and successfully choreographed.

Alternate titles: *Beyond the Living Dead*, *Bracula—The Terror of the Living Dead*, *The Hanging Woman*, *House of Terror*, *La orgia dei morti*.

Revenge of the Dead see ***Zeder***

Revenge of the Evil Dead see ***Return of the Evil Dead***

Revenge of the Living Dead see *Children Shouldn't Play with Dead Things*

Revenge of the Living Zombies see *Flesheater*

Revenge of the Screaming Dead see *Messiah of Evil*

Revenge of the Zombie

Dir: Patrick Regan. *Prod*: Alain Silver. *Screenplay*: Alain Silver, Patrick Regan, Mary Stewart. *Cast*: Fabian Forte, Marilyn Burns, Nell Regan, Patrick Regan III, Jon Cedar, Marvin Miller, Will Rand. Film Ventures International, 1981.

Tame and slow paced, this budgetless vanity showcase for the director to cast his gawky twins as stars is strictly a family affair. In an off-season California coastal resort, Guy Nicholas (Rand) keeps his sickening twins Michael and Beth (Regan and Regan) isolated from the world, for fear that their prodigious ESP powers will become known to authorities. At a loss what to do when their father is killed by passing biker thugs, the children decide they must keep the murder a secret by telekinetically moving Nicholas' body around in some poorly-thought-out scheme to avoid suspicion. They try to continue life as normal with their new puppet father, occasionally sending him off to kill bullies, bill collectors, or anyone who displeases them. At last losing heart, Buffy and Jody say goodbye to their perambulatory pa, and have him dig his own grave. The amateur effort encumbers its interesting premise with a meandering story line, lengthy pauses, and unconvincing child actors. Sadly enough, '60s heartthrob Fabian and *Texas Chainsaw Massacre* heroine Burns appear as a deputy and a social worker. The president of "Film Ventures International" disappeared after a lawsuit, and the movie only gradually made its way out on the video market.

Zombie Nicholas has bluish hands, wears a suit, and has a couple of occult symbols that the children paint on his face. Though he looks and acts like a conventional screen zombie, it's difficult to evaluate his mental status. On the one hand, his body is animated only by the children's telepathy, so there's no reason to think he's sentient. On the other hand, it would seem that what they activate in him is an independent animating principle of some sort, because he drives a car (which they don't know how to do), and he can act and deliberate even when out of their sight. It's never explained how he locates his victims from afar, furthermore, hinting at greater supernatural forces; and in one wildly implausible scene, he exhibits the bizarre power of travelling completely underneath a beach through the sand to spring up on his victims like a shark. Whatever.

Alternate titles: *Kiss Daddy Goodbye*, *Vengeful Dead*.

Revenge of the Zombies

Dir: Steve Sekely. *Prod*: Lindsley Parsons. *Screenplay*: Edmond Kelso, Van Norcross. *Cast*: John Carradine, Gale Storm, Robert Lowery, Bob Steele, Mantan Moreland, Veda Ann Borg, Barry McCollum, Mauritz Hugo, Sybil Lewis, Madame Sul-Te-Wan, James Baskett. Monogram, 1943.

Monogram virtually remakes its earlier hit *King of the Zombies* with a wartime story of an insidious Nazi plot percolating in the Louisiana bayou. Larry Adams (Lowery) and Scott Warrington (Hugo), along with their knock-kneed servant Jeff (Moreland), call in on secretive Dr. von Altermann (Carradine) to investigate the mysterious death of his wife Lila (Borg). Kitchen hand Rosalie (Lewis) warns Jeff of "things walking ain't got no business walking," while Adams and Warrington discover that Altermann is raising an invincible zombie army for Germany. Despite a dramatic score and charismatic Moreland's sincere efforts, the scenic situations and conflicts are stock fare from the Monogram horror-mill. *Revenge of the Zombies* is the first movie to presume the audience knows what a "zombie" is and not provide an explanation.

The undead phenomenon, unlike that of most early zombie movies, is the result of science rather than voodoo. Altermann explains that tissues and cells can be sustained indefinitely by a process of refrigeration, while those areas of the brain controlling volition and independent judgment can be suspended. Thus he intends to raise an undead army that will need no food, and will continue to fight despite fire, gas, and severe bodily damage, so long as the brain remains intact. (In fact, this is the first embryonic mention in a zombie movie that the creature can only be deanimated by destroying the brain.) Though Altermann envisions "many thousands" of undead soldiers, so far his army barely numbers a dozen or so. The sullen zombies in his humble troop are all either emaciated or overweight: in short, an overall unlikely mob to carry the Third Reich to its destiny. Occasionally, an eerie, high-pitched tone is heard from their midst, a sort of zombie call.

The head zombie Lazarus (Baskett) is the zombie equivalent of a house slave: he carries out household tasks such as serving at the dinner table, while the others toil at manual labor outside. The only other character zombie, Altermann's wife Lila, differs from all the other zombies in exerting a will of her own. She wanders off into the swamp, answering flatly when questioned, but otherwise biding her time before summoning her fellow zombies against her evil husband. Once he's dead, the zombies turn around and begin to disperse, but they show no signs of snapping out of their zombie condition. Maybe they're still wandering around the swamps today, calling out their creepy song in the sultry bayou nights, waiting for tighter supporting cast closure.

Alternate title: *The Corpse Vanished.*

Revenge of the Zombies

Dir: Ho Meng-Hua. *Prod*: Run Run Shaw. *Screenplay*: I Kuang. *Cast*: Ti Lung Tanny, Lo Lieh, Liu Hui-Ju, Lily Li, Lin Wei-Tu. World Northal (Hong Kong), 1981.

The Shaw brothers combine black magic, martial arts, and gore in this intense horror-cult favorite. Medical doctor Chen Sing believes black magic is responsible for the strange flesh-eating diseases he sees at the hospital, but his friend Chung Ping is skeptical. Behind it all is sorcerer Kai Chang, who stays immortal by drinking human milk, and who enslaves Chung Ping's friends and even his wife. The nerdy protagonist turns out to be a karate shark, and single-handedly takes on the evil wizard and his motley zombie minions. Budget effects and lackluster martial arts sequences are more than compensated by sustained energy and brazen creativity. Solid conceptual support and periodic surprises keep things festive: an old wizard flogs a zombie woman with a dead weasel, for instance, and then plucks out his own eyes and instructs Chung Ping to eat them for greater powers.

Evil Kai Chang procures corpses, recalls the departed souls with incantations, and then controls the resulting zombie. He keeps them dormant on slabs in his cellar when not in use, and then reanimates them by driving huge nails into their heads with a mallet. The zombies are fairly sedate when first revived, moaning and milling about, but can eventually become quite excited—running, jumping, howling, and zipping around. Kai Chang also keeps some mangy-looking zombie drones in hooded cloaks around the house as guards. Chung Ping deanimates the lot in the closing sequence by burning all the wax dolls that contain their entrapped souls. Between the railroad spikes in their heads and the bouncy somersaults in the fight sequences, these are not your average undead stiffs.

Alternate title: *Black Magic II.*

Revolt of the Dead Ones see ***Vengeance of the Zombies***

Revolt of the Demons see ***Revolt of the Zombies***

Revolt of the Zombies

Dir: Victor Halperin. *Prod*: Edward Halperin. *Screenplay*: Howard Higgins, Rollo Lloyd, Victor Halperin. *Cast*: Dorothy Stone, Dean Jagger, Roy D'Arcy, Robert Noland, George Cleveland, Teru Shimada. Halperin Productions/ Academy, 1936.

Lugosi was originally supposed to star in this uninvolving Halperin follow-up to *White Zombie*, but I doubt even he could have saved it. The movie begins in the thick of World War I, when a regiment of zombified Cambodians proves imperishable in battle; an expedition is subsequently organized and sent to the lost city of Angkor to unearth the "secret of the zombies." General Duval's daughter Claire (Stone) breaks off her engagement with Armand (Jagger) to be with her new love Cliff (Noland). In his grief, Armand cracks the riddle of the zombies, brings everyone under his power, and amasses an army of subservient Cambodian troops. All he really wants, though, is to win Claire's love, which he finds all the power in the world incapable of doing (the theme of *White Zombie* also). He relinquishes his power to prove his love for her, allowing his slave army to rend him to bits. The film is briefly interesting when Armand starts to raise his zombie armies, but they never actually do anything. *Revolt* is only noteworthy in being unusually grandiose for its time—the swiftness with which Armand gains control over the minds of an entire nation anticipates the apocalyptic proportions of later zombie movies.

Though called "zombies" and "human robots," the subjects aren't really revived corpses. Armand turns people into his slaves while they're still alive, and when he relinquishes his power, they simply

Opposite: **The Halperin brothers (creators of *White Zombie*) take the zombie to Cambodia in their dull follow-up, *Revolt of the Zombies* (1936).**

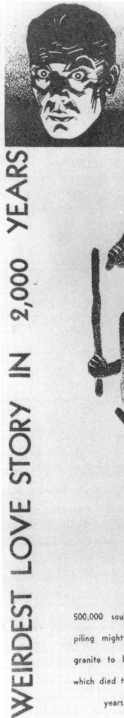

REVOLT OF THE ZOMBIES

WEIRDEST LOVE STORY IN 2,000 YEARS

with

DOROTHY STONE

and

DEAN JAGGER

Zombies—
Not dead, not alive!

500,000 soulless people piling mighty blocks of granite to build a city which died two thousand years ago!

return to their normal waking state. First he turns his servant Buna (Shimada) into a zombie by burning a special powder and fanning the flames toward him, but after that he appears to recruit new subjects with no more than a thought. His "followers," as he calls them, are mostly armies of Southeast Asians with uniforms, rifles, and blank expressions, standing at attention or performing drills. Other than the brief scene at the beginning in the trenches of World War I, when the zombie Cambodians advance on an enemy line with guns and bayonets, the film shows no awareness of what made the zombies of *White Zombie* effective—here they aren't scruffy, dark, inscrutable, or unholy, but clean, sterile, and controlled.

Alternate title: *Revolt of the Demons.*

Roma contra Roma see ***War of the Zombies***

Sanguelia see ***Zombie***

Santo and Blue Demon Against the Monsters

(Orig. *Santo y Blue Demon contra los monstruos*). *Dir*: Gilberto Martínez Solares. *Screenplay*: Rafael García Travesí, Jesús Sotomayor Martínez. *Cast*: Santo, Blue Demon (Alejandro Cruz), Jorge Rado, Carlos Ancira, Hedy Blue. Churubusco-Azteca (Mexico), 1969.

Mad scientists in Mexican wrestling movies will raise the dead as soon as grab the morning paper. Here dastardly Bruno Halder (Ancira) resurrects a small platoon of defunct criminals simply to run errands for him. They hover lamely in the background, while a host of even cheesier fiends are summoned to combat the masked heroes: a vampire, mummy, wolfman, Frankenstein monster, and a Cyclops-gargoyle thing whose rubber face doesn't move but whose eye lights up. Santo and Blue Demon fight the lot of them for 70 endless minutes. This unfortunate installment in our heroes' illustrious careers is sophomoric and directionless, with not much explanation and a whole lot of wrestling.

Halder and his evil dwarf sidekick procure the revived corpses from a cemetery under very hazily defined circumstances. The thuggish, blue-complexioned zombies all wear black T-shirts and pants, and aren't good for much besides holding a flashlight and moving bodies around the lab. They lose interest in their brief scuffle with Santo and B.D. (their only shot at center stage) when one of them gets decapitated: the others don't particularly seem afraid, but they do gather around and gawk at the severed head in dim-witted fascination, while the wrestlers run right by them. Oh well—maybe Halder should just hire some real thugs.

Santo and Blue Demon in the Land of the Dead see ***The Land of the Dead***

Santo contra la magia negra see ***Santo vs. Black Magic***

El Santo contra los zombies see ***Invasion of the Zombies***

El Santo en el mundo de los muertos see ***The Land of the Dead***

Santo vs. Black Magic

(Orig. *Santo contra la magia negra*). *Dir*: Alfredo B. Crevenna. *Prod*: Lic. Borge García Besne, Joseph W. Saliba. *Screenplay*: Fernando Osés. *Cast*: El Santo, Elsa Cárdenas, Sasha Montenegro, Gerty Jones, César del Campo, Fernando Osés, Guillermo Gálvez. Películas Latinoamericanas/Cinematográfica Flama (Mexico), 1972.

Mexican masked wrestler movies are often quirky and entertaining, but even Santo looks confused in the cornucopic tedium of this senseless Caribbean romp. A scientist (Gálvez) has discovered a powerful tactical explosive, which Santo wishes to keep out of the wrong hands. Evil voodoo priestess Yanira (Montenegro) assaults him unsuccessfully with snakes, voodoo dolls, and zombies, but never thinks of just shooting him. After much talking and even more drumming and dancing, Santo conquers the witch woman with the help of a good voodoo priestess (Jones). Shot in Haiti, the picture should provide the perfect setting for an authentic zombie adventure, but instead dissipates its energy (and the viewer's) on lengthy dance rituals at every turn. The letters "FIN" have never looked so beautiful. Not to be confused with the delightful *Dr. Satan vs. Black Magic* (Mexico, 1967).

When Santo first arrives in Haiti, he's beset by a half dozen or so unimpressive zombies. The pathetic African-Caribbeans look like half-wits and fight with all the unbridled fury of Droopy on sedatives. Two of them just stand at the sidelines throughout the fight, looking interested but obviously unclear on the fact that they should be participating. They all flee when Santo threatens them with a tire iron, which is kind of cross-shaped. Fred Sanford could probably take on this sorry troop, and priestess Yanira really should look into a firearm of some sort to carry out her evil schemes.

Santo vs. the Zombies see ***Invasion of the Zombies***

Satan's Satellites see ***Zombies of the Stratosphere***

Scared Stiff

Dir: George Marshall. *Prod*: Hal B. Wallis. *Screenplay*: Herbert Baker, Walter DeLeon. *Cast*: Dean Martin, Jerry Lewis, Lizabeth Scott, Carmen Miranda, George Dolenz, Dorothy Malone, William Ching, Paul Marion, Jack Lambert. Wallis-Hazen/Paramount, 1953.

Marshall's remake of his 1940 hit *The Ghost Breakers* is an annoying Dean Martin and Jerry Lewis stint, which mostly sticks to the original except for the addition of several bad song and dance numbers and even worse comedy routines. Martin plays it straight as Larry, while Lewis is his buffoonish sidekick Myron M. Mertz (the "M" is also for Myron, ha ha). Having an all-white cast sidesteps the racist dimension of the earlier feature, only to replace it with spicy South-of-the-Border songs about enchiladas. Jerry Lewis impersonates a zombie.

Jack Lambert is much less striking as a zombie than Noble Johnson was in the original—he has bad hair, makes an unexplained clicking sound when he walks, and generally looks more confused and groggy than unearthly and menacing. He totes a nastier mace than Johnson did, but is otherwise as scary as Jerry Lewis is funny.

The School That Ate My Brain see ***Zombie High***

Scooby-Doo on Zombie Island

Dir: Jim Stenstrum. *Prod*: Cos Anzilotti. *Story*: Glenn Leopold, Davis Doi. *Screenplay*: Glenn Leopold. *Voices*: Scott Innes, Billy West, Mary Kay Bergman, Frank Welker, B.J. Ward, Adrienne Barbeau, Tara Charendoff, Mark Hamill. Hanna-Barbera/Warner Bros., 1998.

Thirty years after the original show, Hanna-Barbera launches the video release of *Scooby-Doo* episodes with a feature-length movie in which the ghosts are finally real. Leggy Daphne, now a talk show host, rounds up the old crew to explore hauntings in the Louisiana bayou. On creepy Moonscar Island, the gang finds itself caught between zombie pirates and Confederate soldiers on the one hand, and 200-year-old demonic cat-vampires on the other. Shag and Scoob do their patented shtick, but fans will appreciate some insights into the gang's off-hour activities as well as increased attention to the sexual tension between Daphne and Fred. The best scene is Fred trying to pull the "mask" off a zombie he believes is only a criminal in disguise, and wrenching off the whole head by mistake. Fred's voice is the original one from the series (Frank Welker).

The zombies are the generations of victims the cat-vampires have killed, from rebel soldiers with Confederate uniforms to modern tourists with Hawaiian shirts and cameras. They're only trying to warn our heroes, not attack them, but understandably they have a hard time getting the point across since all they can do is lumber forward menacingly with arms outstretched while groaning eerily. With shredded clothes, rusty sabers, and blank eyes, the slimy swamp zombies aren't half bad. The tortured spirits are at last released once the evil cat-vampires are destroyed. "Rombies!"

The Second Coming see ***Messiah of Evil***

The Secret of Dr. Orloff see ***Dr. Orloff's Monster***

El Secreto del Dr. Orloff see ***Dr. Orloff's Monster***

The Serpent and the Rainbow

Dir: Wes Craven. *Prod*: David Ladd, Doug Claybourne. *Screenplay*: Richard Maxwell, A.R. Simoun. *Cast*: Bill Pullman, Cathy Tyson, Zakes Mokae, Paul Winfield, Brent Jennings, Conrad Roberts, Kimberleigh Burroughs. Universal, 1987.

The sensationalized screen version of Wade Davis' relatively sober and informative book, though over-dramatic in many ways, still presents the zombie phenomenon from a refreshingly serious and scientific point of view. Anthropologist Dennis Alan (Pullman) is hired by a pharmaceutical company to track down a sample of the drug used for zombification in Haiti, for its possible use in anesthetics. In Haiti, Alan is aided by locals against corrupt politician and voodoo priest Peitraud (Mokae), while the Duvalier regime crumbles in the background. Alan learns the secret of the zombie powder, fabricated from puffer fish, sea toad, stinging sea worm, and a human corpse (Davis argues in scholarly writings that tetrodotoxin, or puffer fish poison, is the key ingredient in zombie powder). Although colorful, the movie becomes too busy and scattered, with flashy shock-effect horror scenes increasingly supplanting the potential for psychological

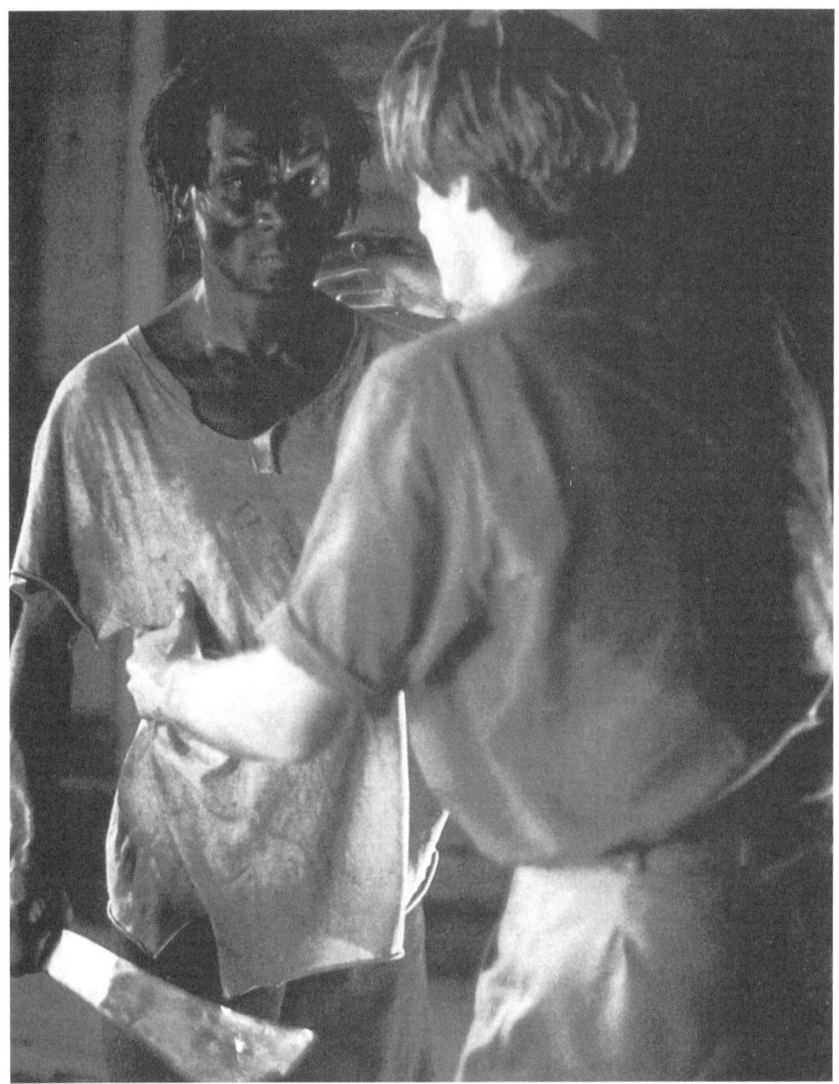

Bill Pullman (right) tries to placate undead Conrad Roberts (left) in *The Serpent and the Rainbow* (1987), one of the few movies to take its zombie conceptualization from folklore and anthropology rather than from Hollywood monster conventions.

anthropology. The dream and drug-trance sequences are all more reminiscent of *Nightmare on Elm Street*, Craven's runaway success from two years earlier, than of Davis' book. After fifty-five years of American zombie movies, this was the first to be shot in Haiti—although the crew reportedly had to flee when 2000 extras revolted, after learning that the crew could afford to pay them more than two dollars each for three hours' work.

The drug Alan discovers induces a temporary death-like abatement of physical processes: for a twelve-hour period, the breathing and heart rate come to a complete stop, but the areas of the brain regulating sensory awareness, thoughts, and emotions are still fully active. Thus the subjects are fully aware throughout their own funerals and burials. Alan encounters a zombie named Margrite (Burroughs) who stares at the wall, and when asked about her ordeal, answers only with a desperate, tortured look. Another zombie, Christophe (Roberts), is slightly more eloquent, though he's also broken in spirit and haunts local graveyards in his off hours. What the film captures best, perhaps, is the profound sense of despair and terror at the heart of the partially-sentient zombies, which is closer to Davis' presentation of actual zombies than other screen interpretations. This is about the only zombie movie to display more than a surface awareness of vodun religion, and it's gratifying to find a film taking its zombie conceptualization from anthropology and folklore rather than from stock Hollywood monster conventions.

The Seven Brothers Meet Dracula see ***The Legend of the Seven Golden Vampires***

Seven Doors of Death see ***The Beyond***

Sexy Nights of the Dead see ***Erotic Nights of the Living Dead***

Shanks

Dir: William Castle. *Prod*: Steven North. *Screenplay*: Ranald Graham. *Cast*: Marcel Marceau, Tsilla Chelton, Philippe Clay, Cindy Eilbacher, Helena Kallianiotes, Don Calfa, Bill Manard, Mondo, Read Morgan. Paramount, 1974.

Modeled after silent film conventions, this dreamlike fairy tale is an exercise in visual and gestural black comedy. The fascinating experiment starring famed French mime Marceau was William Castle's last film. Mute, childlike puppeteer Malcolm Shanks (Marceau) is hired by aged local scientist Mr. Walker (also Marceau) to help him with his experiments in reanimating dead animals. When old man Walker, Malcolm's drunken brother (Clay), and his abusive sister-in-law (Chelton) all turn up dead, Malcolm makes human marionettes out of them using electrode implants and operates them with small remote control boxes. He enacts an ongoing, decidedly macabre puppet show in which the cadavers dance, serve him supper, and generally provide entertainment for him and his underage love interest Celia (Marcia Brady look-alike Eilbacher). Their Nabokovian bliss is disturbed when a biker gang crashes the estate, raping and killing Celia. Lonely and jaded, Malcolm implants the electrode attachments into Celia's corpse, and begins to dance with her reanimated body in a scene left open-ended and loaded with perverse implications. Horror scenes are clashingly accompanied by carnival music, while gruesome shocks intrude suddenly into comical routines. Though slow-paced, the film is continually challenging and well rewards the demands it places on the audience. The playful exterior belies some morbid undercurrents, and a dark vision emerges of how perverse innocence, left to its own devices, really is. The score was nominated for an Oscar, and a man is pecked to death by a zombie chicken.

The three corpses raised in the film are stiff and jerky, like clockwork dolls. When Malcolm directs them to kill, they strangle and drown their victims with formidable strength. In general, however, the zombie-dolls are comical in their stilted performances and Chaplin routines—and even more so when the bikers get a hold of the controls and make them contort into unnatural positions. The reanimated corpses are generally docile, civilized, and show more basic humanity than most of the living characters.

Alternate title: *Shock*.

Shatter Dead

Dir: Scooter McCrae. *Prod*: Scooter McCrae. *Screenplay*: Scooter McCrae. *Cast*: Stark Raven, Flora Fauna, Daniel "smalls" Johnson, Robert Wells. Seeing Eye Dog Productions, 1993.

An intelligent attempt to go one step beyond the normal zombie invasion paradigm, *Shatter Dead* is packed with thoughtful variations on the usual motifs, though ultimately burdened by amateur production values. The walking dead now outnumber the living and society is on the brink of collapse: but the dead don't actively perpetrate violence against the living—they are simply disenfranchised and down-trodden (there's even talk of unionization). Their maimed, corrupt forms linger in shop-fronts and alleyways, panhandling and loitering, harassing the living for handouts and pity. "The freshly dead, embarrassed, frightened, unsure of what to do or even what to make of their own situation," merely wait patiently for the living to join their ever-growing ranks. They have also dug up their long-dead friends and relatives from the cemeteries, answering the muffled calls from beneath the ground. Protagonist Susan struggles for survival amidst a paranoid population of intermixed living and dead, while dead acquaintance Mary tries to convince her to join them. Though the premise is fresh and there is a plentiful supply of good raw ideas, the movie is built around character interaction among amateur actors, leaving it scattered and directionless. It lacks sustained tension and resolution, and directs too much energy away from its fascinating conceptual possibilities in favor of trite exploitation concerns (shower scenes, sex with a pistol, etc.).

Shatter Dead presupposes familiarity with, and consciously reacts against, the traditional Romero mythos. When trying to kill zombie Mary, Susan tries to follow the principle that zombies can be killed by destroying the brain: thus she beats and shoots Mary's head and face repeatedly, but succeeds only in turning them to bloody, mashy pulp. "Sorry, I'm not up there," Mary returns calmly. "It's not the brain but the soul—how do you kill the soul?" The dead don't eat or sleep—all biological functions grind to a halt—while the mental capacities are intact. They still think and feel, though somewhat estranged from their bodies (one mentions that making a face is like placing a long-distance call). Mary laments that no one can die anymore, even if they want to. She adds that no one can even lie down and rest anymore, since staying in one position for too long causes blood to settle in unsightly pools. When she knows she'll have to be around living people and needs to conceal the fact that she's dead, she stands on her head for a while to get color in her cheeks. As well as expanding the traditional zombie mythology with added layers of behavioral complexity, the film succeeds in capturing a vague, unmentioned despair rippling underneath the fine line that separates the living from the dead.

Ship of Zombies see ***Horror of the Zombies***

Shock see ***Shanks***

Shock Waves

Dir: Ken Wiederhorn. *Prod*: Reuben Trane. *Screenplay*: John Harrison, Ken Wiederhorn. *Cast*: Peter Cushing, Brooke Adams, Fred Buch, Jack Davidson,

Luke Halpin, D.J. Sidney, Don Stout, John Carradine. Laurence Friedricks Enterprises/Zopix, 1977.

In this successful zombie experiment, a strange solar phenomenon somehow causes a German ship from World War II to surface from the depths off the coast of an island, complete with its long-dormant crew of genetically engineered storm troopers. Shipwrecked passengers from a small cruise vessel meet the island's only inhabitant (Cushing) in a large, decrepit hotel. The man explains to the party that while he was an SS officer during the war, he was assigned an experimental troop of soldiers designed to exist in any conditions—in this case, underwater soldiers, since they were to man U-boats. The subjects chosen were pathological killers and maniacs, and the experiment failed because they couldn't be controlled. Emerging from swampy wetlands, fresh water rivers, and the sea itself, the aquatic SS zombies from the ship eliminate the cast one at a time. The sole-survivor-gone-mad ending, though now a generic commonplace, is well executed and genuinely disturbing. The control of suspense is excellent, especially in the second half, and the unique zombies themselves are a source of continuous fascination.

The Nazi revenants are blond-haired Aryans whose uniforms are in perfect shape, and who don't look too putrid or picked at, considering they've been in the sea for thirty years (but then, they were genetically engineered for invulnerability). The make-up design is by Alan Ormsby (*Children Shouldn't Play with Dead Things*, *Dead of Night*). Cushing says his troops are "not dead, not alive, but somewhere in between." Their preferred method of killing is drowning victims in the nearest body of water, which in one scene is even a fish tank. They also strangle with a rope or garrote on occasion, which is the only instance of tool use they exhibit. In an admirable show of post–Romero restraint, they don't eat their victims and the condition is not contagious. They spend a good deal of time hiding in the sea, the rivers, or just in the bushes. The inscrutable storm troopers never produce any facial expressions, growls, breathing, or other vocalizations. Their inhumanly detached expressions are sinister when combined with such intensely focused malice.

Perhaps the oddest thing (among many odd things) about these zombies is their stylized, choreographed synchronization. They come across as slick Kraftwerk–Devo Euro-zombies, surfacing or sinking simultaneously and occasionally standing equidistant from one another in a staggered pattern. This rigid composure is consistent with the cold, methodical rigor of the SS, and they would be very powerful if it weren't for the silly goggles they wear at all times. When their goggles are pulled off, they stumble around, make a high-pitched squealing hiss and drop to the ground (this is the only way to deanimate them). There are some good shots of the zombies marching along the bottom of a river and an open-sea coral reef, the actors doing a much better job of keeping air bubbles in than the aqua–Nazi zombies of the later Spanish-French *Zombie Lake.* Although the treatment of the gangrenous antagonists leaves much to be desired in terms of consistency and supporting explanation, *Shock Waves* offers an undeniably creative and innovative approach to the screen presentation of the zombie, at the height of the post–*Night* decade in which such innovation was most lacking.

Alternate titles: *Almost Human, Death Corps.*

Shrunken Heads

Dir: Richard Elfman. *Prod*: Charles Band. *Screenplay*: Matthew Bright. *Cast*: Julius Harris, Meg Foster, Aeryk Egan, Becky Herbst, A.J. Damato, Bo Sharon, Darris Love. Full Moon, 1994.

When a street gang kills three pesky adolescents, kindly newsstand owner Aristide Sumatra (Harris), a former Ton-Ton Makoute and voodoo priest from Haiti, reanimates the heads of the dead boys by stewing them in a bubbling cauldron. The diminutive disembodied heads then fly around the city to avenge themselves on the punks who killed them, while making quirky, deadpan observations in a monotone voice. Sumatra and his creepy shrunken head minions lovingly exaggerate every preposterous line with relish, yielding some outrageous dialogue in an otherwise treadmill production.

The street thugs killed by the shrunken head protagonists come back as zombies, who gurgle and stumble about with great difficulty as they twitchily perform rehabilitory social services such as picking up trash and sweeping. Sumatra says they will walk the earth for a short period of time before deteriorating into brown liquid. The zombies are played entirely for comic effect, and have consistent problems with flatulence.

Sibao

(Episode, *The Saint*). *Dir*: Peter Yates. *Prod*: Robert Baker, Monty Berman. *Teleplay*: Terry Nation. *Original Story*: Leslie Charteris. *Cast*: Roger Moore,

Jeanne Roland, John Carson, Jerry Stovin. New World Production/ITC (England), 1964.

Oily Roger Moore was smug secret agent Simon Templar in the British TV series "The Saint," a '60s cult favorite on both sides of the Atlantic. Here Templar travels to Haiti to topple local boss Theron Netlord (Carson), who is on the verge of tapping into the untold secrets of voodoo magic for his evil ends. The neighborhood houngan's (voodoo priest) daughter Sibao (Roland) helps Templar protect himself against otherworldly powers, while Templar does a pretty good job of protecting himself against worldly ones. Unlike the portrayal of voodoo in American productions of the time, the script validates native beliefs as part of a healthy and intrinsically valuable world view. The strangest anomaly is Sibao herself, though, who comes across more as Polynesian than black Haitian.

A treacherously killed man is brought back from the dead in a communal ceremony, to avenge himself so that he can rest at peace. The disembodied soul—which is explicitly called a zombie—remains entirely invisible during his brief return to the world of the living. He bee-lines through the forest toward the man who ran him over, killing him at once through pure fright. All we see of the zombie are some leaves rustling as he walks through the forest and a vase getting knocked over, but in fact zombies in Haitian folklore are frequently invisible. TV censorship was doubtlessly an issue in understating the zombie, but this is the only screen portrayal I know of—movies or TV—of an important folkloric tradition.

Silent Death **see** ***Voodoo Island***

The Snake People

(Orig. *La muerte viviente*). *Dir*: Juan Ibáñez. *Prod*: Luis Enrique Vergara. *Screenplay*: Luis Enrique Vergara, Jack Hill. *Cast*: Boris Karloff, Julissa, Carlos East, Rafael Bertrand, Tongolele (Yolanda Montes), Quintin Bulnes. Fílmica Vergara/Azteca/Columbia (Mexico, U.S.), 1968.

Shortly before dying, Karloff signed with producer Vergara to appear in a series of substandard Mexican quickies, for which he shot several brief scenes in L.A. and mailed the footage to Mexico. He certainly has one foot in the grave in this trite tale of passion and voodoo magic. Captain Labiche (Bertrand) arrives at the South Pacific "Island of the Serpents" to stamp out native superstition by force, while young

Scriptwriter and Hollywood unit director Jack Hill (left), horror icon Boris Karloff (center), and others struggle to make sense out of *The Snake People* (1968). When the cameras start rolling again, Karloff will either summon the voodoo god Baron Samedi or attend a Tuskan Raider formal.

Anabella (Julissa) falls for dashing Andrew Wilhelm (East). Meanwhile, Anabella's uncle Carl von Molder (Karloff, dressed throughout most of the film like Colonel Sanders) tries to summon the voodoo god Baron Samedi, who will bring forth legions of the walking dead and begin a new era. Though sometimes strange to the point of psychedelic, this tame offering mostly consists of interminable scenes of native rites, women trying to look seductively evil, and shots of snakes.

It's stated at one point that the zombies are only victims of snake venom poisoning, which reduces their metabolism and heart rate and bestows the appearance of death. This venom destroys the brain, such that only the body is actually kept alive, and the person is a walking vegetable. This rational explanation is generally at odds with the supernatural magic that clearly abounds in the movie, however. Though von Molder revives zombies to work in his plantations up in the mountains, his motive isn't capitalist greed, as Legendre's is in *White Zombie*: he's only biding time and amassing his armies of the undead until the right moment, when Baron Samedi will come to claim them as his own. In fact, during the voodoo ceremonies, there is reference made to living death being a privilege—to be a zombie in the service of Baron Samedi is actually an honor. Aside from these working stiffs in the plantations, zombies are occasionally raised on the side without von Molder's permission. In a twisted subplot, his assistant Klinsor (Bulnes) raises a zombie woman for a personal slave, for instance. He has her scratch his back, then fan him, then have presumably listless sex with him (it's rather pathetic to watch him stroke her unresponsive arm as he lays her down on the bed). She is so soulless that in one scene, in order to dance with her, he has to move her arms for her, pinning her hand to his shoulder with his chin to keep it from falling off.

Alternate titles: *Cult of the Damned, La isla de los muertos, Island of the Snake People, Isle of the Snake People.*

Sole Survivor

Dir: Thom Eberhardt. *Prod*: Don Barkemeyer. *Screenplay*: Thom Eberhardt. *Cast*: Anita Skinner, Kurt Johnson, Caren Larkey, Robin Davidson, William Snare. R. & C. Larkey, 1982.

This cumbersome elegy is essentially a reworking of the classic *Carnival of Souls* (1962), except that in this version the dead are decidedly zombies rather than ghosts—they're dimwitted corpses that get up and walk around, rather than cunning spirits that appear capriciously. Denise Watson (Skinner), the only survivor of a plane wreck, is chagrined to find herself pursued by strangely expressionless and hostile people. Her doctor (Johnson) unhelpfully attempts to comfort her by explaining that most sole survivors of large disasters such as herself die within 24 months. There is increasing evidence that the strangers harassing Denise are actually corpses missing from nearby morgues and accident sites: by all rights she should be dead, and they've come to retrieve her. The lurking watchers become increasingly bolder, killing anyone who threatens to keep them from Denise. The movie is slow and funereal, with long pauses and silences punctuated by brief and humorless attack sequences.

There are some ghostly incidents (such as phantasmal shadows and voices from nowhere), but overall what's emphasized is the concrete physicality of the returning departed. Thus the county mortician is puzzled to find that even though the corpses were reclining or sitting at the time of their deaths, all the blood has since drained to their legs. The dead wander the streets, standing around staring at Denise eerily—sometimes for hours on end—waiting until she's alone before attacking. Although these thoroughly malevolent undead have a cool and sober patience (even for zombies) that allows for a few creepy moments, on the whole there isn't much to distinguish them from the weirdos that also hang around city streets staring at people.

Space Zombies see *The Astro-Zombies*

Strange Turf see *Voodoo Dawn*

Los Sueños eróticos de Christine see A Virgin Among the Living Dead

Sugar Hill

Dir: Paul Maslansky. *Prod*: Elliot Schick. *Screenplay*: Tim Kelly. *Cast*: Marki Bey, Robert Quarry, Don Pedro Colley, Betty Anne Rees, Richard Lawson, Zara Cully, Larry D. Johnson. American International Pictures, 1974.

Maslansky's only foray into directing is a humorously dated blaxploitation feature that keeps the familiar elimination-revenge plot afloat with bravado (sorry, I mean with "attitude, Daddy-O"). After her fiancé Langston (Johnson) is beaten to death by local gangsters for not selling his bar, Sugar Hill (Bey) gets local priestess Mama Maitresse (Cully) to summon the voodoo god Baron Samedi (Colley). Appearing as a well-to-do gentleman in a black suit, top hat, and cane, he offers to help with her revenge. The dead promptly crawl from their leafy graves and form a small platoon of hit men who assist in her methodic assassination of those responsible for Langston's death. Robert Quarry (a.k.a. Count Yorga) plays the gang's leader

Marki Bey and her slave zombies take no jive from whitey in *Sugar Hill* (1974).

and gets saved for last. There is little genuine tension—the villains are summarily dispatched, and the protagonists are never really in danger—but retro-hounds will have a field day with the '70s phrases, fashions, and 'fros (Sugar wears her hair down during the day, but wears an afro when she kills). The racist characterization is unimaginatively simplistic, however, leaving the racial moral heavy-handed. The movie was shot in Houston rather than New Orleans, as originally intended, because of trouble with the Teamsters.

The zombies represent a throwback to the classic zombie conceptualization of the '30s and '40s—they don't eat their victims, show no visible decay, are fully subservient to their voodoo masters, and don't generate horror other than through their visual appearance. Their most unusual feature is their eyes: shiny, silver orbs, some with black, reactionless pupils in the center. They have a bluish-white hue, wear tattered pants, and have filmy cobwebs all over them. Quick and silent, the slave zombies kill in a variety of ways, including hacking to pieces, strangling, and throwing a victim into a corral of starving pigs.

The interesting twist on these undead is their history: they are the former slaves who died en route from Guinea in the 1840s, and were buried in mass graves in the swamps. They still carry chains and shackles on their arms and legs. When Samedi first calls them to Sugar's service he tells her, "Put them to evil use—that's all they know or want." This is as close as we get to meditation on zombies in the movie, or even to acknowledgment of them as independent entities. In fact, they are pure weapons or instruments, brought out when needed but otherwise ignored (even in this racially conscious film, the slaves are still unreflectively put to work). Throughout the film the zombies are thrown in for purely gratuitous effect—they aren't even needed half the time they do appear—and suffer from unconvincing make-up on top of cinematic obsolescence.

Alternate titles: *Voodoo Girl*, *Zombies of Sugar Hill*.

The Supernaturals

Dir: Armand Mastroianni. *Prod*: Michael S. Murphy, Joel Soisson. *Screenplay*: Joel Soisson, Michael S. Murphy. *Cast*: Maxwell Caulfield, Nichelle Nichols, Talia Balsam, Margaret Shendal, LeVar Burton, Bobby Di Cicco, Scott Jacoby, Bradford Bancroft. Republic, 1986.

Captain's Log, 1986: TV director/producer Mastroianni creates a nostalgic ghost story about rebel zombies righting old wrongs in rural Alabama. Young Jeremy is the only survivor of a Civil War massacre of POWs committed by the 44th Union regiment. Now he's an ancient, cowering shell of a man, while his mother Melanie (Shendal) continues to haunt the area as a forever youthful ghost. When a group of green modern-day recruits from the U.S. Army, under the command of Sgt. Leona Hawkins (Nichelle Nichols, a.k.a. Lt. Uhura) show up at the old minefield site for maneuvers, Melanie thinks that Private

Ray Ellis (Caulfield) is her long-dead husband returned at last. At her bidding, mud-caked Confederate zombies stir from the ground and from the old underground barracks that have served as their tomb, and slowly mount an offensive against their ancient enemy, the 44th. Though there are a few chilling scenes, such as a race through fields of sharpened wooden spikes angled upwards, the scripting is threadbare and the characters uncharismatic. Geordie Laforge (LeVar Burton) is also on hand, doubtlessly on some mission from the future.

The zombie vestiges of the Confederate prisoners of war still have on the ripped, soiled remains of their CSA uniforms. The moldering cadavers mostly attack by creeping up on their victims and grasping them with their dry, blackened hands, but they also carry rifles with bayonets, and break into a volley of fire once in a while. Weapons have no effect on them, and none of them are deanimated in the course of the movie. There is a terrific shot of the scraggly rebels emerging from the foggy wood framed by Spanish moss, but the film pays far more attention to bland Melanie than to her zombie army.

Swamp of the Blood Leaches see ***The Alien Dead***

Tales from the Crypt

Dir: Freddie Francis. *Prod*: Max Rosenberg, Milton Subotsky. *Screenplay*: Milton Subotsky. *Cast*: Sir Ralph Richardson, Joan Collins, Oliver MacGreevy, Ian Hendry, Angie Grant, Peter Cushing, Robin Phillips, Richard Greene, Barbara Murray, Nigel Patrick. Amicus/Metromedia Producers (England), 1972.

The English production company Amicus, a pioneer of the long-popular horror anthology, entrusts five tourists to the gatekeeper of hell, who confronts them with their various crimes. Based on stories from the comic book of the same name, the episodes turn on ironic twists usually involving supernatural revenge for human sins. In the second segment, wealthy snob Elliot (Phillips) harasses kind but scruffy dustman Arthur Grimsdyke (Cushing) in order to clean up the image of the neighborhood, at last driving him to suicide with an orchestrated series of hate valentine cards. On Valentine's Day a year later, Grimsdyke's moldy body climbs from the grave to return the greeting. He leaves a valentine poem written in blood in which the final word (which needs to rhyme with "start") is the victim's actual heart, ripped out and folded in the page.

The fourth tale is a "Monkey's Paw" variant in which a bankrupt financier's wife (Murray) is granted three wishes which, needless to say, all come true in unexpected and horrifying ways. Since one of her clumsy requests leaves her beloved husband a mutilated corpse from a car wreck, her final wish is that she have him back alive, forever. But his body immediately begins to writhe in pain, while a family friend explains that, since he's been embalmed, the fluids running through his veins are burning him. He will be alive forever, as she directed, but suffering. To help break the tension from this and the last segment, which are particularly cruel, all the characters in the frame story are tumbled off into the burning lake of hell.

Teenage Exorcist

Dir: Grant Austin Waldman. *Prod*: Drew Alan Waldman, Grant Austin Waldman. *Screenplay*: Brinke Stevens. *Story*: Fred Olen Ray. *Cast*: Eddie Deezen, Brinke Stevens, Oliver Darrow, Jay Richardson, Tom Shell, Elena Sahagun, Robert Quarry. Austin Enterprises/Wald-Way Films, 1991.

A demon terrorizes people in an old mansion, keeping them from escaping by calling forth a humble army of the flesh-eating dead to surround the premise. Unable to exorcise the fiends, Father McFarren (Robert Quarry) tries to divert them instead by showing them card tricks. The zombies are so dull-witted that he has to pick their cards for them, and then fools them with simple "What's that over there?" ploys to peek at the card selected. The ghoulish rubes are impressed anyway.

Teenage Psycho Meets Bloody Mary see ***The Incredibly Strange Creatures Who Stopped Living and Became Mixed-Up Zombies***

Teenage Zombies

Dir: Jerry Warren. *Prod*: Jerry Warren. *Screenplay*: Jacques LeCotier. *Cast*: Don Sullivan, Katherine Victor, Steve Conte, J.L.D. Morrison, Bri Murphy, Paul Pepper, Mitzi Albertson, Jay Hawk. Governor, 1957.

In this kitsch epic from matinee-guru Jerry Warren, a bunch of Archie's Gang–style kids with names like Reg, Pam, Skip, and Dottie go out water-skiing and stop for lunch on tiny Mullet Island. A mysterious woman (Victor) living on the island has her mindless servant Ivan throw them all in a cell in her basement instead. "Look—what kind of a creep joint is this?" complains Reg. It seems that foreign powers are scheming to subdue the world through experimental bacteria which, released in the water supply or dropped as gas, will render the entire population mindless and obedient slaves. Their experiments so far have missed the mark, however; subjects have become either utterly unresponsive or too violent. Pam and Julie are given the experimental serum, making them zombies briefly; but our gawky heroes find the antidote and wind up saving the country. Geared toward the Saturday matinee children audience of an earlier era, Warren's productions don't always age well, but this syrupy tale is especially trying. Warren remade the film in 1981 as the far more enjoyable *Frankenstein Island*.

The "zombies" aren't revived corpses but merely drugged subjects in a hypnosis-like trance. At the beginning of the movie there's a brief scene in which entranced workers slowly shuffle by in a line, carrying goods, but other than that, Ivan is the only visible "zombie" until the climax. When not following orders, he stands still, staring blankly ahead, his arms slightly out from his body at each side. At the climax, Pam and Julie are only zombies for three minutes, and since the women are only background figures throughout the movie anyway, their zombie state isn't much of a difference. The title would do better drawing attention to the crazed gorilla or subhuman hunchback also populating the island, rather than to these unexciting adolescents. Watch for the intriguing dock-worker zombie drones in *Frankenstein Island* instead.

Terror Beach see ***Night of the Seagulls***

Terror Creatures from the Grave

(Orig. *Cinque tombe per un medium*). *Dir*: Massimo Pupillo. *Prod*: Frank Merle, Ralph Zucker. *Screenplay*: Robert Nathan, Robin McLorin. *Cast*: Barbara Steele, Walter Brandi, Mirella Maravidi, Alfredo Rizzo, Riccardo Garrone, Luciano Pigozzi. MBS Cinematografica/GIA Cinematografica/International Entertainment Pictures (Italy, U.S.), 1966.

A dead spiritualist avenges himself upon his treacherous wife and business partners by calling back medieval plague-spreaders from their 500-year-old graves. Appearing only in the closing minutes of the film, the bodies climb from their tombs and begin an indiscriminate attack on the living until driven away by rain (they can't tolerate "pure water"). They are only shown briefly in shadow, or in a quick glimpse of the odd grubby hand protruding from a tomb, but nothing more. Though the build-up is phenomenal and the mood is terrifically macabre, the actual slaughter anti-climactically occurs entirely off-screen. Italian zombie movies are no place for Greek tragedy.

The Thirst of Baron Blood see ***Baron Blood***

Those Cruel and Bloody Vampires see ***Tombs of the Blind Dead***

Thriller

Dir: John Landis. *Prod*: George Folsey Jr., Michael Jackson, John Landis. *Screenplay*: John Landis, Michael Jackson. *Cast*: Michael Jackson, Ola Ray. Optimum Productions, 1983.

Moonwalking chart-topper Michael Jackson, after seeing John Landis' *An American Werewolf in London*, called Landis in the middle of the night to ask him to direct a video for the title track of his phenomenally popular "Thriller" album. Although the resulting video followed a zombie rather than a werewolf story line, Jackson insisted on turning into a wolf-man anyway. Walking down a deserted street at night, Jackson and his sweetheart (Ray) are beset by a troop of slick, high-budget ghouls. He responds by becoming a zombie also and leads the others in a coordinated dance routine. Though dizzy with conventional horror frames and devices, the video still treats the basic *Night*–inspired zombie invasion sequence seriously enough to capture the feeling of claustrophobia and helplessness, if only very briefly. Jackson's convulsive dancing style suits the twitching zombies almost too well. *Thriller* was the longest video to be shown regularly on MTV, and the only one to run with film-style (scrolling) credits. Loopy Jackson is so out of touch that the video opens with a disclaimer stating he doesn't actually believe in the occult.

Tomb of the Undead see ***Garden of the Dead***

Tombs of the Blind Dead

(Orig. *La noche del terror ciego*). *Dir*: Amando de Ossorio. *Prod*: José Antonio Perez Giner. *Screenplay*: Amando de Ossorio. *Cast*: Lone Fleming, César Burner, Marian Elena, José Telman, María Silva, Rufino Ingles, Verónica Limera, Juan Cortés. Plata Films/Interfilme (Spain, Portugal), 1971.

Spanish filmmaker de Ossorio earned international fame with this widely popular tale of blind zombie monks, creating a fresh mythology and unforgettable skeletal zombies, all set against imposing scenic backgrounds. Solitary camper Virginia (Elena) trespasses onto the grounds of an ancient Templar monastery in the Portuguese countryside and is promptly devoured by the zombie monks still haunting it. Her friends Roger (Burner) and Elizabeth (Fleming) go to investigate the monastery themselves, bringing along a couple of dangerous outlaws for no apparent reason. The monks kill off everyone except Elizabeth, and by boarding some passing railway cars, proceed to spread their carnage to the local town and possibly beyond: in fact, this (and not Romero's trilogy) is the film that established the unchecked, open-ended apocalypse as a standard zombie movie conclusion. Cruel character dynamics only complement the movie's comfortless mood. De Ossorio presents the entire apocalypse without apology or sentimentality, leaving a nagging suspicion that he expects us to side as much with his zombies as with his characters. Most obviously, however, *Tombs* focuses on the aesthetic rather than the moral elements of apocalypse: it offers breathtaking scenes of the monks, framed by the crumbling archways and dusty ruined cloisters of the monastery, backed by an incredible gothic score by Antón García Abril. De Ossorio made three sequels (*Return of the Evil Dead*, *Horror of the Zombies*, and *Night of the Seagulls*), all featuring his famous monks while varying the settings and background mythology, while other inferior clones predictably appeared as well (e.g., *Cross of the Devil* and *Mansion of the Living Dead*).

De Ossorio's zombies are among the finest (if admittedly overripe) fruits of the genre. In the thirteenth century, the Templar monks apparently came back from the crusades bearing the ankh, the Egyptian symbol of eternal life, instead of the cross. They sacrificed many victims in their dark immortality rites until at last they were caught, excommunicated, and executed—and when their bodies were strung up, crows came and plucked out their eyes (hence the blindness). The cadaverous forms now emerge in musty, mottled-grey cowls, with tightly-drawn, leathery flesh and wispy tufts of beard still clinging to their blackened faces. They glide to their victims slowly, even by zombie standards, in a solemn procession of absolute silence—there is no growling, heavy breathing, or other familiar zombie approach accouterments, only the haunting chords of the monastic chant and the lonely sound of the wind. The blind zombies seek out their victims by sound (generally without fail), hacking at them with large swords and then gnawing at them for blood. Whereas vampires draw blood through two delicate and precise puncture wounds, de Ossorio's monks strip mine for it. No zombie is deanimated in the movie, nor is there a hint of what sort of thing might deanimate them. They are simply unstoppable.

While the zombies themselves are much too slow to pursue a fleeing victim, they have the added advantage of a troop of ghost horses at their command. These spectral steeds gallop gracefully through the courtyards of the monastery and the surrounding fields (effectively shown in slow motion), appearing out of nowhere and disappearing again when not needed. Both on horseback and on foot, the zombie monks are visually stunning, at once reminiscent of the grim reaper as well as the four horsemen, and their slow, inexorable attacks break new ground in scenic tension.

Alternate titles: *The Blind Dead*, *Crypt of the Blind Dead*, *Night of the Blind Dead*, *La noche de la muerta ciega*, *Those Cruel and Bloody Vampires*, *Tombs of the Blind Zombies*.

Tombs of the Blind Zombies see ***Tombs of the Blind Dead***

The Torture Chamber of Baron Blood see ***Baron Blood***

Toxic Zombies

Dir: Charles McCrann. *Prod*: Charles McCrann. *Screenplay*: Charles McCrann. *Cast*: Charles Austin, Beverly Shapiro, Dennis Helfend, Kevin Hanlon, Judy Brown, Philip Garfinkel, John Amplas. CM Productions, 1979.

Drug enforcement officials spray a backwoods Tennessee marijuana field—growers included—with experimental herbicide "Dromax," causing those infected to heave profusely and become rampaging mutant cannibals. Forestry department official Tom Cole (Austin) takes his family on a fishing trip to the area, where they hook up with Amy (Brown) and her simple-minded brother Jimmy (Hanlon—himself something of a zombie in certain scenes), whose parents have fallen prey to the zombies. The band must contend against ignorant locals and government cover-up thugs, in addition to the titular opponents. Though the Dromax is supposedly recalled after the incident is contained, a gas station attendant sneezes suspiciously in the closing scene. The gore is mechanical and the acting uneven in this strange blend of slow-piano pathos and splatter-gore, which despite the title mostly plays it serious. Best line (Amy to brother): "This is fungus—it grows on dead things."

The individuals exposed to Dromax develop open sores, boils, and peeling flesh. They aren't killed in the chemical transformation, and thus aren't technically zombies so much as homicidal maniacs. They are immune to pain, however—one walks barefooted through broken glass unflinchingly. The mutant ghouls sometimes eat the flesh of their victims, but mainly they seem to just suck blood; either way they lose interest in any given kill very quickly, and move on to the next. While they prefer the flesh of uncontaminated persons, one doesn't scruple to nibble at another ghoul for a moment. They wield rocks, machetes, and other weapons, and in fact, these enterprising mutants have mastered the use of fire: in one scene they come out of the forest at night with lit torches—which they must have constructed and ignited themselves somehow—to burn the protagonists out of a cabin. But then again, in other scenes, some of them don't even know how to open a car door. Since they're not really dead, they can be killed just as normal people (stabbed, shot, etc.). Despite inconsistent behavior patterns and embarrassing acting, *Toxic Zombies* has the dubious honor of inaugurating the entire "redneck zombie" sub-genre that would thrive inexplicably in the '80s.

Alternate title: *Bloodeaters.*

The Treasure of the Living Dead see ***Oasis of the Zombies***

La Tumba de los muertos vivientes see ***Oasis of the Zombies***

Twilight of the Dead see ***The Gates of Hell***

Gli Ultimi zombi see ***Zombie***

Valley of the Zombies

Dir: Philip Ford. *Prod*: Dorrell and Stuart McGowan. *Screenplay*: Dorrell and Stuart McGowan. *Story*: Royal K. Cole, Sherman L. Lowe. *Cast*: Robert Livingston, Adrian Booth, Ian Keith, Thomas Jackson, Charles Trowbridge, Earle Hodgins, LeRoy Mason. Republic, 1946.

One of the most promising of zombie movie titles actually conceals a feeble action-thriller with only the barest hint of the supernatural, and featuring neither a valley nor a zombie. Medical students Terry (Livingston) and Susan (Booth) help police investigate a series of murders, of which the pair are suspected. Behind the crimes is Ormand Murks (Keith), a man pronounced dead four years before, now inexplicably parading around in ridiculous Victorian fashions. Murks explains that his work as an undertaker led him to a strange

Evil undertaker Ian Keith keeps himself immortal through regular blood infusions, while hypnotized heroine Adrian Booth assists him despite herself. You don't know where that hand has been, in *Valley of the Zombies* (1946).

quest for the world "in between" life and death, and that he found this dubious boon among the voodoo rites and potions of a certain "Valley of the Zombie" (now maybe *that* part of his life might have made an interesting movie). It seems fairly clear he was never really dead, but only in a cataleptic trance simulating death; in any event, he now needs continuous blood transfusions to counteract certain unstated effects of his ill-defined living-dead "affliction." Murks has been stealing blood from brain surgeon Rufus Maynard (Trowbridge), but with increasing boldness, he takes to killing people of his own blood type and draining their bodies himself. Car chases and shootouts round out the lukewarm thriller from Republic, a studio known for its action serials. The horror elements are only sporadically mixed into its action-detective format, while a continuous stream of witty banter prevents the establishment of any sustained atmosphere. Such is the sad fate of Ian Keith, who was originally up against Lugosi for the part of Dracula.

La Vendetta dei morti viventi see ***Vengeance of the Zombies***

Vengeance of the Zombies

(Orig. *La rebelión de las muertas*). *Dir*: Leon Klimovsky. *Prod*: José Antonio Perez Giner. *Screenplay*: Jacinto Molina (Paul Naschy). *Cast*: Paul Naschy, Rommy, Mirta Miller, Vic Winner (Victor Alcazar), María Kosti, Luis Ciges. Profilmes/Promofilms (Spain, Italy), 1972.

Paul Naschy (pseudonym of prolific Spanish director and screenwriter Jacinto Molina), better known for his werewolf role "El Hombre Lobo" in a long-running movie series, diversifies with a plodding and unengaging zombie mystery. After her family is murdered, upscale Londoner Elvira (Rommy) falls in love with her Indian guru Krishna (Naschy) and goes to stay with him at his country estate. It turns out that Krishna's older brother Kantaka (also Naschy), who wields occult voodoo powers and can raise the dead, is seeking revenge on four British families who almost burned him alive many years ago, for raping and killing a daughter from one of the families. Other members of Kantaka's entourage, also followers of voodoo, become increasingly disappointed in him for selfishly abusing his power, which was granted him in order to "spread voodoo" throughout the world. The most interesting feature of this clunky tale is the jazz-pop score that sounds like game show music, usually at cross-purposes with the scenes of horror and romance that it accompanies. Born of Russian parents, director Klimovsky grew up in Argentina and was a practicing dentist for 15 years before turning to filmmaking.

Kantaka raises corpses using the blood of his victims along with wax dolls, while worshipping the devil (Baron Samedi) in low-key basement black masses. Kantaka seems to raise only women for his undead army, all wearing black robes and slinking around with seductive expressions. They are ashen and livid, but otherwise show no external signs of wounds or decomposition. They don't speak, but mindlessly obey Kantaka's commands, falling to the floor upon his death. Their motions are highly stylized and unnatural, as in a slow-motion ballet, and in the opening credits a zombie woman prances merrily over tombstones. More Novocain, please.

Alternate titles: *Rebellion of the Dead Women*, *Revolt of the Dead Ones*, *La vendetta dei morti viventi*, *Walk of the Dead*.

Vengeful Dead see ***Revenge of the Zombie*** **(1981)**

The Very Important Zombie Affair

(Episode, *The Man from U.N.C.L.E.*). *Dir*: David Alexander. *Prod*: Mort Abrahams. *Teleplay*: Boris Ingster. *Cast*: Robert Vaughn, David McCallum, Linda Gaye Scott, Claude Akins, Leo G. Carroll. Metro-Goldwyn-Mayer, 1965.

In late 1964, the slick, light-hearted, James Bond–inspired *Man from U.N.C.L.E.* series was on the verge of cancellation because of low ratings—but within a year it was topping Nielsen charts, beating out Ed Sullivan, *The Dick Van Dyke Show*, and other primetime staples. "The Very Important Zombie Affair," shot in October and airing in December of 1965, appeared at the crest of the second-season mania—making these the highest profile TV zombies prior to Michael Jackson's *Thriller* video. Too bad they barely have more than a cameo or two. Napoleon Solo (Vaughn) and Illya Kuryakin (McCallum) take a break from fighting THRUSH agents, heading for an unnamed Spanish-speaking island in the Caribbean. There they topple the local dictator El Supremo (Akins), who turns his political opponents into zombies. Solo and Illya are too focused on their mission to worry much about the living dead. Spies are supposed to be cool, but in this case they could at least raise an eyebrow!

El Supremo turns people into zombies from the comfort of his laboratory by playing a tape recording of a voodoo ritual and administering the necessary chemicals. He keeps them on a remote ranch for no apparent reason other than to prolong their suffering, since all they do there is rake listlessly at a dirt path. All the zombies we see are black, wearing tattered work clothes, sun hats, and leg-irons. One of them claims to be dead, and there is nothing in the script to suggest he's wrong—except maybe that character zombie Delgado is "cured" of his zombie stupor in a voodoo ceremony. For all the mystique the title and careful foreshadowing seem to want to evoke, the episode shows little more interest in the zombies themselves than do the two main characters.

The Veteran see *Dead of Night*

The Video Dead

Dir: Robert Scott. *Prod*: Robert Scott. *Screenplay*: Robert Scott. *Cast*: Rocky Duvall, Roxanna Augesen, Sam Davis McClelland, Vickie Bastel, Michael St. Michaels, Jack Stellman, Diane Hadley, Patrick Treadway, Al Millan, Lory Ringuette. Interstate 5/Highlight Production, 1987.

This unsung zombie adventure is a nice surprise, offering gripping action as well as thoughtful meditations on zombies. A beat-up TV intended for the "Institute for Studies in the Occult" is accidentally delivered to the wrong house; zombies pour forth from the screen to harass suburban kids Jeff (Duvall) and Zoe (Augesen) before wandering out into the forest behind the house. With the help of Texas cowboy Joshua Daniels (McClelland), who's had experience fighting the telezombies, Jeff mounts an unsatisfactory offensive against the woods-dwelling undead. More loose ends need tying up—such as the connections between the zombies and the other residents of the mysterious TV (a nymph and a "garbageman"). Though the narrative movements are improbable at best, the movie is vivacious and maintains a successful balance of camp fun and genuine suspense.

The half dozen or so cannibal zombies that emerge from the "Zombie Blood Nightmare" movie are highly tattered and decayed, with black skin and chunks of flesh missing. There are even rats living inside of one, and they scamper out when he's sliced open. The inarticulate undead, who growl like dogs guarding a bone, display rudimentary intelligence and even retain moderate recollections of household objects: one breaks the phone cord when stalking Zoe, while another sits in a car and pretends to be driving it. Most impressively, an undead bride becomes the first screen zombie to wield a chainsaw (others follow her lead in *La Cage aux Zombies*).

These zombies exhibit an unusually complex behavioral and psychological make-up; they are driven by more than mere appetite. They are playful as they wander through the homes in the neighborhood: they sit around a table, fondle household objects, flip through picture books, etc. Two, having just tickled themselves silly by playing with a blender, are further amused at killing a maid, and laugh like school kids. Their childlike playfulness reaches its height when they put a victim upside-down in the washing machine and turn it on, just to watch her legs spin around. They're also capable of lust, jealousy, and a wide range of other emotions. A ghostly white David Bowie look-alike zombie admires a photo of an attractive young woman, for instance; while the bride zombie puts on a wig, and flies into a panic upon seeing her gruesome reflection in a mirror. They avoid mirrors because they can't stand to be reminded of what they have become, and so Daniels has mirrors taped all over the front door.

Daniels explains that the zombies don't feel physical pain, but that nonetheless they often respond with appropriate pain behavior

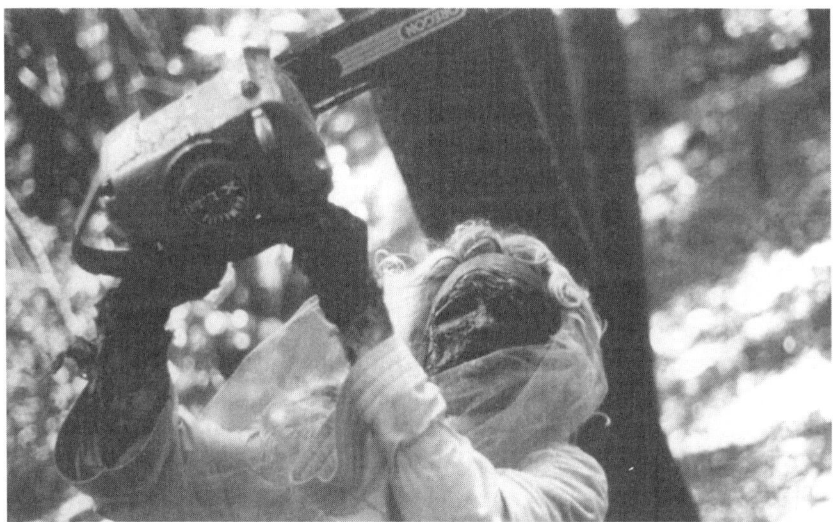

Diane Hadley expresses bridal anxiety in *The Video Dead* (1987).

simply from memory and habit. Thus, though conventional weapons can't kill them, they can make them believe they're dead for a little while. Daniels further explains that their hatred results from their no longer being human: they can't bear to look at themselves in their present state, and they can't stand to be reminded of their otherness through people's reactions of fear or disgust. Therefore a show of friendliness lulls them into submission, and in a masterfully taut scene, Jeff's hysterical sister Zoe has to save herself by inviting the fiends in and pretending not to be afraid of them. They make testy but overall civil houseguests: she seats them at the kitchen table and serves them Campbell's soup (though they don't show much interest in it, and we never actually see them eat anything but people). One bangs his glass, hinting for something to drink, and another puts on the (broken) glasses of one of his victims, wearing them askew for the remainder of the film. These twisted scenes of family life and its daily routines make creative use of the zombie in domestic space, presenting memorable images and thoughtful contrasts. Contemplate, for instance, the zombie bride gleefully pushing buttons on the blender and operating the washing machine—the same mindless occupations that would have been her lot had death not saved her at the threshold.

Une Vierge chez les morts vivants see ***A Virgin Among the Living Dead***

The Vineyard

Dir: Bill Rice, James Hong. *Prod*: Harry Mok. *Story*: Harry Mok, James Hong. *Screenplay*: James Hong, Douglas Kondo. *Cast*: James Hong, Karen Witter, Michael Wong, Cheryl Lawson. New World/Northstar, 1989.

A strong lead from James Hong (also co-director and co-writer) livens up an East Asian vampire tale. Hong is Dr. Elson Po, a world-renowned winemaker who lives on his own island off the coast of California, and who earns immortality from the God of the Wind with the help of a concoction that he brews from human blood. The island is rife with dark secrets: locked upstairs is Po's crazed and ancient mother (looking like someone off a Twisted Sister album cover); downstairs, his dungeon is filled with chained-up women, whom he keeps half alive to maximize his blood supply; and all around, the vineyard is strewn with the bodies of his past victims, now tormented zombies. A group of boneheaded poindexters visit the island and foil him. The mad scientist and the vampire motifs are fresh in the context of Chinese rather than European sorcery, but the film falls into the usual late-'80s horror ruts, preferring isolated shocks to any gradual build-up of mood.

The living-dead bodies strewn throughout the vineyard are continually restless, though they only hover on the periphery of the main action until the final scene. Once culled from Po's vineyard, these full-bodied zombies have a bold yet fruity bouquet and a winsome piquancy. In the meantime, whenever they begin to rise and converge against Po, he keeps them in check with prayers and a bag of "sacred earth." They're generally slow (though at least one has a fast right hook), and several use tools (showing a preference for big sticks). Their brief appearances throughout the movie give the impression that interesting things will eventually happen, but when at last it ripens, the vinegary zombie invasion sequence is fairly mechanical and only lasts a minute or two.

A Virgin Among the Living Dead

(Orig. *Une vierge chez les morts vivants*). *Dir*: Jesús Franco. *Screenplay*: Jesús Franco, Peter Kerut, Henry Brald. *Starring*: Christina von Blanc, Britt Nichols, Howard Vernon, Ann Libert, Rose Kiekens, Paul Muller. Brux International Pictures (Spain, France), 1971.

Director Franco and actor Vernon team up yet again for this

atrophied psychological horror, which is over-stylish and impressionistic to the point of incoherence. To hear the reading of her father's will, Christina (von Blanc) visits the castle of Monserat, where she meets her morbid Uncle Howard (Vernon) and the haunted houseful of usual suspects. Ignoring the warnings from her father's ghost that she ought to flee, she has repeated visions and dreams until finally trapped by the bizarre family and led down into a pond by a certain ill-explained "guardian of night." New characters appear at intervals, often not to be seen again. The end deteriorates into a random series of screams, snippets of scenes from throughout the movie, and dream-within-dream sequences punctuated by her waking up time and again: thus it's never clear what's a dream and what's reality, and certainly not worth the energy to figure it out. There are some interesting mythological background fragments and some lyrical touches, but these are never sustained.

One of Christina's recurring dreams is of a zombie attack (these scenes were supposedly shot by Jean Rollin, and only later spliced into Franco's boring *Christina, princesse de l'érotisme*). Pale hands emerge from the thick coating of autumn leaves on the forest floor while she's out on a walk; a handful of zombies then pursue her back to the estate house and up to her room. The bad-teethed stiffs grimace menacingly, reaching out for her with extended arms and open hands. Breaking into her room, they surround her and grasp at her while she huddles on the floor. They look more goofy than scary as they crowd around the camera, wriggling their fingers and grinning like idiots.

Alternate titles: *A comme apocalypse*; *Among the Living Dead*; *Christina chez les morts vivants*; *Christina, princesse de l'érotisme*; *Christina, Princess of Eroticism*; *Christina, Sex Princess*; *Le labyrinthe*; *La nuit des étoiles filantes*; *Los sueños eróticos de Christine*; *Zombie 4*; *Zombi Holocaust.*

Virus see ***Night of the Zombies***

Virus cannibale see ***Night of the Zombies***

Virus—L'inferno dei morti viventi see ***Night of the Zombies***

Voodoo

Dir: Rene Eram. *Prod*: Donald P. Borchers. *Screenplay*: Brian DiMuccio, Dino Vindeni. *Cast*: Corey Feldman, Joel J. Edwards, Diana Nadeau, Ron

Melendez, Sarah Douglas, Jack Nance, Maury Ginsberg, Amy Raasch, Bryan Michael McGuire. Planet Productions, 1995.

This run-of-the-mill campus thriller crosses *Angel Heart* with *Revenge of the Nerds*, as if that were a niche that really needed filling. Simply looking for a place to sleep, Andy (Feldman) joins strange fraternity Zeta Omega Mu (the "Zombie House"). The entire fraternity is under the control of Cassian Marsh (Edwards), a preppy, white suburban voodoo priest who seeks immortality from the serpent goddess Azili. The other members of the house are all zombies, whom Marsh is collecting for a mass sacrifice. Andy defeats him with a voodoo doll and colored powders. An interesting premise rapidly gives way to stock motifs and plot twists, deteriorating into a completely conventional hero vs. villain show-down. Yes too shabby.

The members of the Zombie House are supposedly all undead, but since they behave normally, the claim is never really tested and doesn't mean much (but one member does watch a lot of TV). They go through the motions of being regular college students, though it's said they have no souls. Interestingly, the movie takes advantage of the fact that zombies can't tolerate salt, a common feature of zombie folklore that doesn't often make it to screen portrayals: Andy slips some in a fellow Zeta's beer, causing him to lapse into a fit of convulsions. But all the zombie elements are largely surface trimming, and the movie is far more concerned with mind games and male bonding than with the undead.

Voodoo Blood Bath **see** ***I Eat Your Skin***

Voodoo Dawn

Dir: Steven Fierberg. *Prod*: Steven Mackler. *Screenplay*: John Russo, Jeffrey Delman, Thomas Rendon, Evan Dunsky. *Cast*: Raymond St. Jacques, Theresa Merritt, Tony Todd, Gina Gershon, Kirk Baily, Billy "Sly" Williams, J. Grant Albrecht. Stillwell Productions, 1989.

College students Miles (Williams) and Kevin (Baily) travel from New York City to a rural Southeastern migrant worker camp to visit their sociologist friend Tony. Among the migrant workers is evil voodoo priest Makouté (Todd), who collects body parts (starting with Tony's head) to make an "Okokiyati," or Voodoo Man. The students meet up with comely Tina (Gershon), whose camp is being terrorized by Makouté. Wise Claude (St. Jacques) and herbalist Madame Duslay

(Merritt) together defeat Makouté and then his Okokiyati monster with a voodoo doll. Though acting and production values are solid, the script is outdated by about forty years and assumes we want to see more witch doctor than zombie. The supposedly Haitian characters don't sound Haitian.

Makouté has the zombies work the fields around his house; thus they use hoes and other gardening implements. They only attack with their hands, though, throwing ill-coordinated punches. Though one bites Claude's arm, there's no indication that they eat flesh (or anything else): the bite appears to have been merely an attack. Inexplicably, a zombie seems to work at a nearby gas station, checking Miles and Claude's oil at the beginning of the film by wiping the searing dipstick on his fingers rather than a rag (but he never does tell them whether or not they need oil). Tina drives a metal rod directly through a zombie from side to side, thus preventing him from going through a doorway—he isn't smart enough to realize he could turn sideways to get through. The ending of the film is the best part: the next day, after Miles and Claude say good-bye to Tina and everyone leaves, a repeated knocking sound emanates from the empty house—inside, we see the same zombie impaled with the sideways rod, still trying over and over to get through the doorway.

Alternate title: *Strange Turf.*

Voodoo Girl **see** ***Sugar Hill***

Voodoo Island

Dir: Reginald LeBorg. *Prod*: Howard Koch. *Screenplay*: Richard Landau. *Cast*: Boris Karloff, Beverly Tyler, Murvyn Vye, Elisha Cook, Rhodes Reason, Jean Engstrom, Glenn Dixon. Bel-Air Productions/United Artists, 1957.

This atrocious South Seas yarn might be fit for Tom Servo, Crow, and the "Satellite of Love" crew, but not much else. A team scoping out locations for a new hotel goes missing in the South Pacific—only one of them turns up, as a mindless vegetable drifting in a boat. Surly hoax-buster Phillip Knight (Karloff, who's never played a more obnoxious character) takes a small crew to investigate. On the mysterious island they battle fake carnivorous plants and crabs whose legs don't move, until at last discovering a lost native tribe dwelling deep in the jungle. The only good scene is that in which two native girls play carelessly in a clearing until one is eaten by a big cabbage. The

Crotchety Boris Karloff (left) wonders whether it would be easier to tilt recently zombified Murvyn Vye (right) or the thatched Polynesian hut forty-five degrees to get them to match, in the rotten rattan adventure *Voodoo Island* (1957).

same year's *Womaneater* also inexplicably connects zombies with carnivorous plants.

There is no apology for locating voodoo in the South Pacific, but the characters call it that by name, as well as calling the charms "ouangas." The zombie Mitchell (Dixon) is controlled by a voodoo doll, closing his eye when the doll's eye is sewn shut. Though all physiological functions are normal, the subjects' minds have been erased, and all they do is sit (or stand) and stare into space. Zombie Mitchell evidently has some glimmer of consciousness deep inside that tries to get out periodically: he gets an intense look on his face once in a while, and twice gets up of his own volition and staggers stiffly for a short distance before collapsing. The other character zombie, Finch, is led off the island with the surviving expedition at the end, presumably never to recover. These zombies are intrinsically disappointing. They serve no narrative function in the movie, but help document Hollywood's confused response to the creature during a period of transition.

Alternate title: *Silent Death*.

Voodoo Man

Dir: William Beaudine. *Prod*: Sam Katzman, Jack Dietz. *Story and Screenplay*: Robert Charles. *Cast*: Bela Lugosi, John Carradine, George Zucco, Wanda McKay, Louise Currie, Michael Ames [Tod Andrews], Ellen Hall, Terry Walker, Henry Hall. Monogram, 1944.

Monogram's zombie repertoire gets increasingly audacious with this nonsense, featuring a pantheon of B–horror stars and not one hypnotized zombie woman (as in both zombie movies of the previous year) but a small platoon of them. Doctor Richard Marlowe (Lugosi), whose wife Evelyn (Hall) has long languished in a half-living zombie stupor, tries to return her to sentience by transferring the souls of women he abducts from a nearby road into her. He must find one who shares a mental or spiritual "affinity" with his wife, but in the meantime, the failed soul transference experiments leave the victims soulless zombies, which collect in the basement. Though Marlowe has a fully-equipped mad scientist laboratory, the soul transferences are actually brought about by means of an absurd religious ceremony conducted by Nicholas (Zucco), gas station owner by day and worshipper of voodoo god Ramboona by night. B–horror writer Ralph Dawson (Ames) helps police uncover the nefarious operation. Zucco is silly, Lugosi diabolically charming, and Carradine is downright frightening as the sniveling, idiotic keeper of the helpless zombie women: he strokes their heads, saying, "Gosh—you've got nice pretty hair," or "You're a very naughty girl." The closing credits entreat the audience to buy war saving stamps and bonds—"on sale in this theatre!"

Marlowe insists that his wife Evelyn has been dead for twenty-two years, and she hasn't aged a day. He initially hypnotizes the women he abducts for the soul transference ceremony, but when the ceremony fails, they lose their souls altogether and remain in the trance indefinitely. There's never a sense that the failed subjects in the basement are dead in any physical way, though Marlowe repeatedly calls them "zombies." They wait with open eyes and empty stares, standing continuously in alcoves along the sides of a corridor. They have coifed hair and wear long, white evening robes reminiscent of Jessica's in *I Walked*. When led out of the cells, they walk in line, their footsteps in sync, and they follow simple directions concerning when to walk and where to stand. Though there's never a flicker of mental or emotional response, there are occasional signs of independent volition—one wanders off randomly from her cell, for instance, when the door is accidentally left open. The movie's whole zombie element primarily comes across as parading women around as visual objects; Marlowe's experiments amount to a veritable machine for female objectification, with women going in one end and women's bodies coming out the other.

Walk of the Dead see ***Vengeance of the Zombies***

War of the Zombies

(Orig. *Roma contra Roma*). *Dir*: Giuseppe Vari. *Prod*: Ferruccio de Martino, Massimo de Rita. *Screenplay*: Piero Pierotti, Marcello Sartarelli. *Cast*: John Drew Barrymore, Susy Andersen, Ettore Manni, Ida Galli, Mino Doro, Matilde Calman, Ivano Staccioli. AIP/Galatea Films (Italy), 1963.

John Drew Barrymore plays the evil sorcerer Adalbar in this tepid Italian sword-and-sandal adventure. In the distant province of Salmatia, as the high priest of an Eastern cult that worships some sort of suspect Cyclops–Buddha goddess, Adalbar leads his people in a rebellion against Rome. Finally he raises an army of ghost legions from fallen Roman soldiers, and pits them against the living legions in a grand battle scene. Brave centurion Gaius stops the undead cohorts by blinding the Cyclops goddess statue. Though overall *War of the Zombies* is primitive and unexceptional, the army of ghost soldiers is pretty disturbing, tinted bluish-purple and advancing to a disjointed choral arrangement. Adalbar wears a fruity magician's robe, and a woman walks over hot coals.

The resurrected zombie Romans fill out an entire army, complete with archers and cavalry. They are mindless juggernauts, utterly incapable of being destroyed until Gaius pulls the plug on their goddess. Actually they're not much like zombies and don't especially act any differently from the living soldiers, but the superimposed filmography and twisted hymnal music lend them a lingering, uncanny impression.

Alternate title: *Night Star—Goddess of Electra*.

Warning Sign

Dir: Hal Barwood. *Prod*: Jim Bloom. *Screenplay*: Hal Barwood, Matthew Robbins. *Cast*: Sam Waterston, Kathleen Quinlan, Yaphet Kotto, Jeffrey De Munn, Richard Dysart, G.W. Bailey. 20th Century–Fox, 1985.

This environmental disaster movie tries to distract attention from its weary story line and trite moralizing with a watered-down zombie subplot. BioTek Agronomics, ostensibly an agricultural research plant but in fact a Department of Defense germ research base, suffers a contamination leak and the entire building is sealed off. Sheriff Cal Morse (Waterston) sneaks into the plant with former employee Dan (De Munn) to rescue Dan's wife Joanie (Quinlan), while evading the other employees who have become murderous fiends from the fugitive germ. Eminently forgettable.

The "borna" virus the plant has been perfecting is transmitted by means of a highly contagious germ ("lacto-bacillus luminensus"), which shows under black light as glowing blue areas on the skin. The virus affects the "rage center" of the brain—at first killing the hosts, but then reanimating them again as raging berserkers sporting bloody, open sores. Although purely aggressive, the subjects are still rational enough to scheme, ambush, etc. The antitoxin that counters the virus in the end comes from a pregnant woman's blood.

Alternate title: *Biohazard.*

Waxwork

Dir: Anthony Hickox. *Prod*: Staffan Ahrenberg. *Screenplay*: Anthony Hickox. *Cast*: Zach Galligan, Deborah Foreman, David Warner, Michelle Johnson, Patrick Macnee, Dana Ashbrook, Miles O'Keeffe. Vestron Pictures, 1988.

A waxwork museum is actually the front for gateways into alternate worlds, through which the characters traipse and confront a variety of classic cinematic monsters. In a black-and-white scene, protagonist Mark (Galligan) finds himself in a graveyard and survives a brief encounter with a horde of zombies that crawl from the ground. He dispels them by announcing that they're only illusory and that he doesn't believe in them.

Waxwork II: Lost in Time

Dir: Anthony Hickox. *Prod*: Nancy Paloian. *Screenplay*: Anthony Hickox. *Cast*: Zach Galligan, Monika Schnarre, Alexander Godunov, Martin Kemp, Bruce Campbell, Michael Des Barres. Electric Pictures, 1991.

A zombie cameo appears during the whirlwind-paced finale montage, in which the hero (Galligan) and the villain (Godunov) conduct a sword fight as they trip through a number of possible worlds via a time door. One of the worlds they briefly pass through is a zombie-infested mall like that in *Dawn of the Dead*, in which a mobilized task force darting through the multi-level shopping complex pause to wonder at the two swashbuckling strangers.

Weekend at Bernie's II

Dir: Robert Klane. *Prod*: Victor Drai, Joseph Perez. *Screenplay*: Robert Klane. *Cast*: Andrew McCarthy, Jonathan Silverman, Terry Kiser, Tom Wright, Steve James, Troy Beyer, Barry Bostwick. Tristar Pictures, 1993.

In this energetic two-day comic-adventure sequel in the Ferris Bueller tradition, Larry (McCarthy) and Richard (Silverman) try to track down the two million dollars that Bernie Lomax (Kiser) embezzled and stashed away on St. Thomas in the Virgin Islands. Though dead throughout the first film, this time around Bernie is partially raised as a zombie by voodoo magic—but because a pigeon is carelessly substituted for a chicken in the ritual, he only animates when there is music playing (apparently Caribbean religious rituals readily lend themselves to zany antics). Eventually discovering that the cash is concealed under water, Larry and Richard don scuba gear and follow the corpse (strutting along to music through a pair of headphones) to the undersea treasure. Against them is Barry Bostwick ("Brad" from *Rocky Horror*). Though not always as humorous or irreverent as it wants to be, there are some entertaining moments and the pace is never slack. Looks like it was funded by the Virgin Islands tourist commission.

The voodoo rituals involve the normal chalk circle, goat's blood, etc., but the zombie behavior is most unprecedented. Bernie's sorely abused corpse twitches and gyrates to life whenever music plays, but plops over again as soon as it stops. His tottering, rhythmic strut conveniently allows him to participate in a conga-line dance, and due to a cord entanglement mishap, the unwitting cadaver even takes to the sky for a brief para-sailing stint. On this most eventful of zombie vacations, he even has a brief affair, and participates in the *second* shark vs. zombie confrontation of the big screen (the first is in *Zombie*). His understated boogying is well-played, and even when Bernie isn't animated, it's hard not to be amused at people dragging his body around: he's repeatedly banged and snagged, dropped and jabbed,

Dearly departed Bernie Lomax (center, Terry Kiser) is a little livelier in the second *Weekend at Bernie's* (1993), thanks to a voodoo spell and to his pals Andrew McCarthy and Jonathan Silverman.

and he rounds off the film with a harpoon transfixed through his head. Now if someone would do the same for the Griswolds.

White Zombie

Dir: Victor Halperin. *Prod*: Edward Halperin. *Screenplay*: Garnett Weston. *Cast*: Bela Lugosi, Madge Bellamy, Joseph Cawthorn, Robert Frazer, John Harron, Brandon Hurst. Amusement Securities/United Artists, 1932.

Though rickety and static-drenched, the first zombie movie remains one of the most successful of the dozen or so from the classical Hollywood period. Madeline (Bellamy) and Neil (Harron) are married at the Haitian estate of Beaumont (Frazer)—but desiring Madeline for himself, Beaumont incurs the aid of voodoo master Murder Legendre (Lugosi) to turn the unlucky bride into a zombie. The soulless companion isn't as much fun as he had imagined, however, and to complicate matters, Neil shows up with a local missionary to retrieve his wayward wife. The villains and zombies all wind up pushing each other over a cliff. Though *White Zombie* is clearly bound by the melodramatic conventions of the stage (the movie was based on a play by Kenneth Webb), and hasn't fully parted from the acting and production conventions of the silent era (actress Bellamy was a silent screen star), these somehow complement the dreamlike Gothic atmosphere the Halperin brothers weave around every scene. The protagonists aren't especially sympathetic, but Lugosi is in top form and there are some powerful moments—particularly the zombies slaving away tirelessly in the sugar mill, themselves indistinguishable from the gears and machinery.

Legendre learned his dark secrets from a voodoo shaman dressed as a Disney-esque magician, who now serves as one of Legendre's zombie valets. The stiff-limbed, wide-eyed undead are "alive in everything" but heart and mind, and Legendre observes that were they to recover their senses, they would tear him to pieces. Well, they could try, but these undead are a clumsy lot: one zombie in the sugar mill trips into the machine works, and at the end, Legendre's entire troop of zombie slaves cartoonishly run themselves over a cliff, when the person they're attacking ducks out of the way at the last moment. The zombies are basically atmospheric garnish.

There is also the case of Madeline, however, the film's one character zombie (the "white" zombie). When Legendre steals her soul, she stares ahead listlessly, in one scene playing the piano without even

Robert Frazer (left) isn't sure he wants to accept the sort of help Bela Lugosi (right) is offering in *White Zombie* (1932). John Peters (center) is the first true zombie of the silver screen.

paying attention to her own music. Unlike the other undead, however, she retains at least a slight degree of autonomy, since she pines away for her beloved Neil. When Legendre is killed, she completely shakes off the trance and returns to normal. While the native zombies are objects of fascination and horror, Madeline is the object of pity, with a spark of subjectivity still evident deep beneath the layers of external subjection and control. Spunky actress Madge Bellamy went on to shoot her millionaire boyfriend in 1943 for marrying another woman, later commenting, "I only winged him, which is all I meant to do. Believe me, I'm a crack shot."

Womaneater

Dir: Charles Saunders. *Prod*: Guido Coen. *Story and Screenplay*: Brandon Fleming. *Cast*: George Coulouris, Vera Day, Peter Wayn, Joyce Gregg, Jimmy Vaughan. Fortress Films (England), 1957.

Monomaniacal Dr. Moran (Coulouris) uses the sap from an absurd carnivorous tree with wacky, flailing branches to resurrect his discontented maid Margaret (Gregg), but is nonplused to find that she comes back only as a mindless zombie. She rises from the table slowly and tries to attack passive heroine Sally (Day), but only makes it a few steps before collapsing to the ground. The Amazonian witch doctor who originally gave Moran the zombie-making technique smugly reveals that his people can raise both the mind and body of the dead, but that they would never divulge to anyone the secrets of reanimating the mind. He might have mentioned that to Moran earlier.

Zeder

Dir: Pupi Avati. *Prod*: Gianni Minervini, Antonio Avati. *Screenplay*: Pupi Avati, Maurizio Costanzo, Antonio Avati. *Cast*: Gabriele Lavia, Anne Canovas, Paolo Tanziani, Cesare Barbetti, Bob Tonelli, Ferdinando Orlandi. AMA Films/IRA (Italy), 1983.

Though the acting, direction, and production values of Avati's stylish Italian mystery are solid, the tight build-up of the first half only deteriorates into irresolution and incoherence. Aspiring Bolognese novelist Salvado (Lavia) pieces together clues surrounding ex-priest Don Luigi Costa, whose death doesn't quite add up. Salvado learns that Costa had himself buried near an Etruscan necropolis, because the ground is an especially powerful "K–zone" (a region in which normal natural laws are suspended and the dead are not truly dead). All the movie's suspense apparently builds to the climactic horror of seeing Costa resurrected: but at the tail end of the Italian zombie movie cycle, after seeing undead armies visit apocalyptic devastation on the earth time and again, just watching one man come back from the dead and walk around for a couple of minutes can hardly produce the intended impact.

Zombie elements begin to appear mostly toward the end, when a pair of ghoulish hands emerge from the ground to strangle someone, and when Costa returns from the dead as a homicidal monster. He smirks toothlessly as he coolly follows Salvado around a hotel construction site. If there are supposed to be other zombies loose in the area (which might help explain the murders committed before Costa revives), they're never shown or accounted for. Salvado's heartthrob Alessandra (Canovas) also returns as a zombie at the very end, just long enough to fall into his arms and kill him in some unseen manner.

Undead Costa and Alessandra apparently just walk around the site aimlessly; what happens to them after the death of Salvado is left open. It's all pretty thin.

Alternate titles: *Revenge of the Dead*, *Zeder—Voices from the Beyond*.

Zeder—Voices from the Beyond see ***Zeder***

Zombi 2 see ***Zombie***

Zombi 3

Dir: Lucio Fulci. *Story and Screenplay*: Claudio Fragasso. *Cast*: Deran Sarafian, Beatrice Ring, Richard Raymond, Alex McBride, Ulli Reinthaler, Marina Loi, Deborah Bergamin, Alan Collins, Mike Monty. Flora Film (Italy), 1988.

Indefatigable Fulci, who helped spark the Euro-zombie wave in 1979 with *Zombi 2*, brings it to a belated close almost a decade later with this concerto-in-gore-major set in the Philippines. Here the accent is on shooting, fighting, and running as a small group of soldiers and dancing women find themselves trapped in the midst of a raging cannibal zombie epidemic caused by the usual bacteriological warfare experiment gone awry. Meanwhile, mellow radio personality "Blueheart" keeps the public informed over the airwaves as the crisis unfolds. The renegade characters move tirelessly through the jungle, avoiding the countless stiffs incessantly pouring out of half-demolished buildings and dark corners. At last two survivors escape in a helicopter, and turn on the radio only to find that Blueheart himself is a zombie. He ushers in a new, enigmatic era of the undead: "Dig on these immortal vibes, people.... New horizons have opened up.... This is now the new world, and the new cycle has begun. For everyone, this is the year zero, so there's lots of work to be done." Most of the movie is a quilt of scenes and motifs shamelessly pasted together from *Dawn of the Dead* and *Return of the Living Dead*, but fast pacing and continuous shooting help distract from the absence of plot or character development. Despite the name, this outing has nothing to do with the characters or events of *Zombi 2*. Bruno Mattei (*Night of the Zombies*) finished directing the picture after Fulci got fed up with it and left.

The "Death-1 compound" virus spreads easily through blood, saliva, and breath; the infected person then develops pustules and begins to deteriorate very quickly. Fulci offers boils of unprecedented grossness, which pulsate and run with rivulets of nasty fluid. The zombies are crooked and bent, and they moan and can even rasp a few words. While they're all pretty ugly, they come in a variety of speeds, from slow and shambling to stealthy and cheetah-fast. The zombies can use tools (ranging from swinging a machete to operating a radio broadcasting station), but don't seem to very often. The characters can generally deanimate them by shooting them repeatedly or damaging them severely, but it isn't specifically necessary to disable the brain (which is notable, because Italians generally cling to that convention more religiously than anyone). The silliest touch is a self-propelled head that flies across the room to sink its teeth into a character, though a close runner-up is the unborn zombie fetus of an infected pregnant woman who tears through its mother's abdomen to grab the victim standing over her. Fulci's zombies are sometimes creative and often entertaining, but his unquenchable drive to provide shocks and to diversify the zombie encounters inevitably leads to glaring inconsistencies.

Zombi 3: Da dove vieni? see ***Let Sleeping Corpses Lie***

Zombi Holocaust see ***Dr. Butcher, M.D.***

Zombi Holocaust see ***A Virgin Among the Living Dead***

Zombie see ***Dawn of the Dead***

Zombie see ***I Eat Your Skin***

Zombie

(Orig. *Zombi 2*). *Dir*: Lucio Fulci. *Prod*: Ugo Tucci, Fabrizio de Angelis. *Screenplay*: Elisa Briganti. *Cast*: Tisa Farrow, Ian McCulloch, Richard Johnson, Al Cliver, Auretta Gay, Stefania D'Amario, Olga Karlatos. Variety Films (Italy), 1979.

Romero's *Dawn of the Dead* was a huge success in Europe, and imitations began appearing almost immediately. Fulci's *Zombi 2* was among the first and the best of these (to cash in on the success of *Dawn*, whose European release title was *Zombi*, Fulci shamelessly named his unrelated movie *Zombi 2*). Fulci takes Romero's mall and suburb zombies back to an exotic island setting, situating them in a creative range of circumstances, and shrouding the whole in a dream-like ambiance. Anne (Tisa Farrow, Mia's younger sister) and reporter Peter West (McCulloch) head to the Caribbean island of Matul to search for Anne's father. The island is besieged by an unstoppable plague of cannibal zombies, however, and the two must fight their way across the island with a couple of friends to make a last stand in a missionary church. The zombie epidemic has meanwhile spread

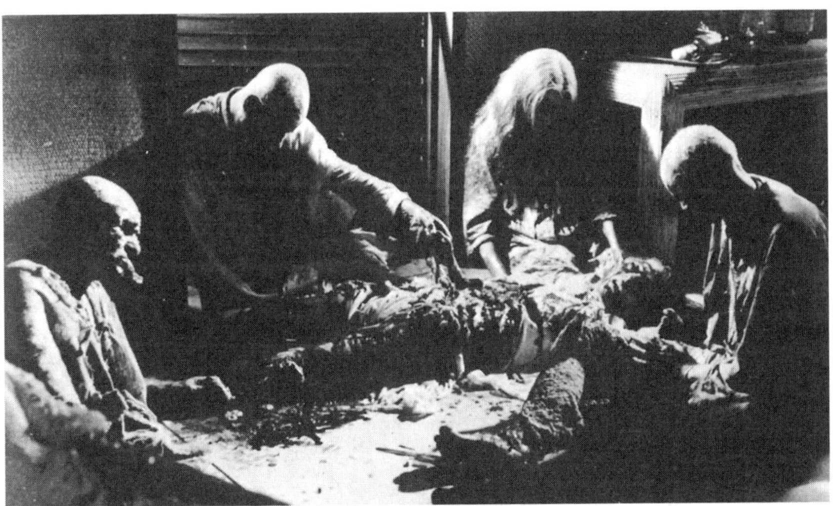

Convivial zombies share a light-hearted moment in Lucio Fulci's cult favorite *Zombie* (1979).

to the mainland, and the closing scene shows the undead roaming freely along the bridges of Manhattan. It's true that Fulci's debt to Romero sometimes borders on theft, but he also offers thoughtful variations on the familiar motifs, with imaginative visual effects such as energetic camera movement, interesting angles, and careful composition. The scene in which Naomi's head is dragged through a broken doorway and her eye pierced with a huge splinter is infamous, a seat-squirming moment by any reckoning. A slew of Italian zombie movies followed in Fulci's footsteps, and he himself made at least three further zombie essays (*The Gates of Hell*, *The Beyond*, *Zombi 3*). In these he experiments with a range of moods and settings rather than repeating the same formula, but *Zombie* is still the most entertaining and influential of the four.

Here Fulci's zombies conform faithfully to Romero's *Night-Dawn* conventions: they eat human flesh, their victims rise as zombies, and they can only be deanimated by destroying the head. But Fulci explores diverse contextual possibilities (such as Spanish conquistador zombies), and focuses on the personal mannerisms of the undead as few other filmmakers do (such as the zombie whose head remains lowered while he brings a tasty morsel to his mouth in a fluid arc that, though it looks unintuitive, actually represents the minimum of required movement). These whitish, crumbly zombies are especially

Things look grim for the Big Apple in the closing moments of Fulci's *Zombie* (1979).

repulsive, with Fulci's characteristic accent on writhing worms. Rather incongruously for cadavers supposedly devoid of body processes, however, they produce heavy breathing sounds of the Darth Vader variety. The most outlandish scene is an underwater grappling match between a great white shark and a zombie who has carelessly wandered down to the ocean floor—they twist and turn in the briny deep around a scenic coral reef, each gnawing sizable chunks out of the other.

Alternate titles: *Island of the Living Dead*, *Sanguelia*, *Gli ultimi zombi*, *Zombie Flesh Eaters*.

The Zombie **[1966] see** ***The Plague of the Zombies***

The Zombie

(Episode, *Kolchak: The Night Stalker*). *Dir*: Alex Grasshoff. *Prod*: Paul Playdon. *Teleplay*: Zekial Marko, David Chase. *Cast*: Darren McGavin, Simon Oakland, J. Pat O'Malley, Paulene Myers, Earl Faison. Universal, 1974.

Before Mulder and Scully there was Kolchak (McGavin), a hapless Chicago reporter in a straw hat who confronts vampires, wolfmen, and other stock fiends. His camera always breaks, so he can never prove his remarkable story. Mobsters accidentally bump off Francois Edmonds (Faison), a Haitian numbers runner whose mother is a voodoo priestess (Myers). She revives her son so he can go around breaking in two all those even vaguely implicated in his death, until Kolchak tracks him to a demolition lot and manages to hang him with a suspended cable. The stories of the *Night Stalker* series are hammy and the monsters are by the book (silver bullets, etc.), but an eye for detail and lighthearted absurdities (such as an implausible inner-city monk informant who's up on illegal Haitian immigrant addresses) provide a certain flair. The real key to the success of the '70s crime-solving bachelor genre, of course, was a strong lead personality (Rockford, Baretta, McCloud, Quincy), and though he's not a great fighter and doesn't pack heat, Kolchak is as surly and antisocial as the best of them.

Francois the hulking, spine-snapping black zombie has no independent volition, but only carries out his mother's directions (he's a good boy). The most graphic of any TV zombie, he is thoroughly decayed, with mottled splotches and exposed, stringy tissue all over. The most noteworthy innovation is the method of deanimating him: his mouth is filled with salt and his lips are sewn shut (like the zombie in *The Four Skulls of Jonathan Drake*). Thus killed once and for all, at the end he's buried for the third time, while Kolchak—desensitized to the occult—sourly adds, "at the taxpayer's expense." Zombies return to Chicago the following year in a feature-length TV movie, *The Dead Don't Die*.

Zombie 3 see *Burial Ground*

Zombie 4 see *A Virgin Among the Living Dead*

Zombie 4: After Death see *After Death*

Zombie 5: Revenge of the House of Usher

(Orig. *El hundimiento de la Casa Usher*). *Dir*: Jesús Franco. *Prod*: Daniel Lesoeur. *Screenplay*: H.L. Rostaine. *Cast*: Howard Vernon, Dan Villers, Jean Tolzac, Joan Virly, Françoise Blanchard, Oliver Mato. Eurociné/Elite (France, Spain), 1982.

Demented 200-year-old Dr. Usher (Vernon) keeps his daughter youthful—albeit in a half-life, half-death stupor—through regular blood infusions from the prostitutes he kidnaps (a plot that was weary in the days of Lugosi). Though Usher's assistant Morpho is pretty ugly, there are no zombies. Obviously the distributors who circulated the English-language video prints under the title *Zombie 5* couldn't find anything of any promotional use in the rambling, pretentious, and outdated yarn itself.

Alternate titles: *The Fall of the House of Usher*, *Los crímines de Usher*, *Neurosis*, *Nevrose*.

Zombie 6: Monster Hunter

(Orig. *Anthropophagus II*). *Dir*: Aristide Massaccesi. *Prod*: Aristide Massaccesi, Donatella Donati. *Story and screenplay*: John Cart. *Cast*: George Eastman (Luigi Montefiore), Annie Belle, Charles Borromel, Katya Berger, Kasimir Berger, Hanja Kochansky, Ian Danby, Ted Rusoff, Edmund Purdom. Filmirage (Italy), 1981.

Massaccesi's boring formula-slasher *Anthropophagus II* has only the thinnest connection with zombies, but was given the deceptive title *Zombie 6* in certain English-language video releases anyway. Mikostanopolis is an escaped laboratory subject rendered murderous and unstoppable through medical experimentation, but he still gets done in by a bratty boy, a baby-sitter, and a woman in traction. His blood regenerates itself at three times the normal rate and coagulates extraordinarily fast—thus, like a zombie, bullets and weapons don't harm him. Furthermore, since brain cells don't regenerate, he can only be killed by destroying the brain. He's also speechless and he takes more punishment than Rasputin, but for all this he still cuts phone lines, removes bodies from plain view, and generally comes across more like Michael Myers than a zombie.

Jess Franco's *A Virgin Among the Living Dead* (1971) was redubbed *Zombie 4* in some release prints. His boring *Neurosis* (better known in English as *Revenge of the House of Usher*) was renamed *Zombie 5* when dubbed into English and put to video, though there's nothing even remotely like a zombie in it. Just for the record, no movie named *Zombie* plus a number has anything to do with any other numbered *Zombie* movie, even those by the same director (Lucio Fulci did both *Zombi 2* and *Zombi 3*). To illustrate how confused matters can get, consider that Bianchi's *Le notti del terrore* (1980) has also circulated as *Zombie 3*, that Fulci's *Zombi 2* was released in North America as *Zombie*, and that Romero's *Dawn of the Dead* was released in Europe as *Zombi*. Ironically, despite all this enumeration, no movie has yet been made whose original title is just plain *Zombie*.

Alternate titles: *Absurd*, *Monster Hunter*.

Zombie '90: Extreme Pestilence

Dir: Andreas Schnaas. *Prod*: Matthias Kerl, Ralf Hess. *Screenplay*: Andreas Schnaas. *Cast*: Matthias Kerl, Ralf Hess, Mathias Abbes, Marc Trinkhaus, Christian Biallas, Wolfgang Hinz. Blood Pictures/Reel Gore (West Germany), 1990.

Andreas Schnaas (known for his *Violent Shit* movies) achieves new depths of aesthetic and cinematic vacuity in this hyper-amateur, tongue-in-cheek effort. A plane goes down carrying an experimental AIDS vaccine, and naturally the bright green liquid that spills out turns everyone into bloodthirsty zombie ghouls (apparently the vaccine still needs a bit of work). The plot is a veritable fugue of baroque complexity: a couple of scientists run around while zombies chase them. Everything takes place out in the woods, to keep down on costs. The zombies follow the usual Romero specs (must be shot in the head, love to squish entrails around before eating them, etc.), except that they also use a fair number of weapons such as chainsaws and machetes. The violence is sick and gratuitous, much of it targeting the genitals (both male and female), and the whole is pervaded by a fascination with bodily excretion. Aside from a grating pre-credit sequence, the most tedious episode is the protracted one between the opening and closing credits.

Zombie and the Ghost Train

(Orig. *Zombie ja Kummitusjuna*). *Dir*: Mika Kaurismäki. *Screenplay*: Mika Kaurismäki. *Cast*: Silu Seppälä, Marjo Leinonen, Matti Pellonpää, Vieno Saaristo, Juhani Niemelä. Marianna Films/Villealfa Filmproductions (Finland), 1991.

Not a horror movie at all, Finland's nominal contribution to our subject is a depressing story of a directionless young rebel gradually being consumed by his own alcoholism. Known to his friends as "Zombie," Antti Autiomaa (Seppälä) wanders around empty, grey city streets in a bleak winter landscape, avoiding societal and personal obligation. Relationships, family, and even an invitation to play with successful band "Harry and the Mule–fukkers" fail to touch his frosty, bottomless soul. The only thing to ever pique his interest, a mysterious band known as the "Ghost Train" that no one has ever seen play, eludes him forever like a fading mirage. Intelligent dialogue and imagery help keep the mono-thematic plot moving, but don't expect the slow-paced tale of deliberately self-destructive drinking in the midst of a stagnant tundra society to be a winner at parties.

Zombie Apocalypse

(Orig. *Cemeterio del terror*). *Dir*: Rubén Galindo Jr. *Prod*: Raúl Galindo. *Story*: Rubén Galindo Jr. *Cast*: Hugo Stieglitz, Usi Velasco, Jose Gómez Parcero, Betty Robles, Erika Buenfil, Edna Bolkan, María Rebeca, Cervando Manzetti, Eduardo Capetillo. Dynamic Films/Producciones Torrentesa (Mexico), 1985.

An unexpected zombie invasion helps liven up the waning interest of this treadmill Mexi–slasher, at least briefly. A bunch of partying imbeciles inadvertently raise burly, Satan–worshipping psycho-killer Devlin from the dead by reading dark prayers from an ancient grimoire. A Dr. Loomis figure (Stieglitz) helps a pack of trick-or-treating kids defeat Devlin and the army of undead who assist him by burning the evil tome. The *Halloween* clone takes the killer's point-of-view through lengthy stalking scenes dubbed over with heavy breathing, while the panic music is right out of *Friday the 13th*.

The movie picks up for the last fifteen minutes, when it switches from a solitary stalker to a zombie invasion format. Though there's no explicit connection between Devlin and the masses of risen dead, he seems to be their leader. They are slow and silent, serenely climbing from the smoky ground and grasping at the shrieking children that prance about hither and thither. They show no sign of emotion or thought as they stumble around with mottled grey and black faces and straggling tufts of white hair. Since the zombies draw their power from hell, they can be repelled by the sign of the cross. It's unfortunate that they all burst into flames before they ever actually kill anyone—especially the whiny children who have had it coming for half the movie.

The Zombie Army

Dir: Betty Stapleford. *Prod*: John Kalinowski. *Screenplay*: Roger Scearce. *Cast*: Eileen Saddow, John Kalinowski, Steven Roberts, Jody Amato, Patrick

Houtman, Steve McConnell, Cindie Acker, Kim Foxx. Cheapshot Productions, 1991.

One of the few zombie movies directed by a woman, this shoddy backyard gore-fest was doubtlessly more fun to make than it is to watch. The U.S. Army buys the building that was formerly the Oak Valley Insane Asylum, where psychotic murderers were subjected to unorthodox treatment. Two inmates accidentally left behind, locked in the basement, are set free when fresh recruits move in, and the pair begin slaughtering the GIs and bringing them back to life with high-powered electro-convulsive "therapy." Psychopathic Jim, with his white (but ever reddening) doctor's coat, carefully records all the kills on a clipboard. Though the gore effects are vibrant and colorful, the movie wilts from home-movie production values and Nebraska-flat acting. It's at least relieving that the moviemakers relish the hamminess of their own creation: Cheapshot Productions originally offered a Jeep-giveaway contest for correctly guessing the number of continuity flaws in the movie.

The script is miserly with explanations, starting with why the resurrected dead would follow Jim as their leader instead of just eating him. It seems improbably convenient, furthermore, that the burning effects of the electroshocks make the revived soldiers look just like conventional screen zombies. Wearing their combat fatigues, the zombie GIs groan loudly and go in search of flesh. There are prolonged scenes of unstrung intestine banqueting; one zombie picks out a victim's eyes and daintily pops them like martini olives. In another scene, a zombie feeds on a cadaver's intestines, then when that cadaver is brought to life, he apologetically coughs them back up and helps the original owner stuff them back into his abdominal cavity. It's never explained what the mad doctor hopes to do with his army of "patients." Though one soldier salutes Jim at one point, a great many opportunities to connect zombies with the military mentality, or to connect them with some of the other interesting ideas raised early in the film (such as "fixation and regression," or "idiot-savant syndrome") are entirely neglected.

Zombie Bloodbath

Dir: Todd Sheets. *Prod*: Todd Sheets. *Story*: Todd Sheets, Jerry Angell. *Screenplay*: Todd Sheets, Roger Williams. *Cast*: Chris Harris, Auggi Alvarez, Frank Dunlay, Jerry Angell, Cathy Metz, Cheryl Metz, T.G. Watkins, Kasey Rausch. Trustinus Productions, 1993.

Though mildly less awful than Sheets' incoherent *Zombie Rampage*, this Midwest undead saga unreflectively tries to keep the late '70s–early '80s zombie invasion plot on life support, wounding it further with home movie production values. Radiation from an underground nuclear facility built on a cursed Native American burial ground sparks off a cannibal zombie epidemic in the south side of Kansas City. A group of oafish suburbanites infiltrate the zombie-infested compound and blow up the facility, but the contagion has already spread uncontrollably. Though society is allegedly crumbling, the low-budget opus never once shows any police or National Guard activity. The violence is minimal, but Sheets' gore is characteristically intense and disgusting even for zombie movies. There are several irreverent church scenes and a nun and priest zombie, but the closing credits still give special thanks to "God for helping us when we needed him."

The gimpy zombies stumble around in lousy make-up to prey on bad actors (watch for the occasional glance at the camera). They crowd around the humans in large, densely packed groups, but all they usually do is paw at them halfheartedly so that the protagonists can break through. The feeble ghouls are easily conquered in hand-to-hand combat, going down from just a sucker punch or karate kick. In fact, these zombies are so ineffectual that half the characters wind up having to shoot themselves to get killed off. The credits claim there were a total of 735 zombies, but it seemed to me that we keep seeing the same few over and over again.

Zombie Bloodbath II: Rage of the Undead

Dir: Todd Sheets. *Story*: Todd Sheets. *Screenplay*: Todd Sheets, Dwen Daggett. *Cast*: Dave Miller, Kathleen McSweeney, Gena Fischer, Nick Stodden, Jody Rovick, Becky Stodden, Rebecca Rose, Byron Nicodemus, Harry Rose, Jerry Angell. Trustinus Productions, 1994.

Unstoppable Todd Sheets, the Ed Wood of Tornado Alley, treats us to yet another small scale, direct-to-video, home movie apocalypse. Donna (McSweeney) and a handful of her friends find themselves trapped by escaped convicts as well as the usual undead ghouls; they flee to a deli while zombies overrun civilization. Some videographed zombie invasions are at least conceptually creative (*The Dead Next Door*, *Shatter Dead*), but Sheets is happy just to present zombies going around eating people for an hour and a half at a time. *Zombie*

Bloodbath II also offers bonus human depravity, and the character dynamics present a virtual pageant of cruelty and ugliness. The dialogue sparkles with crisp philosophical insight: "If I was boss, you'd follow me."

Sheets' flannel-clad, Great Plains undead lumber around with cold cream all over their faces, seeking the flesh of the living and all that. They swat limply as characters run by them and are unable to break through a glass window. They don't really do anything interesting, but Donna manages to deanimate a pack of them by sprinkling them with test tubes of flesh-eating bacteria, which she happens to stumble across in an abandoned pickup truck. A preachy text at the end rather randomly implies that the movie is really about nuclear accidents and satanic cult activity, and tells us once again that the zombies are us.

Zombie Child see ***The Child***

Zombie Cop

Dir: J.R. Bookwalter. *Prod*: Scott P. Plummer, J.R. Bookwalter. *Screenplay*: Matthew Jason Walsh. *Story*: J.R. Bookwalter. *Cast*: Michael Kemper, Ken Jarosz, James R. Black Jr., Bill Morrison. The Suburban Tempe Company, 1991.

This hour-long amateur action feature is about an hour longer than it needs to be. Police officer Robert Gill (Kemper) and evil voodoo priest Dr. Death (Black) kill each other, but both return from the grave through Death's sorcery. Death runs off to pursue some obscure master plan, while Gill joins forces with his former partner Stevens (Jarosz) to stop him. Gill and Death, each impervious to normal attacks, smash and shoot away at each other interminably, culminating in the world's slowest car chase. At last defeating his nemesis, Gill remains a superhero vigilante cop to protect the community. Filmed in "Tempe-vision," which looks suspiciously like home camcorder videography, the movie mainly consists of people running around depressing suburban Ohio locations, interspersed with painfully clichéd dialogue.

Upon first crawling from the grave, Gill is only slightly zombie-like in appearance—a little scruffy and pale, but not too decayed yet. But since he immediately wraps bandages around his whole head and leaves them on for the rest of the movie, he comes across more like Mummy Cop. Gill conforms to expected zombie behavior in no way, and the zombie cop is a bust.

Zombie Creeping Flesh see *Night of the Zombies*

Zombie Flesh Eaters see *Zombie*

Zombie High

Dir: Ron Link. *Prod*: Aziz Ghazal, Marc Toberoff. *Screenplay*: Tim Doyle, Aziz Ghazal, Elizabeth Passarelli. *Cast*: Virginia Madsen, Richard Cox, Kay Kuter, James Wilder, Sherilynn Fenn, Paul Feig, T. Scott Coffey. Priest Hill Productions, 1987.

Actually it's not a high school, but a swanky prep school in which the students are all mindless robot drones. Incoming student Andrea (Madsen) is increasingly distressed by the humorless student body of snooty Ettinger Academy, until she at last discovers that the faculty are vampires who learned the secret of immortality from a Native American medicine man a century ago, and have been turning the student body into zombies and using their blood and cerebral fluids to stay alive ever since. With suit, tie, and tireless study habits, the model pupils present a none-too-subtle satire on yuppie overachievers. A discontented biology professor (Cox) helps Andrea and her boyfriend Barry (Wilder) overcome former Indian scalper Beaurigard (Kuter). The movie plays the concept more seriously than the title lets on, and, in fact, winds up dragging quite a bit. There's a brusquely abrupt cut technique that helps keep you awake but gives you a headache at the same time. The only memorable scene is the Homecoming dance: dozens of lobotomized yuppie couples dance in perfect sync, in an uninspired back and forth slow-step that doesn't change even when the rhythm of the music does.

The students aren't dead, just mind-washed fodder for the blood- and brain-sucking faculty. Though their intellectual faculties seem to be in order, the emotional capacity is utterly eliminated. They only speak when absolutely necessary to maintain a public front, and even their facial expressions seem forced. Though they have no souls, the alumni of Ettinger go on to become successful executives and politicians (maybe, *because* they have no souls). The students on campus are controlled through crystal implants in their brains that respond to special sound waves broadcast all across the school P.A.; Barry and Andrea kill them all by replacing the cassette with a heavy metal tape.

Alternate title: *The School That Ate My Brain.*

Zombie Holocaust

Dir: Gary Whitson. *Screenplay*: W. (Bill) Baylis. *Cast*: Pamela Sutch, Tina Krause, Laura Giglio, Sal Longo, Aven Warren, Kathy Steel, Sidney Nice, Dawn Murphy. W.A.V.E. Productions, 1995.

Set in the year 2008, this abysmal Public Access science-fiction fiasco from home-movie gore factory W.A.V.E. Productions opens on a post-apocalyptic world in which a meteor shower has killed ninety percent of the population (but the water and electricity still seem to be running fine). A psychotic, man-hating she-tyrant called "The Doctor" rules the local community with an iron fist from her force field–protected compound with an army of women. She keeps the male population at bay with a chemical that has turned them into cannibals—if they don't do what she says, she refuses them the periodic inoculations that keep them from deteriorating into mindless, raving monsters. Dissidents Karen (Giglio) and Tracy (Krause) team up with two rebellious men to break the Doctor's reign of terror. The movie plays like an adolescent male fantasy, complete with mud wrestling, slap fighting, a dominatrix scene, and continuous glimpses of women's underwear beneath their short tunics. In fact, the film centers conspicuously around prolonged scenes of women in postures of subjection and victimization. The misogyny might be more offensive if the acting and staging were more convincing; but embarrassing production values and an inability to generate audience sympathy for any character help deflect attention from the questionable ideology. There's a lot of talk about mercenary soldiers, force fields, perimeters, counter-rebellions, and apocalyptic desolation, but really it just looks like a handful of people standing around talking and wrestling in the woods.

The "zombies" promised by the exploitation title are never delivered—there's only the threat that if the men under the Doctor's control don't get their regular shots, they will turn into savage creatures. Rather disappointingly, none of them miss their regular shots. But even with their shots the men need to eat human flesh. In the pre-credit sequence, they bleed cadavers and hang them up in a smokehouse, then cook them on a microwave bed. There's also a lengthy scene of a woman "roasting" on a spit over a sorry fire that's obviously not even large enough to keep her warm. One guy in a flannel shirt and bad mask shows up out of nowhere to hang out with the other characters briefly; I hope he's not supposed to be the zombie, because if so, that's really pathetic. Since zombies are surely the least demanding of screen monsters in terms of acting and make-up effects, it's pretty sad that this film crew couldn't be bothered to write them into their otherwise ambitious "Zombie Holocaust."

Zombie Horror see ***Burial Ground***

Zombie Inferno see ***Night of the Zombies***

Zombie Island Massacre

Dir: John N. Carter. *Prod*: David Broadnax. *Screenplay*: William Stoddard, Logan O'Neill. *Story*: David Broadnax, Logan O'Neill. *Cast*: David Broadnax, Rita Jenrette, Tom Cantrell, Diane Clayre Holub, Ian McMillian, George Peters, Dennis Stephenson, Trevor Reid. Picnic Productions, 1984.

In this run-of-the-mill elimination-stalker a busload of idiot tourists led by chipper guide Reginald Jones (Stephenson) find themselves stranded on the remote Caribbean island of St. Marie, after witnessing a zombie-raising voodoo ritual as part of the tour package. Though convinced the ritual was staged, Paul (Broadnax), Sandy (Jenrette), and the other dull-witted fun-seekers now find the bus disabled, and begin to turn up murdered one after the other. It turns out that hit men sent by Colombian drug-runners are posing as cannibals to frighten the party off; obviously the best way to avoid attracting the attention of authorities is to kill off a score of well-to-do American holidayers. Though up-scale for a Troma release, this is still unbearably tedious and awful, to be avoided by any expedient.

While being stalked, the characters refer to their unknown assailant half-jokingly as "the zombie." Though that's not what's after them, the zombie raised in the initial voodoo ceremony does seem to be genuine (its fingernails grow half an inch instantaneously). Or at least, if it is only played by an actor then it's crummy work, because the gig involves getting hacked in the head with a machete only seconds after being reanimated. Before being sent back to oblivion, though, the zombie sits submissively with head lowered, exuding a faint air of wistfulness and sorrow. There's no further hint of genuine zombies or supernatural activity in the movie, but the statue-like zombie is eerie and engrossing for all the forty seconds he graces the mediocre movie with his presence.

Zombie ja Kummitusjuna see ***Zombie and the Ghost Train***

Zombie Lake

(Orig. *Le lac des morts vivants*). *Dir*: Jean Rollin. *Prod*: Daniel Lesoeur. *Story*: Julian Esteban. *Screenplay*: A.L. Mariaux. *Cast*: Howard Vernon, Pierre Escourrou, Anouchka, Robert Foster, Nadine Pascale, Gilda Arancio. Eurociné/J.E. Films (France, Spain), 1980.

Rollin plays his bare-bones zombie tale as a nostalgic love story, resulting in a mediocre horror piece but a biting parody of sentimental movies. A small French town that slaughtered a platoon of Nazis and dumped their bodies in a lake during the occupation is chagrined to find the dauntless Teutons continuing their depredations a dozen years later. Though the aquatic Aryans receive a steady diet of female swimmers in the lake, they grow increasingly restless and now make forays into the town itself to procure fresh blood. One zombie pays social calls on his daughter, who was born just before he died and who doesn't seem too put off by his rotting flesh or murderous blood-sucking activities. The town mayor (Vernon) convinces the girl to lure daddy and the other fiends into a mill, however, where they're all sprayed with napalm. The opening scene is a hilarious spoof of *Jaws*, with an underwater Nazi zombie substituting for the shark, but after that the only entertainment is the arresting rural French scenery, when it isn't blocked by the obtrusive characters. Rollin later said that he only read the script for the movie on the way to the shoot, and that he had no solid idea what it was about until half way through the filming.

As in *Shock Waves*, the undead reside on the bottom of the pond (though these Nazi zombies are exclusively fresh-water), lurking amidst the weeds and lily pads to grab imprudent bathers from below. On dry land they're much stiffer, slowly shuffling up to actors who don't make very inspired attempts to get away. The unconvincing make-up effects are laughable (with pink skin showing around the outlines of the face paint), and under water it even starts to peel off. Among their supernatural powers can be counted well-coifed hair despite a decade of living as zombies in a lake, and the ability to dry off with remarkable speed. Though unexpressive and inarticulate, the undead Nazis are clearly sentient and emotional: one zombie sour-puss throws a temper tantrum, tipping over tables and smashing things. But they have a soft side too, as when Helena's father holds her hand while the two walk along touchingly, and when he wrestles another zombie to protect her. Two zombies wrestling: now there's heart-stopping action.

Alternate titles: *El lago de los muertos vivientes*, *The Lake of the Living Dead*, *Zombies Lake*.

Zombie Nightmare

Dir: Jack Bravman. *Prod*: Pierre Grisé. *Screenplay*: David Wellington. *Cast*: Manuska Rigaud, Adam West, Jon Mikl Thor, Tia Carrere, Shawn Levy, Frank Dietz, Allan Fisher, Hamish McEwen, Manon Turbide, Francesca Bonacorsa, John Fasano. Gold-Gems Limited/New World (Canada), 1987.

This painful and toilsome feature with woody Adam West (*Batman*) as a thug-turned-police captain is indeed, as the title promises, a nightmare. Ape-like Tony (Thor) is cut down in his prime, run over by a carload of drunken teens. His mother Louise (Bonacorsa) seeks the help of quivery-voiced voodoo priestess Molly (Rigaud) in resurrecting him as a monstrous undead avenger, who then picks the teens off one by one. Meanwhile, police captain Churchman (West) is drawn increasingly into the puzzle, as dark crimes from his own past begin to resurface. The voodoo elements are thinly tacked onto a Bronson-esque elimination-revenge format, garnished with slipshod continuity and teeth-grating acting. Depressing themes of violence and wasted youth are compounded rather than relieved by the ugly avenging zombie and the aloof priestess who controls him.

Molly explains that she can't bring Tony fully back to life, but can only "hold him on this plane until his death has been avenged." When he first rises from the coffin he howls like a wolf-man, and then growls like Lou Ferrigno from *The Incredible Hulk* for the rest of the movie. He kills by snapping necks or whacking people with the baseball bat he carries around with him, and then each night he returns to the makeshift coffin Molly has set up for him in her back yard. Zombies apparently "lose their energy" after avenging themselves, so after slaughtering the last of his own killers, Tony retreats to his permanent grave in the cemetery. In the closing two minutes a second zombie emerges, Tony's long-dead father, to drag Churchman down to hell (what West wouldn't give for his utility belt there, no doubt). This second zombie even pronounces Churchman's name, thus exhibiting more sentience and personality in thirty seconds than Tony does the entire movie.

Zombie Nosh see ***Flesheater***

Zombie of the Savanna see ***Night of the Zombies***

Zombie Rampage

Dir: Todd Sheets. *Prod*: Louis Garrett. *Screenplay*: Todd Sheets, Erin Kehr. *Story*: Roger Williams. *Cast*: Dave Byerly, Erin Kehr, Stanna Bippus, Beth Belanti. Trustinus Productions, 1991.

Quirky one-man zombie movie factory Todd Sheets unleashes the first of his backyard zombie invasions filmed locally in Kansas City, Missouri. The story line hasn't come out of the editing room with much semblance of coherence, but the gist seems to be as follows: acerbic gang leader Tommy (Byerly) tries to raise some recently-deceased gang members from the dead with the aid of a cheap paperback on voodoo (but in fact, zombies start to appear before the rite is even conducted). Faced with an invasion of cannibal ghouls, he teams up with Dave (Kehr) and several others to hide from the escalating undead menace. There is much wearisome in-fighting, broken periodically by random sequences of zombies marauding in the streets. Video filmography gives a new meaning to "low budget," and while it's good to support local filmmaking as an alternative to studio industry productions, *Zombie Rampage* suffers from Scotch Tape editing, inconsistent lighting, bad sound, and some of the worst foley work outside of Public Access. Sheets thanks Jesus Christ in the closing credits, but surely He could have come up with better lighting and stronger continuity.

The uninspired make-up offers a hodgepodge of zombie types, but these are essentially the flesh-eating ghouls familiar from *Dawn* and *Day*, occasionally featuring rivulets of enigmatic fluids (one drips with a fluorescent green ooze). The undead limp along stiff-limbed and contorted, suffering from an epidemic of apoplectic over-acting. They crowd around their victims and tear them apart animalistically, reveling in squishy organs and entrails with delight. A Troma-inspired scene shows the zombies devouring a baby in its stroller as if stopping at a hotdog stand, but on the whole these ghouls are neither scary nor funny, whichever they're trying to be.

Zombie Revival: Ninja Master see ***Zombie vs. Ninja***

Zombie Terror

(Episode, *Ramar of the Jungle*). *Dir*: Spencer Bennet. *Prod*: Rudolph Flothow. *Story and Teleplay*: Robert Pitt. *Cast*: Jon Hall, Ray Montgomery, Kurt Katch, Jo Gilbert, Nick Stewart, Louis Brown, Morris Buchanan. Arrow Productions, 1952.

Ramar of the Jungle was a second-rate TV jungle adventure series about intrepid Tom Reynolds (Hall, known to the natives as "Ramar"), his assistant Howard Ogden (Montgomery), and their black servant Willie (Stewart). With pith helmet and rifle, the two whites trek through starchy jungle sets to confront hostile tribes, stuffed beasts, wildlife footage, women in leopard skin, and other tropical menaces. In this episode, our heroes bring to justice mad Dr. Rennet (Katch), whose thought transference experiments give him the power to control people telepathically. It's all feverishly dull, and it's not really clear what any of these people are supposed to be doing in Africa anyway.

The zombies aren't dead, but only mind-washed. Rennet zombifies subjects with the help of a ray emitter and a few tables of sophisticated electronic apparatus, all of which he has improbably set up in his tent in the middle of the jungle. Ogden is temporarily subjected to the zombification effects, but recovers since his exposure to the ray was not at full dosage. On the other hand, a zombified African who suffers complete brain damage and becomes a blithering killer is possibly the first TV zombie.

Zombie vs. Mardi Gras

Dir: Mike Lyddon, Will Frank, Karl DeMolay. *Prod*: Mike Lyddon, Will Frank, Karl DeMolay. *Screenplay*: Mike Lyddon, Will Frank, Karl DeMolay. *Cast*: Dale Ashmun, Loreli Fuller, John Sinclair, Jeanette Hauser, Veronica Russell. Carnavale Productions, 1996.

I suppose it was only a matter of time before someone did a postmodern Art Zombie movie, but this seems to have been little more than an excuse for a bunch of film school students to hit New Orleans. The "filmmakers" of this black-and-white quasi-documentary go around Bourbon Street and vicinity trying to purchase marijuana, while a ratty zombie bum (a cross between Harpo Marx and Bob Dylan) goes around eating people: as the title implies, the zombie holds a grudge against the entire festival of Mardi Gras. In purgatory, meanwhile, the Renaissance astrologer Galileo is resurrected and sent to Earth to stop the zombie. He makes a couple of halfhearted attempts, but mostly just sits around smoking fags and musing about the space-time continuum instead. It's all relatively painful.

Zombie vs. Ninja

Dir: Godfrey Ho (as Charles Lee). *Prod*: Joseph Lai, Betty Chan. *Screenplay*: Benny Ho. *Cast*: Pierre Kirby, Edowan Bersmea, Dewey Bosworth, Thomas Hartham. IFD Films/Arts Limited (Hong Kong), 1989.

An undertaker's apprentice wishing to avenge his father's death learns kung fu from his buck-toothed master. The undertaker periodically casts spells to reanimate the cadavers that trail about the shop for sparring purposes. The corpses generally wear bright colors, and three of them are decked out in imperial regalia. They all fight with quick, jerky motions, like speeded-up clockwork dolls. They return to their coffins or simply disappear into thin air at sunrise. Though the comical undertaker is good for some entertaining moments, the continuous fighting is monotonous even for a martial arts movie.

Alternate title: *Zombie Revival: Ninja Master*.

Zombies see ***Dawn of the Dead***

Zombies see ***I Eat Your Skin***

The Zombies see ***The Plague of the Zombies***

Zombies Lake see ***Zombie Lake***

Zombies of Mora-Tau

Dir: Edward Cahn. *Prod*: Sam Katzman. *Screenplay*: Raymond T. Marcus, Bernard Gordon. *Story*: George Plympton. *Cast*: Gregg Palmer, Allison Hayes, Autumn Russell, Joel Ashley, Morris Ankrum, Marjorie Eaton, Gene Roth, Leonard Geer, Karl Davis, William Baskin. Columbia Pictures, 1957.

This awkward and talentless movie is nonetheless surprisingly prescient in zombie film history, anticipating a number of motifs that would reappear in later decades. Trying to steal a golden idol from Africa in 1894, a crew of ten European sailors were turned into zombies by local natives, and have been guarding some diamonds in a submerged shipwreck ever since. George Harrison, his wife Mona (Allison Hayes, the original fifty-foot woman), and some others in search of the sunken treasure are welcomed by doomsaying Mrs. Peters, who has already taken the liberty of having graves dug for them. They all fight amongst themselves as well as against the zombies, until Mrs. Peters ends the curse by scattering the diamonds back overboard. The funniest scene is that in which fragile old Mrs. Peters shakes her cane indignantly at a zombie as he passes by her indifferently. Most ironic line in the movie, and perhaps in all of zombie film: "It happened so fast."

The zombies basically look like normal people—Mrs. Peters notes that her husband looks no different now than he did sixty years ago, "except for the eyes" (he has a glassy stare). They are frumpy, middle-aged men with pot-bellies and pattern balding, dressed like dockworkers and sailors. They never close their eyes, and have no blood circulation or body functions. During the day, they mostly lie in coffins in a special crypt, or walk around the ocean floor (the underwater scenes were actually filmed on a studio set, with cardboard seaweed). Sixty years of amphibious wear has been remarkably kind to their clothes; the captain's suit looks like it just came off the rack. They are extremely slow, and dogs bark at them as they silently busy themselves with their ungodly tasks, the odd strand of seaweed neatly draped over their shoulders. Stiff and solid, they are immune to stabbing, shooting, and basically everything except fire. That's why they're afraid of it, Mrs. Peters explains: it's the one thing that can destroy them. Even flares drive them back, and at one point, the characters confine zombie Mona to her room by surrounding her bed with candles.

The zombie sailors, of course, have no free will, and no vestige of humanity or emotion (though at one point they're said to "exist in torment"). They are simply the pawns of some antiquated voodoo curse, whose practitioners are long dead. It's refreshing to see a '50s movie trace voodoo back to its African origins, but then again the cast is all white, including the servants, and no native culture (voodoo or otherwise) enters the story line at all other than through vague references. At least we aren't subjected to lengthy rites of drumming and dancing, as in most jungle/voodoo movies of the period. Judged on its own merits, *Mora-Tau* is ungainly and vacuous, but its enduring influence on the genre is curious: this is the first film in which the zombies clearly exist without a voodoo master or leader controlling them, and the first in which the zombie condition is contagious. It's also the first to claim that zombies are afraid of fire (as they are later in *Night*, for instance). Most outrageous of all, however, is the whole idea of the underwater zombie, a random and incongruous notion to start with, but one that would resurface as a notable sub-genre in the late '70s and early '80s.

Alternate title: *The Dead That Walk.*

Zombies of Sugar Hill see *Sugar Hill*

Zombies of the Stratosphere

Dir: Fred C. Brannon. *Screenplay*: Ronald Davidson. *Cast*: Judd Holdren, Aline Towne, Wilson Wood, Lane Bradford, Stanley Waxman, Leonard Nimoy. Republic, 1952.

Republic fishes out the old Commando Cody flying jet-pack from the prop room yet again to provide the main special effect for a twelve-part action-adventure serial. Martians plot to blow the earth out into deep space, so that they can move their own planet into our orbit through controlled H–bomb explosions and thus enjoy our more favorable climate. They can do all that, but they can't outwit dull government agents Larry and Bob, who foil alien leader Marex again and again as he attempts to obtain uranium and construct a bomb in his secluded cave. The sole surviving Martian, wounded Narab (Leonard Nimoy), treacherously helps our heroes defuse the bomb and save the earth. Expect lengthy and frequent chases in which no one is ever caught and shoot-outs in which no one is ever hit. The science-fiction elements are thin, mostly consisting of the jet-pack, some spark-propelled spaceships without landing gear, and an absurd robot. Have a book of crossword puzzles and maybe some aspirin on hand. The twelve original episodes, each with a recap statement at the beginning and a cliff-hanger ending, were condensed into a movie-length version in 1957 released as *Satan's Satellites*.

Though called "zombies" in the main title, an episode title, and a recap blurb, and though one of the protagonists calls them "zombies" in the closing minutes of the last episode, the unconvincing Martians are simply people in tight, glittery body suits with cheesy zig-zag lightning bolt designs. They are fully rational, speaking without even a trace of a Martian accent. They are, however, able to remain under water or in toxic gas for up to half an hour, since they're accustomed to the oxygen-poor atmosphere of Mars and since it doesn't cost anything to depict. In any case they're hardly "zombies," and for that matter they're not especially from the stratosphere, either.

Alternate title: *Satan's Satellites*.

Zombies on Broadway

Dir: Gordon Douglas. *Prod*: Ben Stoloff. *Screenplay*: Lawrence Kimble. *Story*: Robert Faber, Charles Newman. *Cast*: Wally Brown, Alan Carney, Bela

The word "zombie" soon surpassed the creature itself for market value: neither of the zombies from the flat comedy *Zombies on Broadway* (1945) are portrayed or even billed in this festive title card.

Lugosi, Anne Jeffreys, Sheldon Leonard, Frank Jenks, Russell Hopton, Joseph Vitale, Darby Jones. RKO Radio Pictures, 1945.

In the tradition of *The Ghost Breakers*, nutty Jerry and Mike (Brown and Carney, RKO's attempt to mimic Universal's Abbot and Costello) go up against seriously played villains and monsters. As press agents for ex-gangster Ace Miller (Leonard), the pair have promised to provide an authentic zombie for the opening night of Miller's new night club "The Zombie Hut." They had hoped to make do with a paid actor, but Miller, unimpressed and dogged by an antagonistic journalist, charges them with finding a real one or getting bumped off, see? They travel to San Sebastian in the Virgin Islands, where they team up with singer Jean (Jeffreys) to foil mad scientist Paul Renault (Lugosi), who is attempting to recreate the native zombification rite entirely with chemicals. Mike briefly becomes a zombie through Renault's serum, and then at the end, so does Ace Miller himself—who thus unwittingly appears as the spectacle at his own nightclub. Brown and Carney aren't funny, and it's sad to see Lugosi outwitted by such a pack of morons.

Though there is one brief scene of a wide-eyed native zombie rising from his coffin during a voodoo ceremony, the zombie regular is "Colaga," played by lanky actor Darby Jones, who was also the zombie "Carrefour" in *I Walked with a Zombie*: a thin yet muscular black man with long arms and legs and Ping-Pong ball eyes. Renault, whose artificial serum only produces a temporary zombie-like trance, marvels that even after 20 years, there is still no sign of disintegration in undead Colaga. Renault sends him on his diabolical chores, and has him remain in a coffin when not in use. It's hard to take Colaga seriously most of the time, what with Brown and Carney hamming it up, but the scene in which he kills Renault is memorable enough. Almost overpowered by the protagonists, Renault commands Colaga, "Kill! Kill!" Now, either Colaga is very dense, or else there's some vestige of soul in him encouraging him to twist the meaning of these instructions, because he only follows the order by killing Renault himself—braining him with a spade. Then, entirely on his own initiative, he buries his fallen master, and that's the last we see of him. Jones has a fascinating physique and remains one of the more powerful screen zombies, but is ill-at-ease in the midst of these contrived plot twists and stale vaudeville gags.

Alternate title: *Loonies on Broadway.*

Zombiethon

Dir: Ken Dixon. *Prod*: Ken Dixon. *Cast*: K. Janyll Caudle, Tracy Burton, Paula Singleton, Janelle Lewis, Randolph Roehbling, Chuck Spero. Taryn Productions/Wizard Video, 1986.

Weak and opportunistic, this shameless zombie buffet loosely pastes together snippets from around half a dozen zombie movies for distribution on the video market. This is potentially a good idea, but remarkably, the scavenging perpetrators of this flimsy anti-homage have chosen the most embarrassing moments of the least interesting movies. Dull scenes of massacre and toplessness are presented in lengthy sequences without narration or context, all framed by custom-shot footage of zombies watching the movies in a theater. There is one good scene in the frame footage, maybe—a bratty little girl in the middle of the undead cinema annoying the zombies around her with balloons and a noisemaker. The movies defiled for this hybrid monstrosity are *Zombie*, *Zombie Lake*, *Oasis of the Zombies*, *Fear*, *The Invisible Dead*, *A Virgin Among the Living Dead*, and *The Astro-Zombies*.

Appendix A: Movies Listed by Year

1932	*White Zombie* (V. Halperin)
1935	*Ouanga* (G. Terwilliger)
1936	*Revolt of the Zombies* (V. Halperin)
1940	*The Ghost Breakers* (G. Marshall)
1941	*King of the Zombies* (J. Yarbrough)
1942	*Bowery at Midnight* (W. Fox)
1943	*I Walked with a Zombie* (J. Tourneur) *Revenge of the Zombies* (S. Sekely)
1944	*Voodoo Man* (W. Beaudine)
1945	*Zombies on Broadway* (G. Douglas)
1946	*Valley of the Zombies* (P. Ford)
1952	*Zombies of the Stratosphere* (F. Brannon) "Zombie Terror" (*Ramar of the Jungle*, S. Bennet)
1953	*Scared Stiff* (G. Marshall)
1955	*Creature with the Atom Brain* (E. Cahn)
1957	*Teenage Zombies* (J. Warren) *Voodoo Island* (R. LeBorg) *Womaneater* (C. Saunders) *Zombies of Mora-Tau* (E. Cahn)
1958	*Plan Nine from Outer Space* (E. Wood)
1959	*The Four Skulls of Jonathan Drake* (E. Cahn) *Invisible Invaders* (E. Cahn)

1960 *The Curse of the Doll People* (B. Alazraki)
Doctor Blood's Coffin (S. Furie)

1961 *Invasion of the Zombies* (B. Alazraki)

1962 "The Incredible Doktor Markesan" (*Thriller*, R. Florey)

1963 *The Horror of Party Beach* (D. Tenney)
Monstrosity (J. Mascelli)
War of the Zombies (G. Vari)

1964 *Dr. Orloff's Monster* (J. Franco)
The Earth Dies Screaming (T. Fisher)
I Eat Your Skin (D. Tenney)
The Incredibly Strange Creatures who Stopped Living and Became Mixed-Up Zombies (R.D. Steckler)
The Last Man on Earth (S. Salkow)
"Sibao" (*The Saint*, P. Yates)

1965 "The Very Important Zombie Affair" (*The Man from U.N.C.L.E.*, D. Alexander)

1966 *The Plague of the Zombies* (J. Gilling)
Terror Creatures from the Grave (M. Pupillo)

1967 *Dr. Satan vs. Black Magic* (R. González)

1968 *The Astro-Zombies* (T. Mikels)
Night of the Living Dead (G.A. Romero)
The Snake People (J. Ibáñez)

1969 *The Land of the Dead* (G. Solares)
Santo and Blue Demon Against the Monsters (G. Solares)

1970 *The Mummies of Guanajuato* (F. Curiel)

1971 *Blood of Ghastly Horror* (A. Adamson)
Tombs of the Blind Dead (A. de Ossorio)
A Virgin Among the Living Dead (J. Franco)

1972 *Baron Blood* (M. Bava)
Children Shouldn't Play with Dead Things (B. Clark)
Dead of Night (B. Clark)
Garden of the Dead (J. Hayes)
Horror Express (E. Martin)
Horror Rises from the Tomb (C. Aured)
Invasion of the Dead (R. Cardona)
Messiah of Evil (W. Huyck)
Return of the Zombies (J. Merino)
Santo vs. Black Magic (A. Crevenna)
Tales from the Crypt (F. Francis)
Vengeance of the Zombies (L. Klimovsky)

1973 *Castle of the Mummies of Guanajuato* (T. Novaro)
The House of Seven Corpses (P. Harrison)
The Legend of the Seven Golden Vampires (R.W. Baker)

The Night of the Sorcerers (A. de Ossorio)
Return of the Evil Dead (A. de Ossorio)

1974 *Horror of the Zombies* (A. de Ossorio)
The House on Skull Mountain (R. Honthaner)
Let Sleeping Corpses Lie (J. Grau)
Shanks (W. Castle)
Sugar Hill (P. Maslansky)
"The Zombie" (*Kolchak: The Night Stalker*, A. Grasshoff)

1975 *The Cross of the Devil* (J. Gilling)
The Dead Don't Die (C. Harrington)
Night of the Seagulls (A. de Ossorio)

1977 *The Child* (R. Voskanian)
Shock Waves (K. Wiederhorn)

1979 *Dawn of the Dead* (G.A. Romero)
Erotic Nights of the Living Dead (A. Massaccesi)
The Fog (J. Carpenter)
Toxic Zombies (C. McCrann)
Zombie (L. Fulci)

1980 *The Alien Dead* (F.O. Ray)
Burial Ground (A. Bianchi)
City of the Walking Dead (U. Lenzi)
Dr. Butcher, M.D. (M. Girolami)
Don't Go in the House (J. Ellison)
Frozen Scream (F. Roach)
The Gates of Hell (L. Fulci)
Zombie Lake (J. Rollin)

1981 *The Beyond* (L. Fulci)
Dawn of the Mummy (F. Agrama)
Dead and Buried (G. Sherman)
Frankenstein Island (J. Warren)
Gamma 693 (J. Reed)
Heavy Metal (G. Potterton)
The House by the Cemetery (L. Fulci)
Night of the Zombies (B. Mattei)
Revenge of the Zombie (P. Regan)
Revenge of the Zombies (H. Meng-Hua)
Zombie 6: Monster Hunter (A. Massaccesi)

1982 *Creepshow* (G.A. Romero)
Kung Fu Zombie (H. Hung)
Mansion of the Living Dead (J. Franco)
Oasis of the Zombies (J. Franco)
One Dark Night (T. McLoughlin)
Sole Survivor (T. Eberhardt)
Zombie 5: Revenge of the House of Usher (J. Franco)

1983 *Thriller* (J. Landis)
Zeder (P. Avati)

1984 *Bloodsuckers from Outer Space* (G. Coburn)
Hard Rock Zombies (K. Shah)
I Was a Zombie for the F.B.I. (M. Penczner)
Mutant (J. Cardos)
Zombie Island Massacre (J. Carter)

1985 *Day of the Dead* (G.A. Romero)
The Midnight Hour (J. Bender)
Raiders of the Living Dead (S. Sherman)
Re-Animator (S. Gordon)
Return of the Living Dead (D. O'Bannon)
Warning Sign (H. Barwood)
Zombie Apocalypse (R. Galindo, Jr.)

1986 *Deadly Friend* (W. Craven)
The Gore-met Zombie Chef from Hell (D. Swan)
I Was a Teenage Zombie (J. Michalakis)
Night of the Creeps (F. Dekker)
The Supernaturals (A. Mastroianni)
Zombiethon (K. Dixon)

1987 *Killing Spree* (T. Ritter, V. Miranda)
Redneck Zombies (P. Lewnes)
Return of the Living Dead Part II (K. Wiederhorn)
The Serpent and the Rainbow (W. Craven)
The Video Dead (R. Scott)
Zombie High (R. Link)
Zombie Nightmare (J. Bravman)

1988 *After Death* (C. Fragasso)
Curse of the Blue Lights (J. Johnson)
Dead Heat (M. Goldblatt)
Flesheater (B. Hinzman)
"My Zombie Lover" (*Monsters*, D. Misch)
Raptors (C. Lattanzi)
Waxwork (A. Hickox)
Zombi 3 (L. Fulci)

1989 *Beverly Hills Bodysnatchers* (J. Mostow)
The Chilling (D. Nuse, J. Sunseri)
Chopper Chicks in Zombietown (D. Hoskins)
The Dead Next Door (J.R. Bookwalter)
The Dead Pit (B. Leonard)
From the Dead of Night (P. Wendkos)
Ginseng King (R. Ru-Tar)
Hellgate (W. Levey)
The Laughing Dead (S.P. Somtow)
Linnea Quigley's Horror Work-Out (H. Kennedy)

Monster High (R. Poe)
Night Life (D. Acomba)
Pet Sematary (M. Lambert)
The Vineyard (B. Rice and J. Hong)
Voodoo Dawn (S. Fierberg)
Zombie vs. Ninja (G. Ho)

1990 *The Boneyard* (J. Cummins)
Night of the Living Bread (K. O'Brien)
Night of the Living Dead (T. Savini)
Zombie '90: Extreme Pestilence (A. Schnaas)

1991 *Bride of Re-Animator* (B. Yuzna)
Demoni 3 (U. Lenzi)
Netherworld (D. Schmoeller)
Nudist Colony of the Dead (M. Pirro)
Teenage Exorcist (G.A. Waldman)
Waxwork II: Lost in Time (A. Hickox)
Zombie and the Ghost Train (M. Kaurismäki)
The Zombie Army (B. Stapleford)
Zombie Cop (J.R. Bookwalter)
Zombie Rampage (T. Sheets)

1992 *Dead Alive* (P. Jackson)
"Dial 'Z' for Zombies" (*The Simpsons*, B. Oakley, J. Weinstein, D. McGrath)
Living Dead in Tokyo Bay (K. Komizu)
The Lost Brigade (G. Hickenlooper)
Night of the Day of the Dawn of the Son of the Bride of the Return of the Revenge of the Terror of the Attack of the Evil Mutant Hellbound Flesh-Eating Subhumanoid Living Dead, Part II (L. Mason)

1993 *My Boyfriend's Back* (B. Balaban)
Return of the Living Dead Part III (B. Yuzna)
Shatter Dead (S. McCrae)
Weekend at Bernie's II (R. Klane)
Zombie Bloodbath (T. Sheets)

1994 *The Cemetery Man* (M. Soavi)
Shrunken Heads (R. Elfman)
Zombie Bloodbath II: Rage of the Undead (T. Sheets)

1995 *La Cage aux Zombies* (K. Hughes)
Voodoo (R. Eram)
Zombie Holocaust (G. Whitson)

1996 *Living a Zombie Dream* (T. Reynolds)
Zombie vs. Mardi Gras (M. Lyddon, W. Frank, K. DeMolay)

1997 "Pink Eye" (*South Park*, T. Parker, M. Stone)

1998 *I, Zombie* (A. Parkinson)
Scooby-Doo on Zombie Island (J. Stenstrum)

Appendix B: Foreign Movies by Country

Canada

Dead of Night (B. Clark, 1972)
Heavy Metal (G. Potterton, 1981)
Zombie Nightmare (J. Bravman, 1987)

Egypt

Dawn of the Mummy (F. Agrama, 1981; U.S., Italy co-prod.)

England

Doctor Blood's Coffin (S. Furie, 1960)
The Earth Dies Screaming (T. Fisher, 1964)
Horror Express (E. Martin, 1972; Spain co-prod.)
I, Zombie (A. Parkinson, 1998)
The Legend of the Seven Golden Vampires (R. Baker, 1973; Hong Kong co-prod.)
The Plague of the Zombies (J. Gilling, 1966)
"Sibao" (*The Saint*, P. Yates, 1964)
Tales from the Crypt (F. Francis, 1972)
Womaneater (C. Saunders, 1957)

Finland

Zombie and the Ghost Train (M. Kaurismäki, 1991)

France

The Cemetery Man (M. Soavi, 1994; Italy co-prod.)

Oasis of the Zombies (J. Franco, 1982; Spain co-prod.)
A Virgin Among the Living Dead (J. Franco, 1971; Spain co-prod.)
Zombie 5: Revenge of the House of Usher (J. Franco, 1982; Spain co-prod.)
Zombie Lake (J. Rollin, 1980; Spain co-prod.)

Germany

Baron Blood (M. Bava, 1972; Italy co-prod.)
Zombie '90: Extreme Pestilence (A. Schnaas, 1990)

Hong Kong

Kung Fu Zombie (H.I. Hung, 1982)
The Legend of the Seven Golden Vampires (R. Baker, 1973; England co-prod.)
Revenge of the Zombies (H. Meng-Hua, 1981)
Zombie vs. Ninja (G. Ho, 1989)

Italy

After Death (C. Fragasso, 1988)
Baron Blood (M. Bava, 1972; West Germany co-prod.)
The Beyond (L. Fulci, 1981)
Burial Ground (A. Bianchi, 1980)
The Cemetery Man (M. Soavi, 1994; France co-prod.)
City of the Walking Dead (U. Lenzi, 1980; Spain co-prod.)
Dawn of the Mummy (F. Agrama, 1981; U.S., Egypt co-prod.)
Demoni 3 (U. Lenzi, 1991)
Dr. Butcher, M.D. (M. Girolami, 1980)
Erotic Nights of the Living Dead (A. Massaccesi, 1979)
The Gates of Hell (L. Fulci, 1980)
The House by the Cemetery (L. Fulci, 1981)
Let Sleeping Corpses Lie (J. Grau, 1974; Spain co-prod.)
Night of the Zombies (B. Mattei, 1981; Spain co-prod.)
Raptors (C. Lattanzi, 1988)
Return of the Zombies (J. Merino, 1972; Spain co-prod.)
Terror Creatures from the Grave (M. Pupillo, 1966; U.S. co-prod.)
Vengeance of the Zombies (L. Klimovsky, 1972; Spain co-prod.)
War of the Zombies (G. Vari, 1963)
Zeder (P. Avati, 1983)
Zombie (L. Fulci, 1979)
Zombie 6: Monster Hunter (A. Massaccesi, 1981)
Zombi 3 (L. Fulci, 1988)

Japan

Living Dead in Tokyo Bay (K. Komizu, 1992)

Mexico

Castle of the Mummies of Guanajuato (T. Novaro, 1973)

The Curse of the Doll People (B. Alazraki, 1960)
Dr. Satan vs. Black Magic (R. González, 1967)
Invasion of the Dead (R. Cardona, Sr., 1972)
Invasion of the Zombies (B. Alazraki, 1961)
The Land of the Dead (G. Solares, 1969)
The Mummies of Guanajuato (F. Curiel, 1970)
Santo and Blue Demon Against the Monsters (G. Solares, 1969)
Santo vs. Black Magic (A. Crevenna, 1972)
The Snake People (J. Ibáñez, 1968; U.S. co-prod.)
Zombie Apocalypse (R. Galindo, Jr., 1985)

New Zealand

Dead Alive (P. Jackson, 1992)

Portugal

Tombs of the Blind Dead (A. de Ossorio, 1971; Spain co-prod.)

South Africa

Hellgate (W. Levey, 1989)

Spain

City of the Walking Dead (U. Lenzi, 1980; Italy co-prod.)
The Cross of the Devil (J. Gilling, 1975)
Dr. Orloff's Monster (J. Franco, 1964)
Horror Express (E. Martin, 1972; England co-prod.)
Horror of the Zombies (A. de Ossorio, 1974)
Horror Rises from the Tomb (C. Aured, 1972)
Let Sleeping Corpses Lie (J. Grau, 1974; Italy co-prod.)
Mansion of the Living Dead (J. Franco, 1982)
Night of the Seagulls (A. de Ossorio, 1975)
The Night of the Sorcerers (A. de Ossorio, 1973)
Night of the Zombies (B. Mattei, 1981; Italy co-prod.)
Oasis of the Zombies (J. Franco, 1982; France co-prod.)
Return of the Evil Dead (A. de Ossorio, 1973)
Return of the Zombies (J. Merino, 1972; Italy co-prod.)
Tombs of the Blind Dead (A. de Ossorio, 1971; Portugal co-prod.)
Vengeance of the Zombies (L. Klimovsky, 1972; Italy co-prod.)
A Virgin Among the Living Dead (J. Franco, 1971; France co-prod.)
Zombie 5: Revenge of the House of Usher (J. Franco, 1982; France co-prod.)
Zombie Lake (J. Rollin, 1980; France co-prod.)

Thailand

Ginseng King (R. Ru-Tar, 1989)

Bibliography

Horror Film Guides, Histories, and Encyclopedias

Badley, Linda. *Film, Horror, and the Body Fantastic.* Westport, CT: Greenwood Press, 1995.

Boot, Andy. *Fragments of Fear: An Illustrated History of British Horror Films.* London: Creation Books, 1996.

Britton, Andrew, et al., eds. *The American Nightmare: Essays on the Horror Film.* Toronto: Festival of Festivals, 1979.

Broderick, Mick. *Nuclear Movies.* Jefferson, NC: McFarland & Co., 1991.

Brottman, Mikita. *Offensive Films: Toward an Anthropology of Cinéma Vomitif.* Westport, CT and London: Greenwood Press, 1997.

Bryce, Allan. *Zombie.* Liskeard, England: Stray Cat Publishing, 2000.

Cine Español; Cine de subgeneros. Equipo Cartelera Turia. Valencia: Fernando Torres, 1974.

Clarens, Carlos. *An Illustrated History of the Horror Film.* New York: Capricorn Books, 1967–8.

Crane, Jonathan. *Terror and Everyday Life: Singular Moments in the History of the Horror Film.* Thousand Oaks, CA: Sage Publications, 1994.

de España, Rafael. *Directory of Spanish and Portuguese Film-Makers and Films.* Westport, CT: Greenwood Press, 1994.

Derry, Charles. *Dark Dreams: A Psychological History of the Modern Horror Film.* Cranbury, NJ: A.S. Barnes and Co., 1977.

Douglas, Drake. *Horrors!* (1966). Woodstock, NY: Overlook Press, 1989.

Dyson, Jeremy. *Bright Darkness: The Lost Art of the Supernatural Horror Film.* London and Washington: Cassell, 1997.

Edelson, Edward. *Great Monsters of the Movies.* Garden City, NY: Doubleday & Co., 1973.

Everman, Welch. *Cult Horror Films.* Citadel Press, 1993.

Fischer, Dennis. *Horror Film Directors, 1931–1990.* Jefferson, NC: McFarland & Co., 1991.

Flynn, John. *Cinematic Vampires.* Jefferson, NC: McFarland & Co., 1992.

Frank, Alan. *The Horror Film Handbook.* London: B.T. Batsford, 1982.

Grant, Barry Keith, ed. *Planks of Reason: Essays on the Horror Film.* Metuchen, NJ: Scarecrow Press, 1984.

Halliwell, Leslie. *The Dead That Walk.* London: Grafton Books, 1986.

Hanke, Ken. *A Critical Guide to Horror Film Series.* New York and London: Garland Publishing, 1991.

Hardy, Phil, ed. *Horror: The Aurum Film Encyclopedia.* London: Aurum Press, 1985.

Hoberman, J., and Jonathan Rosenbaum. *Midnight Movies.* New York: Harper & Row, 1983.

Iaccino, James. *Psychological Reflections on Cinematic Terror: Jungian Archetypes in Horror Films.* Westport, CT: Praeger, 1994.

The Internet Movie Database. [http://us.imdb.com/], genre link: "zombie." The Internet Movie Database Ltd., 1990–2000.

Jancovich, Mark. *Rational Fears: American Horror in the 1950s.* Manchester and New York: Manchester University Press, 1996.

Lucanio, Patrick. *Them or Us: Archetypal Interpretations of Fifties Alien Invasion Films.* Bloomington and Indianapolis: Indiana University Press, 1987.

Mank, Gregory William. *Hollywood Cauldron: Thirteen Horror Films from the Genre's Golden Age.* Jefferson, NC: McFarland & Co., 1994.

Marill, Alvin. *Movies Made for Television: The Telefeature and the Mini-Series, 1964–1986.* New York: New York Zoetrope, 1987.

Maxford, Howard. *The A–Z of Horror Films.* London: B.T. Batsford, 1996.

McCarty, John. *The Sleaze Merchants: Adventures in Exploitation Filmmaking.* New York: St. Martin's Griffin, 1995.

_____. *Splatter Movies: Breaking the Last Taboos.* New York: FantaCo, 1981.

Morsiani, Alberto, ed. *Rosso Italiano (1977/1987): Dieci anni di horror con Argento, Bava, Fulci e...gli altri. Sequenze* vol. 7. Verona: Nuova Grafica Cierre, 1988.

Murphy, Michael. *The Celluloid Vampires: A History and Filmography, 1897–1979.* Ann Arbor, MI: Pierian Press, 1979.

Newman, Kim. *Nightmare Movies.* New York: Proteus Books, 1984.

_____, ed. *The BFI Companion to Horror.* London: Cassell and the British Film Institute, 1996.

O'Neill, James. *Terror on Tape.* New York: Billboard Books, 1994.

Peary, Danny. *Cult Movies.* London: Vermilion & Co., 1981.

Pitts, Michael R. *Horror Film Stars.* Jefferson, NC: McFarland & Co., 1991.

Romagnoli, Michele. *L'Occhio del Testimone: Il Cinema di Lucio Fulci.* Bologna: Granata Press, 1992.

Rovin, Jeff. *The Encyclopedia of Monsters.* New York: Facts on File, 1989.

Senn, Bryan. *Drums of Terror: Voodoo in the Cinema.* Baltimore: Midnight Marquess Press, 1998.

_____. *Golden Horrors: An Illustrated Critical Filmography of Terror Cinema, 1931–1939.* Jefferson, NC: McFarland & Co., 1996.

Skal, David J. *The Monster Show: A Cultural History of Horror.* New York and London: W.W. Norton, 1993.

_____. *V is for Vampire: The A–Z Guide to Everything Undead*. New York: Plume (Penguin), 1996.
Tohill, Cathal, and Pete Tombs. *Immortal Tales: European Sex and Horror Movies, 1956–1984*. New York: St. Martin's Griffin, 1995.
Toufic, Jalal. *(Vampires): An Uneasy Essay on the Undead in Film*. Barrytown, NY: Station Hill, 1993.
Tudor, Andrew. *Monsters and Mad Scientists: A Cultural History of the Horror Movie*. Oxford: Basil Blackwell, 1989.
Turner, George, and Michael Price. *Forgotten Horrors: Early Talkie Chillers from Poverty Row*. Cranbury, NJ: A.S. Barnes and Co., 1979.
Twitchell, James. *Dreadful Pleasures: An Anatomy of Modern Horror*. New York and Oxford: Oxford University Press, 1985.
Ursini, James, and Alain Silver. *The Vampire Film*. New York: A.S. Barnes and Co., 1975.
Walker, Mark. *Vietnam Veteran Films*. Metuchen, NJ and London: Scarecrow Press, 1991.
Waller, Gregory, ed. *American Horrors: Essays on the Modern American Horror Film*. Urbana and Chicago: University of Illinois Press, 1987.
Weaver, James B., III, and Ron Tamborini, eds. *Horror Films: Current Research on Audience Preferences and Reactions*. Mahwah, NJ: Lawrence Erlbaum Associates, 1996.
Weaver, Tom. *Interviews with B Science Fiction and Horror Movie Makers*. Jefferson, NC: McFarland & Co., 1988.
_____. *Poverty Row Horrors! Monogram, PRC and Republic Horror Films of the Forties*. Jefferson, NC: McFarland & Co., 1993.
_____. *Science Fiction Stars and Horror Heroes*. Jefferson, NC: McFarland & Co., 1991.
Weisser, Thomas. *Asian Cult Cinema*. New York: Boulevard Books, 1997.
Weldon, Michael. *The Psychotronic Encyclopedia of Film*. New York: Ballantine Books, 1983.
Williams, Tony. *Hearths of Darkness: The Family in the American Horror Film*. Cranbury, NJ: Associated University Presses, 1996.
Willis, Donald. *Horror and Science Fiction Films: A Checklist*, 3 vols. Metuchen, NJ: Scarecrow Press, 1972, 1982, and 1984.
Wolfe, Sebastian, ed. *Reel Terror*. New York: Carroll and Graf, 1992.
Zillmann, Dolf, and Rhonda Gibson. "Evolution of the Horror Genre," in Weaver and Tamborini, eds. (1996): 15–31.

Studies of Particular Zombie Movies and Directors

Allen, Tom. "Knight of the Living Dead," *Village Voice* (Apr. 23, 1979): 44–46.
Balun, Charles. *Lucio Fulci: Beyond the Gates*. Key West: Fantasma Books, 1997.
Beard, Steve. "No Particular Place to Go," *Sight and Sound* 3.4 (1993): 30–31.

Bérard, Yves. "Les Morts-Vivants," *L'Avant Scène Cinéma* 187 (1977): 23–38.

Boss, Pete. "Vile Bodies and Bad Medicine," *Screen* 27.1 (1986): 14–24.

Burrell, Nigel. *Knights of Terror: The Blind Dead Films of Amando de Ossorio*. Midnight Media, 1995.

Caputi, Jane. "Films of the Nuclear Age," *Journal of Popular Film and Television* 16 (1988): 100–7.

Dillard, R.H.W. "*Night of the Living Dead*: It's Not Like Just a Wind That's Passing Through," in Waller, ed. *American Horrors* (1987): 14–29.

Draper, Ellen. "Zombie Women When the Gaze Is Male," *Wide Angle* 10.3 (1988): 52–62.

Flippo, Chet. "When There's No More Room in Hell, the Dead Will Walk the Earth," *Rolling Stone* (March 23, 1978): 46–49.

Gagne, Paul R. *The Zombies That Ate Pittsburgh: The Films of George A. Romero*. New York: Dodd, Mead, & Co., 1987.

Gires, Pierre. "Zombie, d'hier et d'aujourd'hui," *L'Ecran Fantastique* 31 (Feb. 1983): 10–57.

Grant, Barry Keith. "Taking Back *The Night of the Living Dead*: George Romero, Feminism & the Horror Film," *Wide Angle* 14.1 (1992): 64–76.

Higashi, Sumiko. "*Night of the Living Dead*: A Horror Film about the Horrors of the Vietnam Era," in Linda Dittmar and Gene Michaud, eds. *From Hanoi to Hollywood: The Vietnam War in American Film* (Rutgers University Press, 1990): 174–88.

London, Rose. *Zombie: The Living Dead*. New York: Bounty Books, 1976.

Lowry, Ed, and Louis Black. "*Dawn of the Dead*: Cinema of Apocalypse," *Take One* 7.6 (May 1979): 17–18.

Lowry, Ed, and Richard deCordova. "Enunciation and the Production of Horror in *White Zombie*," in Grant, ed. *Planks of Reason* (1984): 346–89.

McGuinness, Richard. "The Night of the Living Dead," *The Village Voice* (Dec. 25, 1969): 54.

Mercer, Kobena. "Monster Metaphors: Notes on Michael Jackson's *Thriller*," *Screen* 27.1 (1986): 26–43.

Newman, Kim. "Night of the Living Dead," *Sight and Sound* 3.4 (Apr. 1993): 51–52.

Russo, John. *The Complete Night of the Living Dead Filmbook*. Pittsburgh: Imagine, 1985.

Sevastakis, Michael. "*White Zombie*: 'Death and Love Together Mated,'" ch. 3 in *Songs of Love and Death: The Classical American Horror Film of the 1930s* (Westport, CT: Greenwood Press, 1993): 41–56.

Stein, Elliott. "The Night of the Living Dead," *Sight and Sound* 38 (Spr. 1970): 105.

Telotte, J.P. "Narration and Incarnation: *I Walked with a Zombie*," *Film Criticism* 6.3 (1982): 18–31.

Waller, Gregory. *The Living and the Undead: From Stoker's Dracula to Romero's Dawn of the Dead*. Urbana and Chicago: University of Illinois Press, 1986.

Williams, Tony. "*White Zombie*: Haitian Horror," *Jump Cut* 28 (1983): 18–20.
Winter, Douglas. *Prime Evil: New Stories by the Masters of Modern Horror* (New York and Scarborough, Ontario: New American Library, 1988): 1–9.
Wood, Robin. "Apocalypse Now: Notes on the Living Dead," in Britton, ed. *American Nightmare* (1979): 91–97.
_____. "Return of the Repressed," *Film Comment* 14.4 (July-Aug., 1978): 25–32.
Yakir, Dan. "Morning Becomes Romero," *Film Comment* 15.3 (May-June 1979): 60–65.

Zombies and the Living Dead: Folklore and Anthropology

Ackermann, Hans-W., and Jeanine Gauthier. "The Ways and Nature of the Zombi," *Journal of American Folklore* 104 (1991): 466–94. [This succinct article is the most complete overview of folkloric characterizations of zombies to date.]
Bourguignon, Erika. "The Persistence of Folk Belief: Some Notes on Cannibalism and Zombis in Haiti," *Journal of American Folklore* 72 (1959): 36–46.
Campbell, Joseph. *The Hero with a Thousand Faces* (1949). Princeton University Press, 1973.
Camporesi, Piero. *The Incorruptible Flesh: Bodily Mutation and Mortification in Religion and Folklore*, trans. Tania Croft-Murray. Cambridge: Cambridge University Press, 1988.
Courlander, Harold. *A Treasury of Afro-American Folklore* (1976). New York: Marlowe and Company, 1996.
Davis, Wade. *Passage of Darkness: The Ethnobiology of the Haitian Zombie*. Chapel Hill: University of North Carolina Press, 1988.
_____. *The Serpent and the Rainbow*. New York: Simon and Schuster, 1985.
Deren, Maya. *Divine Horsemen: Voodoo Gods of Haiti* (1953). New York: Chelsea House, 1970.
Dewisme, C.-H. *Les zombis, ou le secret des morts-vivants*. Bernard Grasset, ed. Paris: *Bilan de mystère* 2, 1957.
Finucane, Ronald. *Ghosts: Appearances of the Dead and Cultural Transformation*. Amherst, NY: Prometheus Books, 1996.
Frazer, Sir James G. *The Fear of the Dead in Primitive Religion* (London: Macmillan and Co., 1933, 1934, and 1936). Reprinted as 1 vol., New York: Arno Press, 1977.
Freud, Sigmund. *Totem and Taboo*, trans. A.A. Brill. New York: Vintage Books, 1918.
Hurston, Zora Neale. *Tell My Horse: Voodoo and Life in Haiti and Jamaica*. New York: Harper & Row, 1938.
Laroche, Maximilien. "The Myth of the Zombi," in Rowland Smith, ed.

Exile and Tradition: Studies in African and Caribbean Literature. New York: Africana Publishing Co. (Homes & Meier)/Dalhousie University Press, 1976.

Métraux, Alfred. *Le Vaudou haïtien.* Paris: Gallimard, 1958.

Parsons, Elsie C. *Folk-lore of the Antilles, French and English.* 3 vols. New York: American Folk-lore Society, 1933, 1936, and 1943.

_____. "Spirit Cult in Hayti," *Journal de la Société des Américanistes de Paris.* n.s. 20 (1928): 157–79.

Pradel, Jacques, and Jean-Yves Casgha. *Haïti: la république des morts vivants.* Monaco: Du Rocher, 1983.

Seabrook, William. *The Magic Island.* New York: Harcourt, Brace and Co., 1929.

Toynbee, Arnold, et al., eds. *Man's Concern with Death.* St. Louis, New York, and San Francisco: McGraw-Hill, 1968.

Index

A comme apocalypse see *A Virgin Among the Living Dead*
Abbes, Mathias 199
Abbott, Bruce 28, 139
Abrahams, Mort 177
Abril, Antón Garía 172
Absurd see *Zombie 6: Monster Hunter*
Acker, Cindie 201
Ackerman, Forrest J 127
Acomba, David 117
Acuff, Charis Kirkpatrick 65
Adams, Brooke 159
Adamson, Al 23, 24
After Death 12, **17**
Agar, John 89
Agrama, Frank 44
Agrasánchez, Rogelio 30, 112
Aguilar, Luz María 61
Ahn, Robert Yun Ju 26
Ahrenberg, Staffan 187
Akins, Claude 177
Alazraki, Benito 41, 88
Albertson, Jack 49
Albertson, Mitzi 169
Albrecht, J. Grant 182
Alcazar, Victor 176
Alchimede, Diego 36
Alexander, David 177
Alexander, Frank 105
Alexander, Terry 45
"Alice" 21
Alien 143
The Alien Dead 2, 11, **18**
Allen, Bob 138
Allen, Woody 119
Almost Human see *Shock Waves*
Alvarez, Auggi 201
Alves, Maria 57
Amati, Edmondo 103
Amato, Jody 200
American Graffiti 109
An American Werewolf in London 171
Ames, Michael 185
Among the Living Dead see *A Virgin Among the Living Dead*
Amplas, John 38, 45, 173
Ancira, Carlos 152
And You'll Live in Terror! The Beyond see *The Beyond*
Andersen, Susy 186
Anderson, Clyde *see* Fragasso, Claudio
Anderson, McKee 123
Anderson, Melody 49
Andreu, Simón 124
Andrews, Geno 76
Andrews, Tod 185
Angel Heart 182
Angell, Jerry 201, 202
Ankrum, Morris 211
Anouchka 207
Anthony, Carl 136
Anthropophagus II see *Zombie 6: Monster Hunter*
Antinori, Antonietta 29
Anton, Katja 30
Anzilotti, Cos 154
Apocalipsis canibal see *Night of the Zombies*
Arancio, Gilda 207
Archer, John 26, 96
Argento, Dario 57
Armstrong, Ron 70
Army of Darkness 102
Arnold, Alfonso 41
Arnold, Mike 61
Asali, Donna 138
Asbury, James 41
Ashbrook, Dana 144, 187
Ashley, Joel 211
Ashmun, Dale 210
Aspen, Giles 95
Astin, John 117
The Astro-Zombies 4, **19**, 216
El Ataque de los muertos sin ojos see *Return of the Evil Dead*
Atkins, Tom 66, 117
The Atomic Brain see *Monstrosity*
Attack of the Blind Dead see *Return of the Evil Dead*
Attack of the Eyeless Dead see *Return of the Evil Dead*
Audret, Caroline 128
Augesen, Roxanna 177
Aured, Carlos 81
Austin, Charles 173

Avati, Antonio 192
Avati, Pupi 192
The Awful Dr. Orloff 61
Azaria, Hank 58
The Aztec Mummy 5, 41

Backus, Richard 53
Badley, Linda 11, 140
Bagdad, William 19
Baily, Kirk 182
Baker, Herbert 154
Baker, Robert 161
Baker, Roy Ward 102
Balaban, Bob 114
Ball, David 76
Ballen, Ruth 31
Balme, Timothy 47
Balogh, Joe 57
Balsam, Talia 167
Bamber, Judy 111
Bancroft, Bradford 167
Band, Charles 116, 161
Bang, Joy 109
Barb, Beautiful 98
Barbeau, Adrienne 38, 66, 154
Barbetti, Cesare 192
Barbi, Vincent 19
Bark, Peter 29
Barkemeyer, Don 164
Barker, Clive 28, 145
Barnett, Laurel 31
Barnett, Vince 26
Baron Blood **21**
Barrett, Edith 91
Barrymore, John Drew 186
Barwood, Hal 186
Baskett, James 148
Baskin, William 211
Bastel, Vickie 177
Bartholomew, Sunny 70
"Batman" 130, 208
Baughn, Jeff 75
Bava, Lamberto 57
Bava, Mario 21
Baylis, W. (Bill) 205
Beard, Steve 11
Beatty, Diane 45
Beaudine, William 185
Bechina, Marty 41
Bechtel, Joan 54
Beck, Billy 85
Bécquer, Gustavo Adolfo 40
Belafonte-Harper, Shari 110
Belanti, Beth 209
Bell, James 91
Bell, Jasmina 108
Bellamy, Madge 190
Belle, Annie 198
Bender, Jack 110
Bendetti, Michael 116
Bennet, Spencer 209
Benson, William 141
Bérard, Yves 1, 11
Berdahl, Blaze 132
Bergamin, Deborah 193
Berger, Kasimir 198
Berger, Katya 198
Bergman, Mary Kay 154
Berman, Monty 161
Bernsen, Corbin 106
Bernt, Eric 111
Bersmea, Edowan 211
Bertrand, Rafael 162
Besne, García 153
Best, Willie 73
Bettoia, Franca 99
Beverly Hills Body-snatchers **21**
"Bewitched" 85
Bey, Marki 165
Beyer, Troy 188
The Beyond 11, **22**, 139, 195
Beyond the Living Dead see *Return of the Zombies*
Biallas, Christian 199
Bianchi, Andrea 29, 198
Bianchi, Guillermo 98
Billock, Rik 65
Biohazard see *Warning Sign*
Bippus, Stanna 209
The Birds 64
Bishop, Edward 141
Black, Gerry 140
Black, James, Jr. 203
Black, Louis 11
Black, Terry 51
Black Magic II see *Revenge of the Zombies* (1981)
Black Zombies see *Demoni* 3
Blair, Linda 33
The Blair Witch Project 129
Blake, Frank see Braña, Frank
Blanchard, Françoise 197
Blanco, Hugo 61
Bledsoe, Tempestt 115
Bleich, William 69, 110
The Blind Dead see *Tombs of the Blind Dead*
The Blob 118
Bloch, David 111
Bloch, Robert 50
Blondell, Joan 50
The Blood Baron see *Baron Blood*
Blood of Ghastly Horror **23**
Bloodeaters see *Toxic Zombies*
Bloodfeast of the Blind Dead see *Night of the Seagulls*
Bloodsuckers from Outer Space 8, 9, **25**
Bloodsucking Nazi Zombies see *Oasis of the Zombies*
Bloom, Jim 186
Blount, Lisa 49
Blue, Hedy 152
Blue Angel 30
Blue Demon 87, 98, 112, 152
Blum, Len 77
Blumenfeld, Alan 117
Bodkin, Tain 68
Bolkan, Edna 200
Bonacorsa, Francesca 208
Bonavia, Mike 18
Bond, Wells 82
The Boneyard **25**
Book of Enoch 72
Bookwalter, J.R. 52, 203
Booth, Adrian 174
Booth, Jim 47
Borchers, Donald P. 181
Borg, Veda Ann 148
Borge, Lic. 153
Borromel, Charles 198
Boss, Pete 11

Bostwick, Barry 188
Bosworth, Dewey 211
Bottin, Rob 66
Bowery at Midnight **26**
Bowser, Jeffrey 104
Boxleitner, Bruce 69
Bracula—The Terror of the Living Dead see *Return of the Zombies*
Bradford, Lane 213
Bradford, Thomas 116
Braindead see *Dead Alive*
Brald, Henry 180
Braña, Frank 141
Brandi, Walter 170
Brandner, Gary 69
Brandon, Philip 130
Brandt, Carolyn 86
Brannon, Fred C. 213
Bravman, Jack 208
Breakfast at the Manchester Morgue see *Let Sleeping Corpses Lie*
Bride of Re-Animator **28**
Brides of Dr. Jeckyll see *Dr. Orloff's Monster*
Briganti, Elisa Livia 81, 194
Bright, Matthew 161
Brissac, Virginia 73
Broadnax, David 206
Brodie, Steve 68
Brophy, Jed 47
Brophy, Richard 25
Brown, Judy 173
Brown, Louis 209
Brown, Wally 213, 214
Bruce, Jim 127
Bruns, Philip 144
Bryan, Peter 133
Bryce, Allan 1
"Bub" 18, 47
Buch, Fred 159
Buchanan, Morris 209
Buchanan, Sherry 60
Buenfil, Erika 200
Bulnes, Quintin 41, 162
El Buque maldito see *Horror of the Zombies*
Burial Ground 2, 7, **29**, 198
Burlington-Smith, Anthony 141
Burner, César 171
Burnett, Bill 115
Burns, George 114
Burns, Marilyn 147
Burr, Robert 116
Burroughs, Kimberleigh 155
Burton, LeVar 110, 167
Burton, Tracy 215
Bush, Peter 93
Butler, William 123
Byerly, Dave 209
Byrd, Eugene 115
Byron, Jean 89

La Cage aux Zombies **98**, 178
Cahn, Edward L. 37, 67, 89, 211
Calderón, Guillermo 41
Calderón, Pedro 41
Calfa, Don 34, 142, 157
Calman, Matilde 186
Campbell, Bruce 187
Campbell, Joseph 15
Campos, Rafael 19
Canalejas, José 141
Cannibal Virus see *Night of the Zombies*
Canovas, Anne 192
Cantafora, Antonio 21
Cantrell, Tom 206
Capetillo, Eduardo 200
Caporali, Roberto 29
Caputi, Jane 11
Carbone, Raymond 96
Cardan, Carlos 87
Cárdenas, Elsa 112, 153
Cardille, Lori 45
Cardona, Rene, Sr. 87
Cardos, John "Bud" 113
Carlen, Catherine 34
Carlin, Lynn 53
Carlson, Richard 73
Carney, Alan 213, 214
Carnival of Souls 69, 164
Carpenter, John 66
Carradine, John 19, 23, 68, 82, 89, 148, 160, 185
Carrere, Tia 208
Carrol, Regina 24
Carroll, Leo G. 177
Carson, John 133, 162
Cart, John 198
Carter, John N. 206
Cartwright, Nancy 58
Casey, C.W. 75
Castellaneta, Dan 58
El Castillo de las momias de Guanajuato see *Castle of the Mummies of Guanajuato*
Castle, William 157
Castle of the Mummies of Guanajuato **30**
Cat People 91
Caudle, K. Janyll 215
Caulfield, Maxwell 167
Cavanaugh, Paul 67
Cawthorn, Joseph 190
Cedar, Jon 147
Cemeterio del terror see *Zombie Apocalypse*
The Cemetery Man **30**
Chamber of Tortures see *Baron Blood*
Chan, Betty 211
Charendoff, Tara 154
Charles, Robert 185
Charteris, Leslie 161
Chase, David 196
Chelton, Tsilla 157
Chi, Shum Yan 97
Chiang, David 102
Chicago, Billy 116
The Child **31**
Children Shouldn't Play with Dead Things **32**, 53, 110, 160
The Chilling 11, **33**
Ching, William 154
Chirizzi, Gian Luigi 29
Chong, Billy 97
Chopper Chicks in Zombietown 9, **34**
Christina chez les morts vivants see *A Virgin Among the Living Dead*
Christina, Princess of Eroticism see *A Virgin Among the Living Dead*
Christina, princesse de l'érotisme see *A Virgin Among the Living Dead*

Christina, Sex Princess see *A Virgin Among the Living Dead*
Christopher, Robert 68
Cicchetti, Tony 127
Ciges, Luis 176
Cinque tombe per un medium see *Terror Creatures from the Grave*
Citizen Kane 97
City of the Dead see *The Gates of Hell*
City of the Living Dead see *The Gates of Hell*
City of the Walking Dead 7, **36**, 57
Clare, Diane 133
Clark, Benjamin 32
Clark, Bob 32, 53
Clarke, J.R. 98
Clarke, Marilyn 79
Clarke, Mindy 145
Clarke, Robert 68
The Class of Nuke 'Em High 141
Clavel, Aurora 61
Clay, Philippe 157
Claybourne, Doug 155
Clayton, Xernona 83
Clement, Marc 113
Cleveland, George 150
Cliver, Al 194
Coburn, Glen 25
Coch, Gary 32
Coe, Jennifer 76
Coen, Guido 191
Coffey, T. Scott 204
Coffin, Tristram 37
Cohen, Emma 40, 81
Cohen, Rob 10
Cole, Alexandra 60
Cole, Rosalie 31
Cole, Royal K. 174
Collatina, Silvia 82
Colley, Don Pedro 165
Collins, Alan 21, 193
Collins, Joan 168
Colman, Henry 50
Colombo, Enrico 146
Combs, Jeffrey 28, 139
Comer, Anjenette 116
Conroy, Jarlath 45
Conté, María Pía 146
Conte, Steve 169
Contello, Ellena 18
Continenza, Sandro 103
Conway, Tom 91
Cook, Elisha 183
Cook, Elisha, Jr. 109
Cooper, Stanley *see* Rosi, Stelvio
Cordero, Joaquín 61
Corey, Wendell 19
Corman, Leonard 138
The Corpse Vanished see *Revenge of the Zombies* (1943)
Corsi, Tilde 30
Cortés, Juan 171
Corti, Antonio 36
Cortona, Sergio 125
"The Cosby Show" 115
Coscia, Marcello 103
Costanzo, Maurizio 192
Coster, Candy 107
Cotten, Joseph 21
Coulouris, George 191
Court, Hazel 59
Couyoumdijan, Gianfranco 60
Cox, Richard 204
Coy, Walter 83
Crabbe, Buster 18
Craig, Charles 121
Crampton, Barbara 139
Craven, Wes 55, 155
Creature with the Atom Brain 6, **37**
Creeps see *Night of the Creeps*
Creepshow 2, **38**
Crevenna, Alfredo B. 153
Crime of Voodoo see *Ouanga*
Los Crímines de Usher see *Zombie 5: Revenge in the House of Usher*
Crisanti, Gabriele 29
Cristal, Linda 50
Cristal, Pearl 61
Criswell 136
Critchlow, Keith 117
Cronenberg, David 13
Cronin, Paul 32
Crosby, Denise 132
Cross, Henry 63
The Cross of the Devil 2, **40**, 172
Crowe, Rick 94
Cruz, Alejandro *see* Blue Demon
La Cruz del diablo see *The Cross of the Devil*
Crypt of the Blind Dead see *Tombs of the Blind Dead*
Cully, Zara 165
Cult of the Damned see *The Snake People*
Cummins, James 25
Cummins, Leslie 138
Cunilles, J.M. 125
Cunningham, Sean S. 114
Curcio, E.J. 76
Curiel, Federico 112
Curran, Petrea 78
Currie, Louise 185
Curse of the Blue Lights 10, **41**
The Curse of the Doll People **41**
Curtis, Jamie Lee 66, 67
Curtis, Sonia 57
Cushing, Peter 7, 78, 102, 159, 168

Dadashian, Robert 31
Daggett, Dwen 202
Dai, Kei 106
Daily, Elizabeth 129
Daly, Candice 17
Daly, Jane 32, 53
D'Amario, Stefania 194
Damato, A.J. 161
D'Amato, Joe *see* Massaccesi, Aristide
Danby, Ian 198
Danieli, Emma 99
Daniell, Henry 67
Daniels, David Mason 129
Dano, Royal 109
Danson, Ted 38
D'Arcy, Roy 150
Dardick, Ruth 63
Dark Eyes of the Zombie see *Raptors*
Darrow, Oliver 169
Davidson, Jack 159
Davidson, Robin 164

Davidson, Ronald 213
Davis, Karl 211
Davis, Wade 3, 155, 157
Davison, Alex 134
Dawn, Vincent *see* Mattei, Bruno
Dawn of the Dead 7, 8, 9, 11, **42**, 46, 52, 118, 123, 188, 193, 195, 197, 198, 209
Dawn of the Living Dead see *Dawn of the Dead*
Dawn of the Mummy **44**
Day, Vera 191
Day of the Dead 6, 9, 11, 18, 28, **45**, 52, 90, 123, 138, 209
Dead Alive 10, **47**
Dead and Buried **49**
The Dead Don't Die **50**, 197
Dead Heat **51**
The Dead Next Door 11, **52**, 202
Dead of Night **53**, 160
Dead People see *Messiah of Evil*
The Dead Pit 10, **54**
The Dead That Walk see *Zombies of Mora-Tau*
Deadly Friend 10, 55, 93
De Angelis, Fabrizio 22, 60, 81, 194
Deans, Darla 141
Death Corps see *Shock Waves*
Deathdream see *Dead of Night*
De Blas, Manuel 80
De Castro, J.L. Bermúdez 80
De Cordoba, Pedro 73
Dee, Frances 91
Deezen, Eddie 169
De Haven, Lisa 141
Dekker, Fred 117
Del Campo, César 153
DeLeon, Walter 73, 154
Delgado, José Luis 36
Della morte, del'amore see *The Cemetery Man*
Delli Colli, Alexandra 60
Delman, Jeffrey 182
Del Pozo, Angel 78
DeLuise, Peter 110
De Martino, Ferruccio 186
DeMejo, Carlo 72
De Mendoza, Alberto 78
DeMolay, Karl 210
Demon Wind 14
Demoni 14, 57
Demoni 3 4, **56**
Demons '95 see *The Cemetery Man*
De Munn, Jeffrey 186
De Nava, Giovanni 82
Denning, Richard 37
Dennis, John 71
DeNoble, Alphonse 70
De Ossorio, Amando 7, 40, 80, 102, 108, 123, 124, 141, 146, 171
Depp, Johnny 137
Depuay, Theo 75
Deren, Maya 3
De Rieux, Jack A. 33
De Rita, Massimo 186
Derleth, August 85
De Rossi, Giannetto 29
Des Barres, Michael 187
El Desierto de los zombies see *Oasis of the Zombies*
Deveau, Robert 138
DeVencenty, Deborah 41
Devenie, Stuart 47
Dever, Janice 26
Diabolical Dr. Voodoo see *The Incredibly Strange Creatures Who Stopped Living and Became Mixed-Up Zombies*
"Dial 'Z' for Zombies" **58**
Di Cicco, Bobby 167
"The Dick Van Dyke Show" 177
Dickey, Paul 73
Dierkop, Charles 109
Dietlein, Marsha 144
Dietz, Frank 208
Dietz, Jack 26, 185
DiLeo, Antone 45
Diller, Phyllis 26
Dillman, Dean, Jr. 111
DiMuccio, Brian 181
Dishy, Bob 114
Dixon, Glenn 183
Dixon, Ken 215
Dobrin, Ronald 44
Doctor Blood's Coffin 5, **59**
Dr. Butcher, M.D. **60**, 125
Dr. Jeckyll's Mistress see *Dr. Orloff's Monster*
Dr. Orloff's Monster 6, **61**
Dr. Satan vs. Black Magic **61**, 153
El Dr. Satán y la magia negra see *Dr. Satan vs. Black Magic*
Doi, Davis 154
Dolenz, George 154
Dollar-Smith, Cindy 26
Domergue, Faith 82
Donahue, Troy 33
Donati, Donatella 198
Donelson, Nancy 94
Don't Go in the House **63**
Don't Open the Window see *Let Sleeping Corpses Lie*
Dooley, Paul 114
Doria, Daniela 72
Doro, Mino 186
Douglas, Gordon 213
Douglas, Jerry 50
Douglas, Sarah 145, 182
Dow, Barbara 127
Doyle, Tim 204
Dracula and the Seven Golden Vampires see *The Legend of the Seven Golden Vampires*
Dracula 2
"Dragnet" 94
Druddi, Rossella 17
Drums of the Jungle see *Ouanga*
Duggan, Andrew 68

Dullaghan, John 71
Dunlay, Frank 201
Dunsky, Evan 182
Durand, Jean 83
D'Usseau, Arnaud 78
Duvall, Rocky 177
Dysart, Richard 186

...E tu vivrai nel terrore! L'aldilà see *The Beyond*
The Earth Dies Screaming **63**, 64
East, Carlos 162
Eastman, George 64, 198
Eastman, Marilyn 121
Eastman, Rodney 21
Easton, Sid 130
Eaton, Marjorie 111, 211
Eaton, Premika 101
Eberheardt, Thom 13, 164
Ebert, Roger 6
Ecclesiastes 14
Ed Wood 137
Edmond, J. Trevor 145
Edwards, Joel J. 181
Effner, Ryan 101
Egan, Aeryk 161
Ege, Julie 102
"Eight Is Enough" 110
Eilbacher, Cindy 157
Elena, Marian 171
Elfman, Richard 161
Ellis, Laura 25
Ellison, James 91
Ellison, Joseph 63
Elsey, Amon 105
Emge, David 42
Engstrom, Jean 183
Enyo, Erina 86
Eram, Rene 181
Erotic Nights of the Living Dead 2, **64**
Erzule 83
Escaño, Mabel 107
Escape from New York 106
Escourrou, Pierre 207
El Espanto surge de la tumba see *Horror Rises from the Tomb*
Esteban, Julian 207
Estrada, Blanca 80
Eustermann, James 25
Evans, Mike 83
Evans, Robin 129
Everett, Gimel 54
Everett, Rupert 30
Evil Dead 14, 48, 52
Ewing, Floyd, Jr. 52
The Exorcist 34

Faber, Robert 213
Faiad, Zulma 30
Faison, Earl 196
Faison, Ellene 45
Fajaro, Eduardo 40
Falchi, Anna 30
The Fall of the House of Usher see *Zombie 5: Revenge of the House of Usher*
Farentino, James 49
Farrow, Tisa 194
Fasano, John 208
Fauna, Flora 158
Fear 216
The Fear see *The Gates of Hell*
Fear in the City of the Living Dead see *The Gates of Hell*
Fear of the Dead 12
Feig, Paul 204
Feldman, Corey 181
Fell, Norman 25
Felt, Asbestos 96
Fenn, Sherilynn 204
Fentress, Robert 49
Ferrer, Mel 36
Ferrigno, Lou 208
Ferrin, Doug 69
Ferry, Peter 52
Field, Virginia 63
The Fiend with the Atomic Brain see *Blood of Ghastly Horror*
The Fiend with the Electronic Brain 24
The Fiend with the Synthetic Brain see *Blood of Ghastly Horror*
The Fiends 91
Fierberg, Steven 182
Fin de semana para los muertos see *Let Sleeping Corpses Lie*
Finneran, Kate 123
Fischer, Gena 202
Fisher, Allan 208
Fisher, Terence 63
Flagg, Cash *see* Steckler, Ray Dennis
Flanagan, John 33
Fleming, Brandon 191
Fleming, Lone 141, 171
Flesheater **65**, 121
Florey, Robert 85
Floria, Holly 116
Flothow, Rudolph 209
The Fog 2, **66**
Folsey, George, Jr. 171
Fonoll, Luis 126
Forbes-Robertson, John 102
Ford, Anitra 109
Ford, Philip 174
Foree, Ken 42
Foreman, Deborah 187
Formica, Fabiana 30
Forsythe, Henderson 53
Forte, Fabian 147
Forte, Vincent 21
Foster, Meg 161
Foster, Robert 107, 207
Foster, Steffen Gregory 54
The Four Skulls of Jonathan Drake **67**, 192
Fowler, Frank 111
Fowler, George 59
Fox, Matthew 114
Fox, Tom 142, 144
Fox, Wallace 26
Foxx, Kim 201
Fragasso, Claudio 17, 125, 193
Francis, Freddie 168
Francks, Don 77
Franco, Jesús 61, 107, 126, 128, 180, 197, 198
Frank, A.M. *see* Franco, Jesús; Lesoeur, Daniel
Frank, Diana 111
Frank, Nick 61
Frank, Will 210
Frankenstein 2, 55
Frankenstein Island **68**, 170

Franz, Eduard 67
Frazer, Sir James 12
Frederick, Vicki 34
French, Valerie 67
French, Victor 83
Frezza, Giovanni 82
Friday the 13th 114, 200
Fritzell, Kent 41
Frizzi, Fabio 22
From the Dead of Night **69**
Frost, Lee 71
Frost, Lindsay 51
Frozen Scream **69**
Fry, Rick 28
Frye, William 85
Fuhrer, David 111
Fulci, Lucio 8, 22, 23, 29, 43, 60, 72, 81, 126, 193, 194, 198
Fuller, Loreli 210
Funari, Dirce 64
Furie, Sidney J. 59
Furio, Sonia 61

Gaines, Jim 17
Galbo, Christine 103
Gale, David 28, 140
Gale, Ed 34
Galindo, Raúl 200
Galindo, Rubén, Jr. 200
Gallardo, Juan 112
Galli, Ida 186
Galligan, Zach 187
Gálvez, Guillermo 153
Gamma 693 2, **70**
Garden of the Dead **71**
Garfield, Frank see Giraldi, Franco
Garfinkel, Philip 173
Gargiulo, Giuseppe 56
Garlington, Rick 25
Garrett, Louis 209
Garrone, Riccardo 170
The Gates of Hell 8, 22, **72**, 195
Gathright, Lin 138
Gay, Auretta 194
Gay, Gregory 37
Gay, Ramón 41
Geary, Anthony 117
Geer, Leonard 211
Gelin, Manuel 128
Gemser, Laura 64
Gentile, Denise 116
George, Christopher 72
Gershon, Gina 182
Gerstle, Frank 111
Getz, Geha 54
Ghazal, Aziz 204
The Ghost Breakers **73**, 96, 154, 214
Ghost Brigade see *The Lost Brigade*
The Ghost Galleon see *Horror of the Zombies*
Ghost Ship of the Blind Dead see *Horror of the Zombies*
Gibson, Rhonda 12
Giglio, Laura 205
Gilbert, Jo 209
Gillen, Jeffrey 32
Gillick, John 94
"Gilligan's Island" 20
Gilling, John 40, 41, 133
Gillis, Jamie 70
Giner, José Antonio Pérez 124, 171, 176
Ginsberg, Maury 182
Ginseng King 2, **75**
Giordano, Maria Angela 29
Giraldi, Franco 126
Gires, Pierre 1
Girolami, Marino 60
Girotti, Massimo 21
Gladsjo, Eric 98
Gochnauer, Danny 54
Goddard, Charles 73
Goddard, Paulette 73
Godsell, Vanda 63
Godunov, Alexander 187
Gohar, Ali 45
Goldberg, Dan 77
Goldberg, Sheila 138
Goldblatt, Mark 51
Golladay, Becky 41
González, Rogelio A. 61
Gordon, Bernard 78, 211
Gordon, Charles 117
Gordon, Christine 91
Gordon, Stuart 28, 139
The Gore-met Zombie Chef from Hell **75**
Gorshin, Frank 21
Gowen, Thomas 70
Graham, Ranald 157
Graham, Roger 52
Granger, Michael 37
Grant, Angie 168
The Grapes of Death 13
Grasshoff, Alex 196
Grau, Jorge 103
Grave Misdemeanors see *Night Life*
The Grave of the Living Dead see *Oasis of the Zombies*
Grazián, Albino 107–108
Grease 110
Greenberg, Matt 106
Greene, Richard 168
Greenquist, Brad 132
Greer, Michael 109
Gregg, Joyce 191
Grey, Samantha 70
Grey Knight see *The Lost Brigade*
Griffin, Claire 95
Grimaldi, Dan 63
Grimes, Scott 117
Grisé, Pierre 208
"Grizzly Adams" 34
Groening, Matt 58
Gross, Jerry 84
Grossi, Michael 52
Guffey, Cary 113
Gulager, Clu 142
Gwynne, Fred 132

Hadji-Lazaro, Francois 30
Hadley, Diane 177
Haggerty, Dan 33
Haines, Sean 111
Hale, Richard 85
Halevy, Julian 78
Hall, Ellen 185
Hall, Henry 185
Hall, Jon 209
Hall, Laurence 94
Hall, Willard 41
Halliwell, Leslie 1, 5
Halloween 66, 200
Halloween III: Season of the Witch 94
Halperin, Edward 2, 150, 190
Halperin, Victor 2, 150, 190

Halpin, Luke 160
Hamill, Mark 154
Hamilton, George 50
Hammill, Ellen 63
Hammond, Celeste 69
Hammond, Marcus 134
Hampton, Orville H. 67
The Hanging Woman see *Return of the Zombies*
Hanlon, Kevin 173
Hanners, Richard 31
Hansa, Kali 124
Hard Rock Zombies 2, 8, 9, **76**
Hardman, Karl 121
Hare, Lumsden 67
Harmon, Renee 69
Harper, Steve 115
Harras, Patricia 104
Harrington, Curtis 50
Harris, Chris 201
Harris, Ed 38
Harris, Julie 161
Harris, Katie 120
Harris, Teresa 91
Harris, Winifred 130
Harrison, John 159
Harrison, Paul 82
Hartham, Thomas 211
Harvey, Randall 104
Hauser, Jeanette 210
Hauser, Wings 113
Hawes, Michael 129
Hawk, Jay 169
Hayase, Heiko 106
Hayes, Allison 211
Hayes, John 71
Headley, Mark 127
Heaven Can Wait 115
Heavy Metal **77**
Helfend, Dennis 173
Hell of the Living Dead see *Night of the Zombies*
Hell of the Living Death see *Night of the Zombies*
Hellbound 54, 78
Hellgate **78**
Hellraiser 78
Helpern, David 51
Hendry, Ian 168
Henstell, Diana 55
Herbst, Becky 161
Herminghausen, Steve 120
Hess, Ralf 199
Heston, Charleton 99
Hewitt, Heather 83
Hickenlooper, George 106
Hickox, Anthony 187
Higashi, Sumiko 11
Higgins, Howard 150
Highsmith, William 75
Hilbeck, Fernando 103
Hill, Debra 66
Hill, Jack 162
Hill, Mariana 109
Hilliard, Richard 79
Hilliard, Ryan 70
Hinz, Wolfgang 199
Hinzman, Bill 65, 121, 122
Hirsh, Richard 93
Hitchcock, Alfred 121
Ho, Benny 211
Ho, Godfrey 211
Hoberman, J. 11
Hodgins, Earle 174
Holbrook, Hal 38, 66
Holdren, Judd 213
Holub, Diane Clayre 206
Homecoming Night see *Night of the Creeps*
Hong, James 180
Honthaner, Ron 83
Hoover, Jospeh 19
Hope, Anna 26
Hope, Bob 73
Hopkins, Bo 113
Hopton, Russell 214
Horn, Erica 104
Hornblow, Arthur, Jr. 73
Horror Express **78**
The Horror of Party Beach 4, **79**
Horror of the Zombies **80**, 142, 172
Horror Rises from the Tomb **81**
Hoskins, Dan 34
Hotton, Donald 129
Houghton, Don 102
The House by the Cemetery **81**
The House of Seven Corpses **82**
House of Terror see *Return of the Zombies*
The House on Skull Mountain **83**
The House Outside the Cemetery see *The House by the Cemetery*
Housely, James 141
Houseman, John 66
Houtman, Patrick 200
Howes, Basil 85
Huerta, Rudolfo *see* El Santo
Hughes, Kelly 98
Hughes, Miko 132
Hugo, Mauritz 148
Hui-Ju, Liu 149
El Hundimiento de la Casa Usher see *Zombie 5: Revenge of the House of Usher*
Hung, Hwa I 97
Hunter, Henry 85
Hunter, Ian 59
Hurst, Brandon 190
Hutton, Robert 89
Huyck, Willard 109

I Am Legend 99
I Drink Your Blood 84
I Eat Your Skin **83**
I Walked with a Zombie 3, 10, **91**, 185, 215
I Was a Teenage Zombie 9, 10, 12, **93**, 145
I Was a Zombie for the F.B.I. **94**
I, Zombie: The Chronicles of Pain **95**
Iandoli, Dean 111
Ibáñez, Juan 162
"The Incredible Doktor Markesan" 5, **85**
"The Incredible Hulk" 208
Incredibly Mixed-Up Zombie see *The Incredibly Strange Creatures Who Stopped Living and Became Mixed-Up Zombies*

The Incredibly Strange Creatures Who Stopped Living and Became Mixed-Up Zombies 4, **86**, 111
Incubo sulla città contaminata see *City of the Walking Dead*
Inferno dei morti viventi see *Night of the Zombies*
Ingles, Rufino 171
Ingster, Boris 177
Innes, Scott 154
Interlenghi, Antonella 72
Invaders from Mars 14, 38
La Invasión de los muertos see *Invasion of the Dead*
La Invasión de los zombies atómicos see *City of the Walking Dead*
Invasion of the Atomic Zombies see *City of the Walking Dead*
Invasion of the Body Snatchers 14, 38, 94
Invasion of the Dead **87**
Invasion of the Zombies **88**
The Invisible Dead 216
Invisible Invaders 4, 64, **89**, 101
The Invisible Man 2
Ireland, John 82
Isbell, Anthony 94
La Isla de los muertos see *The Snake People*
The Island of the Last Zombies see *Dr. Butcher, M.D.*
Island of the Living Dead see *Zombie*
Island of the Snake People see *The Snake People*
Island of the Zombies see *Erotic Nights of the Living Dead*
Isle of the Snake People see *The Snake People*
It Fell From the Sky see *The Alien Dead*
Itchy Kitchen 9
Izay, Victor 19

J'Accuse! 14
Jack, Wolfman 110
Jackson, Michael 8, 110, 171, 177
Jackson, Peter 10, 47
Jackson, Thomas 174
Jackunas, Jolie 52
Jacobs, Michael 33
Jacoby, Scott 167
Jaffe, Seth 21
Jagger, Dean 150
James, Julie 123
James, Lee 70
James, Steve 188
Jane Eyre 91
Janson, Frank 31
Jarosz, Ken 203
Jasmer, Brent 104
Jaws 207
Jeffreys, Anne 214
Jenks, Frank 214
Jennings, Brent 155
Jenrette, Rita 206
Johann, Zita 138
Johnson, Daniel "smalls" 158
Johnson, John Henry 41
Johnson, Kurt 164
Johnson, Larry D. 165
Johnson, Michelle 187
Johnson, Noble 73, 74, 154
Johnson, Richard 194
Johnson, Tor 136
Jones, Claude Earl 28
Jones, Darby 91, 214
Jones, Duane 121
Jones, Gerty 153
Jones, John 71
Jones, Michael 113
Jones, Prince 104
Jordan, France 128
Joseph, Adrianne 17
Joyce, Babe
Joyce, William 83
Julissa 162
Julius, Bettina 41
Juran, Jerry 59

Kagan, Larry 101
Kalinowski, John 200
Kallianiotes, Helena 157
Kaltreider, Sallie Middleton 26
Kantos, Igo 113
Kaplan, Mamie 108
Karay, Selan 126
Karen, James 142, 144
Karlatos, Olga 194
Karloff, Boris 5, 85, 162, 183
Katch, Kurt 209
Katz, Gloria 109
Katzman, Sam 26, 185, 211
Kaurismäki, Mika 199
Kavner, Julie 58
Kayser, Allan 117
Kearney, Carolyn 85
Keene, Tom 136
Kehr, Erin 209
Keim, Krista 101
Keith, Ian 174
Keith, Woody 28
Keller, Patrick 41
Keller, Sarah 22
Kelly, James 59
Kelly, Lew 26
Kelly, Thomas J. 82
Kelly, Tim 165
Kelsey, George 18
Kelso, Edmond 96, 148
Kemp, Martin 187
Kemper, Michael 203
Kendall, Brenda 47
Kendall, Tony *see* Stella, Luciano
Kennedy, Arthur 103
Kennedy, Hal 104
Kennis, Dan Q. 138
Kent, Peter 140
Kent, Robert E. 67, 89
Kenworthy, Michael 144
Kera 106
Kerl, Matthias 199
Kerut, Peter 180
Khan, Ibrahim 44
Khunne, D. 107
Kiekens, Rose 180
Kill and Go Hide see *The Child*
Killing Birds see *Raptors*
The Killing Box see *The Lost Brigade*
Killing Spree **96**

Killough, Jon 52
Kimble, Lawrence 213
King, Atlas 86
King, Bárbara 124
King, Brenda 44
King, Stephen 38, 132
King of the Zombies 2, **96**, 148
Kinmont, Kathleen 28
Kirby, Pierre 211
Kirk, Tommy 24
Kirkconnell, Clare 51
Kiser, Terry 188
Kiss Daddy Goodbye see *Revenge of the Zombie*
Klane, Robert 188
Klar, G. Howard 45
Klimovsky, Leon 176
Klisser, Evan 78
Knox, Mickey 30
Koch, Howard 183
Kochansky, Hanja 198
Kocol, Lynne 70
Kokai, Robert 52
"Kolchak: The Night Stalker" 196, 197
Komizu, (Gaira) Kazuo 106
Kondo, Douglas 180
Kosti, María 123, 124, 176
Kotto, Yaphet 186
Krause, Tina 205
Krevoy, Brad 106
Kruize, John 113
Kulis, Juni 70
Kung Fu Zombie **97**
Kunicki, Kelley 75
Kuter, Kay 204

La Cage aux Zombies **98**, 178
Laborteaux, Matthew 55
Le Labyrinthe see *A Virgin Among the Living Dead*
Le Lac des morts vivants see *Zombie Lake*
LaCouter, Jacques 68
Ladd, David 155
El Lago de los muertos vivientes see *Zombie Lake*
Lai, Joseph 211
The Lake of the Living Dead see *Zombie Lake*
L'aldilà see *The Beyond*
Lambert, Henry 128
Lambert, Jack 154
Lambert, Mary 132
The Land of the Dead 88, **98**
Landau, Richard 183
Landis, John 171
Landson, Myriam 128
Lang, Lisa 111
Langsdon, Roy 111
Larkey, Caren 164
Laser, J.A. *see* Rollin, Jean
Lassander, Dagmar 82
The Last Man on Earth 5, 64, **99**
Latt, Rachel 127
Lattanzi, Claudio 138
Lau, Chan 97
The Laughing Dead **101**
Launer, S. John 37
Laurel, Allan 79
Lavia, Gabriele 192
The Lawnmower Man 54
Lawson, Cheryl 54, 180
Lawson, Richard 165
Lazar, Veronica 22
LeBorg, Reginald 183
LeCotier, Jacques 169
Lee, Charles *see* Ho, Godfrey
Lee, Christopher 7, 78
Lee, Joanna 136
Lee, Jonna 110
The Legend of the Seven Golden Vampires **102**
Leicester, William 99
Leigh, Janet 66
Leinonen, Marjo 199
Lemos, Carlos 80
Lenzi, Umberto 36, 56
León, Carlos 98
León, Eva 107
Leonard, Brett 54
Leonard, Sheldon 130, 214
Leone, Alfred 21
Leopold, Glenn 154
Lercara, Courtney 96
Lesoeur, Daniel 129, 197, 207
Let Sleeping Corpses Lie **103**
Letts, Dennis 25
Levey, William A. 78
Levy, Joan 44
Levy, Shawn 208
Lewis, Herschell Gordon 6
Lewis, Janelle 215
Lewis, Jerry 73, 154
Lewis, Linda 18
Lewis, Paul 82
Lewis, Sybil 148
Lewnes, Pericles 141
Lewton, Val 91
Li, Lily 149
Libert, Ann 180
Liberty, Richard 45
Liebman, Wayne 70
Lieh, Lo 149
Lifante, José Ruiz 103
Lik, Pak Sha 97
Limera, Verónica 171
Lind, Robert 111
Lind, Traci 114
Linder, Christa 87
Lindfors, Viveca 38
Liné, Helga 78, 81
Link, Ron 204
Linnea Quigley's Horror Work-Out **104**
Linton, Betty Hyatt 83
Lippert, Robert 63, 99
Lippincott, Charles 117
Lively, Jason 117
Living a Zombie Dream **105**
Living Dead at the Manchester Morgue see *Let Sleeping Corpses Lie*
Living Dead in Tokyo Bay **106**
Livingston, Robert 174
Lloyd, Rollo 150
Loggia, Kristina 34
Loi, Marina 193
London, Rose 1
Long, Patrick 61
Longo, Sal 205
Loonies on Broadway see *Zombies on Broadway*

López, Alberto 88
Lorey, Dean 114
The Lost Brigade **106**
Love, William 98
The Love Wanga see *Ouanga*
Lovecraft, H.P. 140
Lovelock, Ray 103
Lowe, Sherman L. 174
Lowery, Andrew 114
Lowery, Marcella 115
Lowery, Robert 148
Lowry, Ed 11
Lucas, Ralph 31
Lugosi, Bela 2, 26, 76, 136, 150, 175, 185, 190, 198, 213, 214
Lukas, Paul 73
Lyddon, Mike 210
Lyon, Alice 79

Macaulay, Charles 82
MacColl, Katherine 22, 72, 81
MacGreevy, Oliver 168
Mackler, Steven 182
Macnee, Patrick 187
Madame Sul-Te-Wan *see* Sul-Te-Wan
Madden, Cassie 93
Madsen, Virginia 204
Maggiore, Sal, Jr. 138
The Magic Island 2
Malco, Paolo 81
Malone, Dorothy 154
Mamches, Valerie 32
"The Man from U.N.C.L.E." 177
The Man with the Synthetic Brain see *Blood of Ghastly Horror*
Manard, Bill 157
Manlove, Dudley 136
Mann, Sam 76
Manni, Ettore 186
La Mansión de los muertos vivientes see *Mansion of the Living Dead*
Mansion of the Living Dead 2, **107**, 172
Manz, Mick 76
Manzetti, Cervando 200
Maravidi, Mirella 170
Marceau, Marcel 157
Marcus, Raymond T. 211
Marcus, Richard 55
Mariaux, A.L. 128, 207
Marion, Paul 154
Marko, Zekial 196
Markovic, Maria 52
Marley, John 53
Marluzzo, Giorgio 22, 81
Marriott, David 111
Marshall, Betty 98
Marshall, E.G. 38
Marshall, George 73, 154
Marshall, Steve 117
Marsillac, Adolfo 40
Martin, Dean 73, 154
Martin, Eugenio 78
Martin, Frank *see* Girolami, Marino
Martin, James 93
Martínez, Jesús Sotomayor 98, 152
Martino, Chris 23
Matheson, Richard 99
Mascelli, Joseph 111
Masciarelli, Stefano 30
Masefield, Joseph 63
"MASH" 20
Maslansky, Paul 165
Mason, LeRoy 174
Mason, Lowell 119
Massaccesi, Aristide 64, 198
Massini, Giovanni 72
Mastroianni, Armand 167
Mathews, Thom 142, 144
Mato, Oliver 197
Mattei, Bruno 125, 193
Mattioli, Simone 29
Maxford, Howard 1
Maxwell, Richard 155
Mazes, Michael 53
Mazur, Heather 123
McBride, Alex 17, 193
McCallum, David 177
McCarthy, Andrew 188
McCarthy, Kevin 110
McCaw, Clayton 41
McClelland, Sam Davis 177
McCollum, Barry 148
McConnell, Steve 201
McCord, Kent 145
McCoy, Steve 93
McCrae, Scooter 158
McCrann, Charles 173
McCulloch, Ian 60, 194
McEachin, James 50
McEwen, Hamish 208
McGavin, Darren 51, 196
McGowan, Dorrell 174
McGowan, Stuart 174
McGrath, Dan 58
McGuire, Bryan Michael 182
McKay, Wanda 26, 185
McKenzie, Heather Jean 104
McKenzie, Mary J. Todd 83
McKinnon, Mona 136
McLorin, Robin 170
McLoud, Duncan 71
McLoughlin, Thomas 129
McMillian, Ian 206
McPherson, Heather 127
McSweeney, Kathleen 202
Medford, Jody 113
Meeker, Ralph 50
Melendez, Ron 181
Meltzer, Michael 51
Mendelson, Braddon 127
Mendez, Luis 36
Meng-Hua, Ho 149
Merino, José Luis 146
Merle, Frank 170
Merritt, Theresa 182
Messiah of Evil **109**
Mestre, Jeannine 103
Metrano, Art 21
Metz, Cathy 201
Meyers, Thom 25
Michalakis, John Elias 93
Michelle, Janee 83
Midkiff, Dale 132
The Midnight Hour **110**
Mikels, Ted 19, 20
Mil Máscaras 112
Millan, Al 177

Milland, Ray 50
Miller, Dave 202
Miller, Marvin 147
Miller, Mirta 176
Miller, Peter 59
Milliken, Claude *see* Lattanzi, Claudio
Milton, H.A. 71
Minervini, Gianni 192
Ming, Pal 97
Miranda, Carmen 154
Miranda, Vincent 96
Misch, David 115
Mistresses of Dr. Jeckyll see *Dr. Orloff's Monster*
Mitchell, Cameron 68
Mok, Harry 180
Mokae, Zakes 155
Molina, Jacinto 7, 40, 81, 146, 176
Las Momias de Guanajuato see *The Mummies of Guanajuato*
Mondo 157
"The Monkey's Paw" 53, 132, 168
Monster High **111**
Monster Hunter see *Zombie 6: Monster Hunter*
Monsters 115
Monstrosity **111**
Montefiore, Luigi *see* Eastman, George
Montenegro, Sasha 153
Montes, Yolanda 162
Montgomery, Jeff 128
Montgomery, Lee 110, 113
Montgomery, Ray 209
Monty, Mike 193
Moody, Elizabeth 47
Moon, Kwon Young 97
Moore, Duke 136
Moore, Eulabelle 79
Moore, Kieron 59
Moore, Roger 161
Moreland, Mantan 96, 148
Morell, Andre 133
Moreno, Luis Laso 124
Morgan, Read 157
Morghen, John 72
Morrison, Bill 52, 203
Morrison, J.L.D. 169
Morton, Roy 24
Mosley, Bill 123
Mostow, Jon 21
Mowood, John 65
Mozarowsky, Sandra 123
La Muerte viviente see *The Snake People*
Muller, Paul 180
The Mummies of Guanajuato 88, **112**
The Mummy 2
The Mummy's Hand 24
El Mundo de los muertos see *The Land of the Dead*
Muñecos infernales see *The Curse of the Doll People*
Murayama, Noe 61
Murphy, Brianne 169
Murphy, Dawn 205
Murphy, Michael S. 167
Murray, Barbara 168
Murray, K. Gordon 41, 42
Murray, Philip 57
Muser, Wolf 70
Mutant **113**
My Boyfriend's Back 10, 12, 93, **114**, 145
"My Zombie Lover" 10, 114, 115, 145
Myers, Michael 198
Myers, Paulene 196

Nadeau, Diana 181
Naff, Lycia 34
Nagle, Kevin 93
Nakashima, Lex 101
Nalder, Reggie 50
Nance, Jack 182
Napoles, Peter 127
Naschy, Paul *see* Molina, Jacinto
Nathan, Robert 170
Nation, Terry 161
Neal, Tom 26
Nelson, Ed 25
Nelson-Keys, Anthony 133
Netherworld **116**
Neurosis see *Zombie 5: Revenge of the House of Usher*
Nevrose see *Zombie 5: Revenge of the House of Usher*
Newell, Stephen R. 120
Newman, Charles 213
Newman, Melissa 129
Newman, Samuel 89
Newton, Cyndi 104
Newton, Margit Evelyn 125
Newton, Peter *see* Massaccesi, Aristide
Nice, Sidney 205
Nicholas, Martin Alan 18
Nichols, Britt 180
Nichols, Nichelle 167
Nicodemus, Byron 202
Nicolosi, Al 96
Nielsen, Leslie 38
Niemelä, Juhani 199
The Night Andy Came Home see *Dead of Night*
A Night in the Crypt see *One Dark Night*
Night Life **117**
Night of Anubis see *Night of the Living Dead* (1968)
Night of the Blind Dead see *Tombs of the Blind Dead*
Night of the Blood Cult see *Night of the Seagulls*
Night of the Comet 13
Night of the Creeps **117**
Night of the Day of the Dawn of the Son of the Bride of Return of the Revenge of the Terror of the Attack of the Evil Mutant Hellbound Flesh-Eating Subhumanoid Living Dead, Part II **119**
Night of the Death Cult see *Night of the Seagulls*
Night of the Flesh Eaters see *Night of the Living Dead* (1968)

Night of the Living Bread **120**
Night of the Living Dead (1968) 5, 6, 7, 8, 9, 11, 13, 33, 42, 43, 44, 46, 64, 66, 81, 87, 91, 94, 99, 101, 103, 119, 120, **121**, 142, 143, 161, 171, 195, 212
Night of the Living Dead (1990) **123**
Night of the Seagulls **123**, 172
The Night of the Sorcerers **124**
Night of the Wehrmacht Zombies see *Gamma 693*
Night of the Witches see *The Night of the Sorcerers*
Night of the Zombies 8, **125**, 193; see also *Erotic Nights of the Living Dead; Gamma 693*
Night of the Zombies II see *Gamma 693*
Night Star—Goddess of Electra see *War of the Zombies*
Night Walk see *Dead of Night*
Nightbreed 145
Nightmare see *City of the Walking Dead*
Nightmare City see *City of the Walking Dead*
A Nightmare on Elm Street 54, 156
Nimoy, Leonard 213
No profanar el sueño de los muertos see *Let Sleeping Corpses Lie*
La Noche de la muerta ciega see *Tombs of the Blind Dead*
La Noche de los brujos see *The Night of the Sorcerers*
La Noche de los gaviotas see *Night of the Seagulls*
La Noche del buque maldito see *Horror of the Zombies*
La Noche del terror ciego see *Tombs of the Blind Dead*
Noland, Robert 150
Non sì deve profanare il sonno dei morti see *Let Sleeping Corpses Lie*
Norcross, Van 148
Norris, William J. 139
North, Steven 157
North by Northwest 87
La Notte dei zombi see *Erotic Nights of the Living Dead*
La Notte erotiche dei morti viventi see *Erotic Nights of the Living Dead*
La Notti del terror see *Burial Ground*
Le Notti erotiche dei morti viventi see *Erotic Nights of the Living Dead*
Novaro, Tito 30
Noyard, Frank 78
Nudist Colony of the Dead **127**
La Nuit des étoiles filantes see *A Virgin Among the Living Dead*
Nuñez, Miguel 142
Nuse, Deland 33
Nye, Carrie 38

Oakland, Simon 196
Oakley, Bill 58
Oasis of the Zombies 2, 8, 45, **128**, 216
O'Bannon, Dan 49, 78, 142, 144
Obrecht, Kathi 104
O'Brian, Donald 60
O'Brien, Kevin S. 120
O'Dea, Judith 121
O'Hara, Brett 86
Ohtsuki, Kenzi 106
O'Keeffe, Miles 187
Oliver, Bill 70
Oliveros, Ramiro 40
Omaggio, Maria Rosaria 36
O'Malley, Pat 196
The Omega Man 99
One Dark Night **129**
O'Neal, Peter 60
O'Neil, Patrick 68
O'Neil, Robert 126
O'Neill, James 84
O'Neill, Logan 206
O'Neill, Michael 75
Orellana, Antonio 88
La Orgía de los muertos see *Return of the Zombies*
La Orgia dei morti see *Return of the Zombies*
Orlandi, Ferdinando 192
Ormsby, Alan 32, 53, 160
Ormsby, Anya 32, 53
O'Rourke, Michael 78
Gli Orrori del castello di Norimberga see *Baron Blood*
Ortin, Polo 87
Orton, Peter 113
Osés, Fernando 153
Osth, Robert 63
Ouanga 3, **130**
Pace, Tom 19

Palillo, Ron 78
Palk, Anna 63
Palmer, Gregg 211
Palmer, Gretchen 34
Paloian, Nancy 187
Panic in the Trans-Siberian Train see *Horror Express*
Pánico en el transiberiano see *Horror Express*
Paoli, Dennis 139
Paquette, Bruce 96
Parcero, Jose Gómez 200
Pares, Mildred 83
Parker, Trey 133
Parker, Willard 63
Parkinson, Andrew 95
Parsons, Elsie 2
Parsons, Jack 63

Parsons, Lindsley 96, 148
Pascale, Nadine 207
Pasdar, Adrian 106
Passarelli, Elizabeth 204
Patrick, John 19
Patrick, Nigel 168
Paura nelle città dei morti viventi see *The Gates of Hell*
Paxton, Marie 130
Pearce, Jacqueline 133
Pecic, Bogdan "Don" 52
Peck, Brian 142
Peck, George 44
Pehar, Olga 56
Pellicer, Pilar 98
Pellonpää, Matti 199
Peña, Julio 78
Peñalver, Diana 47
Penczner, Marius 94
Pendleton, Austin 114
Penney, John 145
Pepper, Paul 169
Perschy, María 80
Pet Sematary **132**
Peters, Erika 111
Peters, George 206
Peterson, Nina 34
Petit, Víctor 123
Peyton, Chuck 17
Pfeiffer, Dedee 110
Phillips, Robin 168
Pieroni, Ania 81
Pierotti, Piero 186
Pigozzi, Luciano 170
Pilato, Joe 45
Pingüino, Jorge 112
"Pink Eye" **133**
Piper, Brett 138
Piranha, P. Floyd 141
Pirro, Mark 127
Piscopo, Joe 51
Pitt, Robert 209
The Plague of the Zombies 5, 11, 13, 40, 59, **133**
Plan Nine from Outer Space 4, 118, **136**
Plana, Ramón 141, 146
Platt, John 111
Playdon, Paul 196
Plumer, Daniel 61
Plummer, Scott P. 203
Plympton, George 211
Poe, Edgar Allan 68
Poe, Rüdiger 111
Pollak, Cheryl 117
Pollexfen, Jack 111
Pollock, Gene 86
Portillo, Rafael 5, 41
Porto, Juan José 40
Poston, Dick 23
Potterton, Gerald 77
Price, Daria 44
Price, Dennis 63
Price, Lorin E. 70
Price, Vincent 51, 99
Proctor, Marland 71
Proctor, Phil 117
Prosky, Robert 69
Psycho 50
Psycho a Go-Go 24
Psychomania 31
Pullman, Bill 155
Pupillo, Massimo 170
Purcell, Dick 96
Purdom, Edmund 198

Quarry, Robert 165, 169
Queen of the Cannibals see *Dr. Butcher, M.D.*
Quella villa accanto al cimitero see *The House by the Cemetery*
Quigley, Linnea 104, 142
Quincey, Charles 146
Quinlan, Kathleen 186
Quintana, Elvira 41

Raasch, Amy 182
Rabal, Francisco 36
Rabid 13
Rado, Jorge 152
Raho, Humi 21
Raiders of the Living Dead **38**
Raimi, Sam 52
Ramar of the Jungle 210
Ramirez, Raul 87
Ramsey, Anne 55
Rand, Will 147
Randall, Mónica 40
Randolph, Beverly 142
Randolph, Bill 65
Raptors **138**
Rasberry, James 94
Raspberry, Larry 94
Rassimov, Rada 21
Rausch, Kasey 201
Raven, Joseph 61
Raven, Stark 158
Raw Meat 49
Raxel, Antonio 98
Ray, Esther see Esperanza Roy
Ray, Fred Olen 18, 169
Ray, Ola 171
Raymond, Richard 193
Re-Animator 8, 9, 12, 26, 28, 55, 138, **139**
Re-Animator II see *Bride of Re-Animator*
Reason, Rhodes 183
Rebeca, María 200
La Rebellion de las muertas see *Vengeance of the Zombies*
Rebellion of the Dead Women see *Vengeance of the Zombies*
Redfield, Dennis 49
Redneck Zombies 9, 11, **141**
Reed, Joel 70
Rees, Betty Anne 165
Regan, Nell 147
Regan, Patrick 147
Regan, Patrick III 147
La Regina dei cannibali see *Dr. Butcher, M.D.*
Regnoli, Piero 29, 36
Reiniger, Scott H. 42
Reinthaler, Ulli 193
Reis, Whitney 34
Reltman, Ivan 77
Remmealy, Phil 71
Rendon, Thomas 182
Renom, Gabby 126
The Reptile 40, 134
Resident Evil 10
Rest in Peace see *One Dark Night*
Return of the Blind Dead see *Return of the Evil Dead*
Return of the Evil Dead **141**, 172

Return of the Living Dead 8, 9, 11, 25, 26, 41, 58, 78, 104, 133, 138, 140, **142**, 144, 193; see also *Messiah of Evil*
Return of the Living Dead Part II 9, **144**
Return of the Living Dead Part III 10, **145**
Return of the Zombies **146**
Revenge of the Dead see *Zeder*
Revenge of the Evil Dead see *Return of the Evil Dead*
Revenge of the Living Dead see *Children Shouldn't Play with Dead Things*
Revenge of the Living Zombies see *Flesheater*
Revenge of the Nerds 182
Revenge of the Screaming Dead see *Messiah of Evil*
Revenge of the Zombie **147**
Revenge of the Zombies (1943) 2, 6, 11, 139, **148**
Revenge of the Zombies (1981) **149**
Revolt of the Dead Ones see *Vengeance of the Zombies*
Revolt of the Demons see *Revolt of the Zombies*
Revolt of the Zombies **150**
Rey, Bárbara 80
Reyes, Pia 145
Reynolds, Todd 105
Rhys, Jean 91
Rice, Bill 180
Richards, Grant 67
Richardson, Jay 169
Richardson, Ralph 168
Riche, Clive 30
Rickman, Allen 93
Rico, Luis Quintanilla 112
Ridley, Judith 121
Rigaud, Manuska 208
Ring, Beatrice 193
Ringuette, Lory 177
Ritter, Brent 41
Ritter, Tim 96
Rivera, Robert G. 41
Rizzo, Alfredo 170
Roach, Frank 69
Robbins, Matthew 186
Robbins, Tacey 24
Roberts, Conrad 155
Roberts, Raymond 18
Roberts, Steven 200
Robles, Betty 200
Rochelle, Bob 70
The Rocky Horror Picture Show 188
Roehbling, Randolph 215
Rogers, Wayne 19, 20
Roland, Jeanne 162
Rollin, Jean 13, 181, 207
Roma contra Roma see *War of the Zombies*
Romero, George 7, 8, 9, 12, 13, 28, 38, 42, 45, 50, 51, 52, 58, 61, 65, 91, 99, 106, 121, 123, 136, 143, 159, 160, 172, 194, 195, 198, 199
Rommy 176
Romoli, Gianni 30
Rosas, Enrique 87
Rose, Deborah 25
Rose, Harry 202
Rose, Jamie 34
Rose, Rebecca 202
Rosemary's Baby 49
Rosenbaum, Jonathan 11
Rosenberg, Max 168
Rosi, Stelvio 146
Roskowick, Patrick 101
Ross, Daniel see Stroppa, Daniele
Ross, Gaylen 42
Rossi-Stuart, Giacomo 99
Rostaine, H.L. 197
Roth, Gene 211
Roubal, Cathy 98
Rovick, Jody 202
Roy, Esperanza 141
Royston, Roy 134
Ruben, Michael 93
Rubin, Bruce Joel 55
Rubinstein, Richard 38, 42, 45, 132
Rusoff, Ted 198
Russell, Autumn 211
Russell, Veronica 210
Russo, John 121, 123, 143, 182
Ru-Tar, Rotar 75

Saaristo, Vieno 199
Sabin, Robert 93
Sacchetti, Bob 138
Sacchetti, Dardano 22, 72, 81
Saddow, Eileen 200
Sahagun, Elena 169
"The Saint" 161
St. Jacques, Raymond 182
Saint John, Antoine 22
Saint-Just, Eric 128
St. Michaels, Michael 177
Salazar, Alfred (Abel) 41
Saliba, Joseph W. 153
Salkow, Sidney 99
Salomé, Mara 30
Salvo, John 44
Sampson, Robert 116, 140
Sancho, Fernando 141
Sanford, Donald 85
Sanguelia see *Zombie* (L. Fulci)
El Santo 88, 98, 112, 152, 153
Santo and Blue Demon Against the Monsters **152**
Santo and Blue Demon in the Land of the Dead see *The Land of the Dead*
Santo contra la magia negra see *Santo vs. Black Magic*
El Santo contra los zombies see *Invasion of the Zombies*

El Santo en el mundo de los muertos see *The Land of the Dead*
Santo vs. Black Magic 88, **153**
Santo vs. the Zombies see *Invasion of the Zombies*
Santo y Blue Demon contra los monstrous see *Santo and Blue Demon against the Monsters*
Santos, José Angel 123
Sarafian, Deran 193
Sartarelli, Marcello 186
Satana, Tura 19
Satan's Satellites see *Zombies of the Stratosphere*
Sattels, Barry 44
Saunders, Charles 191
Saunders, Wolfgang S. 120
Savalas, Telly 78
Savini, Tom 43, 53, 123
Scared Stiff 73, **154**
Scearce, Roger 200
Schick, Elliot 165
Schmoeller, David 116
Schmoeller, Gary 145
Schnaas, Andreas 199
Schnarre, Monika 187
Schnitzer, Gerald 26
Schon, Kyra 121
The School That Ate My Brain see *Zombie High*
Schorer, Mark 85
Schroeder, Michael 129
Schwartz, Scott 138
Sclavi, Tiziano 30
Scooby-Doo on Zombie Island **154**
Scott, George 141
Scott, John 79
Scott, Linda Gaye 177
Scott, Lizabeth 154
Scott, Robert 177
Seabrook, William 2
The Second Coming see *Messiah of Evil*
The Secret of Dr. Orloff see *Dr. Orloff's Monster*
El Secreto del Dr. Orloff see *Dr. Orloff's Monster*
Sekely, Steve 148
Selko, Warren 21
Seminara, George 93
Seppäla, Silu 199
The Serpent and the Rainbow **155**
The Seven Brothers Meet Dracula see *The Legend of the Seven Golden Vampires*
Seven Doors of Death see *The Beyond*
Sevilla, Carmen 40
Sexy Nights of the Dead see *Erotic Nights of the Living Dead*
Shah, Krishna 76
Shanks 7, **157**
Shannon, Mark 64
Shapiro, Beverly 173
Sharrett, Michael 55
Shatter Dead 11, **158**, 202
Shaw, Run Run 149
Shaw, Vee King 102
Shearer, Harry 58
Sheen, Martin 106
Sheets, Todd 10, 201, 202, 209
Shell, Tom 169
Shen, Chan 102
Shendal, Margaret 167
Sherman, Gary A. 49
Sherman, Howard 45
Sherman, Robert M. 55
Sherman, Samuel 23, 138
Shimada, Teru 150
Ship of Zombies see *Horror of the Zombies*
Shock see *Shanks*
Shock Waves 2, 7, 19, 70, 144, **159**, 207
Short Circuit 55
Shreck, Max 32
Shrunken Heads **161**
Shusett, Ronald 49
"Sibao" **161**
Sidney, D.J. 160
Siegler, Bill 115
Silent Death see *Voodoo Island*
Silliphant, Robert 86
Silva, María 171
Silver, Alain 147
Silverman, Jonathan 188
Simonds, P.K. 21
Simoun, A.R. 155
"The Simpsons" 9, 58
Sinclair, John 210
Sinclair, Stephen 47
Singh, Anant 78
Singleton, Paula 215
Siodmak, Curt 37, 91
Sipling, Dean 95
Sir Lancelot 91
Sisson, Bryan 41
Sixteen Candles 93
Skinner, Anita 164
Slate, Jeremy 54
Smedley, Richard 24
Smellman, Fester 141
Smith, Lisa 65
Smith, Mike 105
Smith, Yeardly 58
The Snake People **162**
Snare, William 164
Snyder, Maria 34
Snyder, Suzanne 144
Soavi, Michele 30
Softley, Ellen 95
Soisson, Joel 167
Solares, Gilberto Martínez 98, 152
Sole Survivor 69, **164**
Solomon, Bruce 117
Sommer, Elke 21
Somtow, S.P. 101
Soney, Michael 69
"South Park" 9, 133
Spaak, Agnes 61
Space Zombies see *The Astro-Zombies*
Spalding, Harry 63
Speights, Leslie 129
Spenser, David 63
Spero, Chuck 215
Stabler, Steve 106
Staccioli, Ivano 186
Stacey, Patricia 96
Stader, Peter 132
Stapleford, Betty 200
Stapleton, Dan 83
Stark, Philip 133

Steckler, Ray Dennis 4, 86, 111
Steel, Kathy 205
Steele, Barbara 170
Steele, Bob 148
Stell, William Calderón 41
Stella, Luciano 141
Stellman, Jack 177
Stenstrum, Jim 154
Stephenson, Dennis 206
Stern, Deborah 127
Stevens, Angela 37
Stevens, Brinke 169
Stewart, Mary 147
Stewart, Mel 28
Stewart, Nick 209
Stewart, Robin 102
Stiglitz, Hugo 36, 200
Stockman, Paul 59
Stoddard, William 206
Stodden, Betty 202
Stodden, Nick 202
Stoloff, Ben 213
Stone, Dorothy 150
Stone, Matt 133
Storey, Ray 83
Storm, Gale 148
Stouch, Eric 133
Stough, Ray 93
Stout, Don 160
Stovin, Jerry 162
Strange Turf see *Voodoo Dawn*
Stratford, Willie, Jr. 26
Streiner, Russell 121, 123
Strickler, Jerry 82
Stroppa, Daniele 138
Strycula, Mark 65
Suárez, Carlos 98
Suay, Ricardo Muñez 81
Subotsky, Milton 168
Los Sueños eróticos de Christine see *A Virgin Among the Living Dead*
Sugar Hill 4, 7, 57, **165**
Sullivan, Don 169
Sullivan, Ed 177
Sullivan, Tim 101
Sul-Te-Wan 96, 148
Sumner, Chuck 18
Sunseri, Jack A. 33
The Supernaturals 11, **167**
Superzán 30
Sutch, Pamela 205
Sutterfield, James 138
Suzuki, Cutei 106
Swamp of the Blood Leeches see *The Alien Dead*
Swan, Don 75
Swanson, Kristy 55, 56
Swanson, Logan 99
Sylvestre, Armando 88
Szu, Shih 102

Tales from the Crypt **168**
Tallman, Patricia 123
Tanamera, Juan 127
Tanny, Lung 149
Tanziani, Paolo 192
Tau, Chang 97
Tayback, Vic 21
Taylor, Jack 80, 124
Taylor, Kent 23
Taylor, Wally 117
Teasedale, Boo 141
Teenage Exorcist **169**
Teenage Psycho Meets Bloody Mary see *The Incredibly Strange Creatures Who Stopped Living and Became Mixed-Up Zombies*
Teenage Zombies 4, 68, **169**
Telles, Rico 104
Telman, José 171
Tenney, Dell 4, 79, 83
Terror Beach see *Night of the Seagulls*
Terror Creatures from the Grave 12, **170**
Terwilliger, George 130
The Texas Chainsaw Massacre 5, 147
Texeira, Juliana 57
Thelman, Joseph 124
They Shoot Horses, Don't They? 50
The Thirst of Baron Blood see *Baron Blood*
Thomas, Robin 69
Thor, Jon Mikl 208
Those Cruel and Bloody Vampires see *Tombs of the Blind Dead*
Thriller (music video) 8, 110, **171**, 177
"Thriller" (series) 5, 85
Thrower, Steve 1
Tibetan Book of the Dead 82
Tichy, Gerard 146
Tilly, Meg 129
Tinieblas 30
Toberoff, Marc 204
Todd, Michael 52
Todd, Tony 123, 182
Toglistos, George 77
Tolzac, Jean 197
Tomb of the Undead see *Garden of the Dead*
Tombs of the Blind Dead 2, 7, 108, 141, 142, **171**
Tombs of the Blind Zombies see *Tombs of the Blind Dead*
Tonelli, Bob 192
Tonge, Philip 89
Tongolele see Yolanda Montes
Tortosa, Silvia 78
The Torture Chamber of Baron Blood see *Baron Blood*
Tourneur, Jacques 91
Tovar, Loretta 141
Tower, Lorena 124
Towles, Tom 123
Towne, Aline 213
The Toxic Avenger 141
Toxic Zombies 11, **173**
Trane, Reuben 159
Travesí, Rafael García 98, 152
Treadway, Patrick 177
The Treasure of the Living Dead see *Oasis of the Zombies*
Tressler, Dieter 21
Trichardt, Carel 78
Trinkhaus, Marc 199
Trotter, Laura 36
Trowbridge, Charles 174
Tucci, Ugo 194
La Tumba de los muer-

tos vivientes see *Oasis of the Zombies*
Turbide, Manon 208
Twilight of the Dead see *The Gates of Hell*
Twomey, Anne 55
Tyler, Beverly 183
Tyson, Cathy 155

Udenio, Fabiana 28
Gli Ultimi zombi see *Zombie*
Underwood, Dennis 18

Valley of the Zombies **174**
Vampira 136
Van Hoven, Keith 57
Van Patten, Dick 110
Vari, Giuseppe 186
Vaughan, Jimmy 191
Vaughn, Robert 138, 177
Velasco, Usi 200
Velázquez, Lorena 88
La Vendetta dei morti viventi see *Vengeance of the Zombies*
Vengeance of the Zombies **176**
Vengeful Dead see *Revenge of the Zombie*
Vergara, Luis Enrique 162
Vernon, Howard 180, 197, 207
"The Very Important Zombie Affair" **177**
The Veteran see *Dead of Night*
Victor, Henry 96
Victor, Katherine 169
The Video Dead **177**
Une Vierge chez les morts vivants see *A Virgin Among the Living Dead*
Village of the Damned 14
Villemaire, James 138
Villers, Dan 197
Vincent, Ron 33
Vindeni, Dino 181
The Vineyard 10, **180**
Violent Shit 199
A Virgin Among the Living Dead 7, **180**, 198, 216
Virly, Joan 197
Virus see *Night of the Zombies*
Virus—L'inferno dei morti viventi see *Night of the Zombies*
Virus cannibale see *Night of the Zombies*
Vitale, Joseph 214
Von Blanc, Christina 180
Voodoo **181**
Voodoo Blood Bath see *I Eat Your Skin*
Voodoo Dawn **182**
Voodoo Girl see *Sugar Hill*
Voodoo Island **183**
Voodoo Man **185**
Voskanian, Robert 31
Vye, Murvyn 183

Wagner, Lindsay 69
Walcott, Gregory 136
Waldman, Drew Alan 169
Waldman, Grant Austin 169
Walk of the Dead see *Vengeance of the Zombies*
Walker, Terry 185
Wallace, Basil 145
Wallis, Hall B. 154
Walsh, Frances 47
Walsh, Matthew Jason 203
Walsh, Sharon 86
Walters, Thorley 63
War of the Zombies **186**
Warbeck, David 22
Ward, B.J. 154
Ward, Joanne 78
Warda, Arne 24
Ware, Vince 120
Warner, David 187
Warning Sign **186**
Warren, Aven 205
Warren, Jennifer 113
Warren, Jerry 42, 68, 169
Warren, Kenneth J. 59
Washington, Fredi 130
Waterston, Sam 186
Watkin, Ian 47
Watkins, T.G. 201
Watt, Timothy 138
Waxman, Stanley 213
Waxwork **187**
Waxwork II: Lost in Time **187**
Wayn, Peter 191
Wayne, Keith 121
Weaver, Fritz 38
Webb, Kenneth 2, 190
Webb, Wendy 101
Weekend at Bernie's II **188**
Weinstein, Josh 58
Wei-Tu, Lin 149
Welker, Frank 154
Well, Karin 29
Wellford, Christina 94
Wellington, David 208
Wells, Carol 82
Wells, Robert 158
Wells, Ted 76
Wendel, Lara 138
Wendell, Howard 67
Wendkos, Paul 69
West, Adam 129, 208
West, Billy 154
Weston, Garnett 190
Wexler, Paul 67
What's Up, Tiger Lily? 119
Wheeler, Ed 115
Whipper, Leigh 96
White, Michelle 105
White Zombie 2, 3, 11, 13, 132, 150, 152, 164, **190**
Whitlow, Jill 117
Whitson, Gary 205
Whitten, Marguerite 96
Wide Sargasso Sea 91
Wiederhorn, Ken 144, 159
Wilcox, Steve 127
Wilder, James 204
Williams, Billy "Sly" 182
Williams, Brook 133
Williams, Cynda 106

Williams, Roger 201, 209
Williams, Treat 51
Wilson, Don 17
Wilson, Roger 106
Winfield, Paul 155
Winner, Vic 81, 176
Wise, Ray 106
Witter, Karen 180
Wolcott, Abigail 78
The Wolfman 2
Wolfman, Martin 141
Womaneater 184, **191**
Wong, Michael 180
Wood, Edward, Jr. 67, 136
Wood, Wilson 213
Woodbury, Joan 96
Woolley, Clayton 104
The Wrath of Khan 118
Wray, Ardel 91
Wright, Tom 188
Wynkoop, Joel 96

Yanovsky, Zal 77
Yarbrough, Jean 96
Yates, Peter 161
Ying, Cheng Ka 97
York, Dick 85
Young, Denise 25
Yuzna, Brian 28, 139, 145

Zavada, Ervin 110
Zeder **192**
Zeder—Voices from the Beyond see *Zeder*
Zellner, Alan 94
Zillmann, Dolf 12
Zombi 2 see *Zombie* (L. Fluci)
Zombi 3 **193**, 195, 198
Zombi Holocaust see *Dr. Butcher, M.D.*; *A Virgin Among the Living Dead*
Zombie (stage production) 2
Zombie see *Dawn of the Dead*; *I Eat Your Skin*
Zombie (L. Fulci) 2, 8, 22, 29, 43, 60, 126, 188, **194**, 198, 216
The Zombie see *The Plague of the Zombies*
The Zombie **196**
Zombie 2 see *Zombie* (L. Fulci)
Zombie 3 see *Burial Ground*
Zombie 3: Da dove vieni? see *Let Sleeping Corpses Lie*
Zombie 4 see *A Virgin Among the Living Dead*
Zombie 4: After Death see *After Death*
Zombie 5: Revenge of the House of Usher **197**, 198
Zombie 6: Monster Hunter **198**
Zombie '90: Extreme Pestilence 12, **199**
Zombie and the Ghost Train **199**
Zombie Apocalypse **200**
The Zombie Army **200**
Zombie Bloodbath 11, **201**
Zombie Bloodbath II: Rage of the Undead **202**
Zombie Child see *The Child*
Zombie Cop 52, **203**
Zombie Creeping Flesh see *Night of the Zombies*
Zombie Flesh Eaters see *Zombie* (L. Fulci)
Zombie High 119, **204**
Zombie Holocaust **205**
Zombie Horror see *Burial Ground*
Zombie Inferno see *Night of the Zombies*
Zombie Island Massacre **206**
Zombie ja Kummitusjuna see *Zombie and the Ghost Train*
Zombie Lake 2, 8, 70, 161, **207**, 216
Zombie Nightmare 130, **208**
Zombie Nosh see *Flesheater*
Zombie of the Savanna see *Night of the Zombies*
Zombie Rampage 202, **209**
Zombie Revival: Ninja Master see *Zombie vs. Ninja*
Zombie Terror **209**
Zombie vs. Mardi Gras **210**
Zombie vs. Ninja **211**
Zombies see *Dawn of the Dead*; *I Eat Your Skin*
The Zombies see *The Plague of the Zombies*
Zombies Lake see *Zombie Lake*
Zombies of Mora-Tau 2, 4, **211**
Zombies of Sugar Hill see *Sugar Hill*
Zombies of the Stratosphere 4, **213**
Zombies on Broadway **213**
Zombiethon **215**
Zontar, the Thing from Venus 1
Zoofeet 141
Zorn, Danny 114
Zovek 87
Zucco, George 185
Zucker, Ralph 170
Zurakowska, Dianik 146